Practices for Network Management

Jukka Vesalainen • Katri Valkokari • Magnus Hellström
Editors

Practices for Network Management

In Search of Collaborative Advantage

palgrave
macmillan

Editors
Jukka Vesalainen
University of Vaasa
Vaasa, Finland

Magnus Hellström
Åbo Akademi University
Åbo, Finland

Katri Valkokari
VTT Technical Research Centre of Finland
Tampere, Finland

ISBN 978-3-319-49648-1 ISBN 978-3-319-49649-8 (eBook)
DOI 10.1007/978-3-319-49649-8

Library of Congress Control Number: 2016962496

Cover illustration: ordi clave garsot / Alamy Stock Photo

Printed on acid-free paper

This Palgrave Macmillan imprint is published by Springer Nature
The registered company is Springer International Publishing AG
The registered company address is: Gewerbestrasse 11, 6330 Cham, Switzerland

Foreword

In the network era we live in today, many organizational actors in positions of management or expertise increasingly play important roles in building, organizing, coordinating, and developing business relationships, networks, or even entire ecosystems. In doing so, they face challenges for how to influence the actions of their partner firms as well as how to align their own firms with their business partners. These "boundary spanners" strive to build a shared understanding between the members in a network. The DIMECC REBUS (Towards relational business practices) research program was inspired by the *relational* view introduced first by Dyer and Singh in 1998. The research program also wanted to result in concrete deliverables that would have practical value for network management, that is, developing and then studying relational business practices in industrial networks. Therefore, the research utilized design science approach.

The idea for a book that combined the central findings of these research and development efforts arose from the recognition of the multidisciplinary nature of network management. All coauthors of this book have written numerous papers for scientific journals and conferences on their research results. However, writing for highly focused scientific journals has not allowed a full exploration of the multidisciplinary nature of this work and the systemic nature of network dynamics. In real business life, relational network management practices are strongly connected between themselves and other business practices, and not much has been written about that aspect. Further still, the text and style in the focused scientific papers follow the lingo of each particular discipline and may be difficult for an expert from another discipline to understand fully. In this book, therefore, we have tried to explain the multidisciplinary content in a way that can be understood by those from different backgrounds. Indeed, the book targets a wide range of academic readers but also reflective practitioners from industry.

Altogether, 36 authors have contributed to this edited collection of ideas. The content of the book was formed through numerous group discussions between all the authors during the research effort. For each part (I–III) named persons were responsible for introducing the respective category of practices and papers. Mika Viljanen and Peter Zetting were responsible for the introduction to Part I titled, "*Networks-as-Coordinated Social Systems*". Rainer Breite wrote the introduction to Part II titled "*Networks-as-Knowledge-Creating Platforms*". Magnus Hellström was responsible for the introduction to Part III, which focused on "*Networks-as-Value-Generating Entities*". All the chapters discussing the tools were peer reviewed by at least two other contributors. As editors, we have put our combined efforts into shaping the book into a coherent and high-quality scholarly presentation that presents a novel system framework for network dynamics. Further still, the book establishes a clear path toward the use of the network-as-practice view in studying inter-organizational relationships.

The editors thank all 33 coauthors for their contributions related to the tools presented in the three main sections of the book. We also thank all the participating boundary-spanning managers in the 22 innovative organizations in our consortium (and some adjacent ones) that shared their networking experiences and practices with us during the research effort. It was part of the research program, "Towards Relational Business Practices" (REBUS), one of the research programs in the portfolio of the open innovation vehicle DIMECC (the Digital, Internet, Materials & Engineering Co-Creation Company). The DIMECC REBUS program was funded by TEKES—the Finnish Funding Agency for Innovation, 22 participating companies, and seven participating research institutions. We also thank them for their valuable contributions.

August 30, 2016 Jukka Vesalainen
Tampere Katri Valkokari
Magnus Hellström

Contents

Notes on Contributors

Sampo Autio MSc (Econ. & Bus. Adm.), works as a project researcher in the research group "Networked Value Systems" at the University of Vaasa. He takes a special interest in supply network performance management. He also runs his own company that helps small- and medium-sized companies to improve their business processes and business models.

Rainer Breite has worked as an engineer in several engineering companies. His main industrial experience derives from water turbines. Since 1998, he has been working as a lecturer and researcher in Tampere University of Technology. His research interest is focused on knowledge sharing in supply chains and networks.

Kent Eriksson received his PhD in 1994 and is professor, chair in Applied Business Studies at KTH, Sweden. He is since 2013 a visiting professor at Global Projects Center, Stanford University, USA, and since 2014 also at Åbo Akademi University, Åbo, Finland. He is also a member of the board of directors of Första APfonden in Sweden. His research concerns engineering project business. His recent work is on infrastructure and logistics service delivery.

Magnus Gustafsson is an Associate Professor in Industrial Management, especially Project Business and Industrial Marketing, at Åbo Akademi University. His areas of expertise are (1) business relationships, network trust, sustainable production networks, and how to build business models oriented toward the business challenges. He has published more than 130 articles, reports, and books. In 2010, he was awarded the Research Award by the International Project

Management Association for ground-breaking research that contributes to business.

Nina Helander works as an Associate Professor in the field of Knowledge Management at the Department of Information Management and Logistics at the Tampere University of Technology. In addition, she is an Adjunct Professor of Information System Sciences at the University of Jyväskylä. She has received her PhD in 2004 on the subject of value creation in business networks. Her research interests are related to value creation, knowledge management, digital business, and business networks.

Magnus Hellström works as a Senior Lecturer and Docent in Industrial Management at Åbo Akademi University, Finland. He has 5+ years' experience from work within the engineering works industry. His research interests include modularity, industrial services, and business ecosystems.

Anna Hurmerinta works as a doctoral candidate at the Faculty of Law, University of Turku. Her research interests lie in the field of contract law. Her doctoral dissertation will focus on the interplay between relational contract theory, transaction cost economics, and functional use of contracts. She has also been an active researcher in the REBUS project.

Maria Ivanova-Gongne works as a postdoctoral researcher in International Marketing at Åbo Akademi University. Her research interests include business-to-business marketing management, particularly the aspects of business interaction, managerial sensemaking and culture in international business-to-business relationships and networks. She has received her PhD in economics and business administration in 2014.

Valtteri Kaartemo is a university teacher at Turku School of Economics, University of Turku, Finland. He is a coauthor of several books, book chapters, conference papers, and peer-reviewed articles. His research interests include market shaping, service research, innovation management, international entrepreneurship, value co-creation, and particularly various processes in and around these phenomena. Aside his research activities, he runs his own company and advices two startups to develop their value propositions in markets that are yet to be created.

Elisa Kallio is a doctoral candidate at Turku School of Economics at the University of Turku and has been working in research projects focusing on marine and pharmaceutical industries. Her doctoral research focuses on exploring changing organizational schemata through organizational practices during strategic change.

Outi Kettunen MSc (Tech.), works as a senior scientist at VTT. She has 16 years of experience in research projects in the area of Industrial Engineering and Management. Her expertise areas are supply chain management, value networks, and logistics efficiency, with growing emphasis on the circular economy.

Susanna Kunttu MSc, works as a research scientist at VTT. She has been working more than 10 years in the area of engineering asset management and life-cycle management. Her main research interest is on decision support by data analysis.

Johnny Långstedt (MA) works as a postgraduate student in comparative religion at Åbo Akademi University, Finland. His main interests are leadership, intercultural communication, and human values.

Johanna Liinamaa works as a Postdoctoral Researcher and Lecturer in Industrial Management at Åbo Akademi University. Her research interests include strategic management and innovation, especially systems integration and integration management, industrial service innovations, and business model development. She defended her doctoral thesis entitled *Integration in Project Business* in 2012.

Hanna Luotola (MA) is finalizing her doctoral thesis in Industrial Management at Åbo Akademi University. Her research specializes on designing industrial solutions. Her research interests include developing of industrial solutions and value-driven sales processes. Her areas of expertise combine both industrial management and creative arts and design thinking.

Sari Mäenpää works as a postdoctoral researcher and a project manager in Tampere University of Technology, Finland. She defended her doctoral thesis about managing network relations in project business context in 2013. She is especially interested in knowledge integration, relationship quality, and digitalization among manufacturing networks and business ecosystems. She also has several years of experience from working within the construction industry.

Danijela Majdenic is currently a doctoral candidate in International Business at the Turku School of Economics, University of Turku, in Finland. Her research focuses on global virtual teams.

Jonathan Van Mumford is currently a doctoral candidate in International Business at the Turku School of Economics, University of Turku, in Finland. He is investigating stakeholder commitments in international new venture creation.

Tomi Nokelainen works as a research manager at Åbo Akademi University. His research interests include strategic management, particularly competitive dynamics and inter-organizational collective strategy work, and technology management. He has earned his PhD in Strategic Management from Tampere University of Technology, in 2008, where he served as an Associate Professor in Strategic Management before joining the Åbo Akademi University faculty.

Mika Perho received an MSc in Industrial Engineering and Management and Information Technology, and BSc in Machine Automation. He has extensive knowledge and work experience in multidisciplinary R&D and technology fields. He has worked as supply network researcher in Tampere University of Technology, specialist in Nokia software product development, and machine design engineer.

Anni Rajala works as a doctoral candidate at the Department of Management, University of Vaasa. Her research interests are related to business networks, buyer–supplier relationship, boundary spanning, and quantitative research methods.

Antti Saurama is a director of the Centre for Collaborative Research at Turku School of Economics at the University of Turku. He designs and coordinates multi-stakeholder corporate-academia research projects and facilitates academic research results to business managers. His current research work focuses on industrial value creation.

Víctor A. Sifontes Herrera has a background in chemical engineering. His activities in industrial management began on 2014 with focus on business ecosystems for the shipping industry and business models for project-based organizations. He is currently working as a researcher at the Laboratory of Industrial Management at Åbo Akademi University.

Anu Suominen is currently a doctoral student at Tampere University of Technology in Finland, where she has a work-in-progress doctoral thesis on network legitimation. She has both academic and practical working experience in the field of Industrial Management and Engineering. Her research interests focus on inter-organizational networks and their governance, and innovation especially from knowledge management aspect.

Anastasia Tsvetkova defended her doctoral dissertation in 2014 at Åbo Akademi University. Her main research interests include the structure and dynamics of business ecosystems and boundary-spanning business models. She is especially interested in generating actionable knowledge within the context of sustainable business and industrial ecology. She currently works as a researcher at the Laboratory of Industrial Management, Faculty of Science and Engineering, Åbo Akademi University and as a senior researcher at PBI Research Institute, Turku.

Tero Välisalo MSc (Tech.) has worked at VTT as a research scientist since 1997. He has worked with Finnish mobile machine manufacturers developing and applying safety, reliability and life-cycle cost analysis methods into their product-development processes.

Tiina Valjakka is a team leader of the VTT Business Renewal in Organizations and Networks team. She received MSc in Operations and Production Management at Michigan Technological University. She has carried out several projects developing collaboration and published articles on business network research. Her expertise covers network integration and value co-creation.

Katri Valkokari works as a principal scientist at VTT in the Business Ecosystems, Value Chains and Foresight research area. Currently, she also works as a program manager of FIMECC REBUS Program. Over the past 15 years, she has carried out several business-development projects concerning different SME networks (i.e. supply, R&D, distribution, service, and innovation networks). She has published several international and national articles in the research areas of business networks, innovation management, and sustainability.

Jukka Vesalainen is a Professor of Management and Organization at University of Vaasa. His current research has addressed networking and business relationships. He has published research articles in top international journals like *Industrial Marketing Management*, *Journal of Business & Industrial Marketing*, *Entrepreneurship and Regional Development*, and *International Small Business Journal*.

Mika Viljanen works as the Acting Professor of Obligation Law at the Faculty of Law, University of Turku. In his research, he focuses on the regulation of financial markets, private law theory and contract and tort law. He is also working for a number of interdisciplinary research projects, such as REBUS.

Vilma Vuori works as an assistant professor in the research group "Networked Value Systems" at the University of Vaasa. Her research focuses on knowledge management and value creation in networks. She is particularly interested in knowledge sharing in inter-organizational networks as well as the role of social media in intra-organizational knowledge sharing.

Robin Wikström works as a Researcher in Industrial Management at Åbo Akademi University, Finland. His research interests circle around decision-making and analytics.

Joakim Wincent is a Professor in Entrepreneurship and Management at Luleå University of Technology/Hanken School of Economics. He is also a visiting professor at the University of Vaasa. His research focuses largely on strategic interfirm relations, as well as effectiveness implications of start-ups and various change programs in larger companies.

Milla Wirén works as a doctoral candidate in the University of Turku. Her research area is behavioral strategy in international business, a research stream that explores the impact of individual level drivers and assumptions on the strategy process and performance on the firm level. She has an extensive previous career in music, communications, and management consulting, and continues as a board member in the SME sector.

Juho Ylimäki is an assistant professor in the research group "Networked Value Systems" at the University of Vaasa. He takes a special interest in relational business practices such as customer and supplier involvement in new product and service development. As a founder of Improve Research Ltd. he has conducted dozens of projects helping small- and medium-sized companies to collect and analyze customer information to facilitate their product and service development.

Peter Zettinig is currently a University Research Fellow and Adjunct Professor in International Business at the University of Turku, in Finland. One of his current collaborative research projects within the REBUS program is focused on strategizing processes of Multinational Corporations which attempt to shift power asymmetries and build inter-firm strategies within their industrial networks.

List of Figures

List of Tables

1

Introduction

Jukka Vesalainen, Katri Valkokari, and Magnus Hellström

Engaged Scholarship in Network Management Studies

A network as a form of organizing economic activity has been traditionally positioned in between markets and hierarchies. Markets are coordinated by the *invisible hand*, a metaphor that refers to the power of market mechanism. Hierarchies, again, are developed by the *visible hand*, referring to the intra-organizational power that derives its legitimacy

J. Vesalainen (✉)
University of Vaasa, Vaasa, Finland

K. Valkokari
VTT Technical Research Center of Finland, Tampere, Finland

M. Hellström
Åbo Akademi University, Turku, Finland

J. Vesalainen et al. (eds.), *Practices for Network Management*,
DOI 10.1007/978-3-319-49649-8_1

from organizational authority. In this setting, a network is considered a hybrid model coordinated by both invisible and visible hands (Powell 1990). In fact, networks are coordinated by three different mechanisms. In addition to hierarchical power residing in inter-organizational dependencies and the use of market mechanism, trust has been considered the third independent coordination mechanism in networks (Adler 2001). Trust, unity, commitment, and so-called relational norms constitute the basis for *relational business practices* (as opposed to *transactional*). It is, however, important to observe that these practices are always intertwined with other practices that do not have relational origins, but competitive and hierarchical ones. Thus, network management is a mix of all these mechanisms with varying emphasis. While this book approaches inter-organizational relationships and interaction from the relational perspective, it examines relational practices within the comprehensive context constituted by the three mechanisms of organizing economic activity mentioned above.

Today network management and *relational view* (Dyer and Singh 1998) are established concepts in the academic field and there are several partially overlapping academic discussions on (inter-organizational) relationships, alliances, networks, and other collaborative business settings.[1] Still, firms struggle with implementing the approach and easily turn to a transactional business conduct, not the least due to failing attempts to convince their business partners (i.e. their networks) of the benefits of a relational approach. Moreover, the hybrid form of organizing is all the time finding new, specific areas of application, such as innovation ecosystems or, more generally speaking, various meta-organizational contexts (Gulati et al. 2012).

One of the key problems with applying network theories (and looking beyond the single-firm perspective) in practice and managing them as one entity is the fact that networks and their management are a multi-level and systemic phenomenon. At least three levels can be found. *First*, they manifest themselves at the dyadic level of interaction in a partnership type of buyer–seller relationship. *Second*, networks are triadic

[1] Throughout the book we use the term "network" as a general expression for various network constellations (dyadic business relationships, groups of firms, and even business ecosystems). If the term "network" refers to a certain type of network, it is defined more closely.

and multi-firm constellations, which look for collaborative advantage by joining forces against competitors. *Third*, at the ecosystems level, the symbiosis of different firms and their relationships constitutes a competitive platform (especially in an innovation context), and their objective is to outperform other ecosystems or firms outside these systems by superior mutual strategic and operational fit. It is worth noting, however, that a network or business relationship is not usually considered a managed entity. Even if the actors in these relationships have common goals, the managerial power to implement those goals is much weaker than in an intra-organizational context. The wider the network, the less manageable it is as an entity.

Hence, there seems to be a need for more actionable knowledge and tools for managing business networks over inter-organizational boundaries. To our knowledge, there are very few research-based tools[2] addressing the challenges managers face, in particular the ones that are used as a kind of boundary object in the relationship or network. This book aims to fill that gap in the network management literature by presenting a set of research-based tools that managers may find helpful in managing networks. Pursuing engaged scholarship (Van de Ven 2007), however, does not mean a mere managerial contribution, but can at best provide new insights for theory building. As the relational approach and network organization are applied in new areas, we can, through the tools, obtain new information, for example, on the impact of contextual factors. Increase in digitalization and globalization (and hence competition) also calls for new, often practice-based, network management theories. Moreover, for knowledge to be actionable, it must bear on what and how managers do in reality, that is, praxis at the micro-level. Not only is such reality at best embedded in these tools but it also manifests itself in their sometimes unexpected use (Jarzabkowski and Kaplan 2015). Tools-in-use offers an interesting new point of view within the emerging strategy-as-practice discourse (Jarzabkowski and Kaplan 2015). Furthermore, research on tools-in-use may offer a deeper understanding on what is considered to be important when crossing inter-organizational boundaries at the network level and, conversely, what is not. In other words, certain tools are selected

[2] The term "tool" is defined as a generic name for frameworks, concepts, models, or methods.

for creating common language about networks' goals as well as offering spaces for the negotiation of interests. This brings out new understanding on the relational business practices, that is, instrumental aspects and institutional norms guiding the praxis of managers. Advocating a practice view within network management can thus be seen as one of the first steps toward something we term *network-as-practice* approach(cf. Chakrabarti et al. 2013). This is also the grand theoretical aim of the book. We shall elaborate the concept further in the concluding chapter of this book.

The Purpose of the Book: Novel Tools for Better Networking Praxis

Traditionally, management has been an intra-organizational function that gets its legitimacy from organizational hierarchy. However, in the network-era, many organizational actors in positions of management or expertise increasingly play roles in building, organizing, coordinating, and developing business relationships, networks, or even entire ecosystems. In doing so, they face challenges on how to influence on the action of the partner firms as well as to how to align their own firms with partners. Such "boundary spanners" strive to build shared understanding among the other members in a network. Further, each function within an organization (from sourcing to sales) typically has its own views about how to act in business networks. In order to avoid such one-sided functional and firm-based views on managing within business relationships, there is a need for a novel and comprehensive managerial thought process for approaching networks as systems. This systems view of networks is one of the key principles underpinning this book and also forms the basis for the "networks dynamic"-framework presented further below.

As indicated above, it is our firm contention and belief that this complexity, brought about by the systemic nature of networks, can be rendered more manageable through suitable managerial tools. All managers are familiar with strategy-making tools such as SWOT analysis, BCG matrix, or Balanced Scorecard, which are used in daily managerial praxis to support situation analysis and to develop and analyze strategic choices. As argued above, there seems to be a lack of scientifically grounded

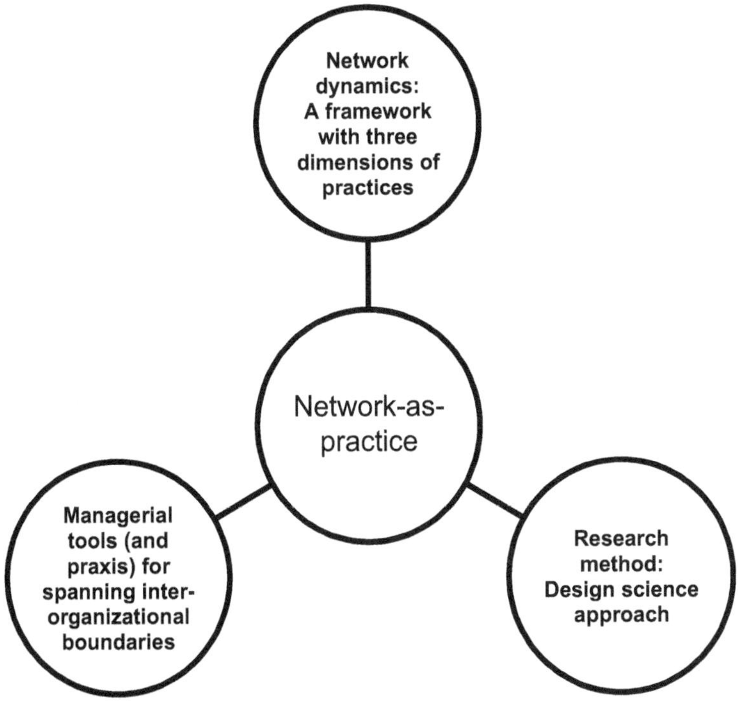

Fig. 1.1 Network-as-practice view of the book

network management tools that enable spanning inter-organizational boundaries. Our three-year participative research program, DIMECC REBUS[3] was set up to fill this void by addressing relational business practices. It has produced new practice-oriented knowledge on network management in the form of tools and practices; this book is the result of that development work. The DIMECC REBUS program (especially the tool development), as well as this book, is based on *three perspectives* that also form the basis for the *network-as-practice* view as shown in Fig. 1.1.

First, we defined a novel framework which shows networking in a new light, highlighting the comprehensiveness and systemic nature of the

[3] Dimecc, the Digital, Internet, Materials & Engineering Co-Creation Company, manages joint research and pre-emptive development actions. The program was funded by TEKES—the Finnish Funding Agency for Innovation, 22 participating companies, and 7 participating research institutions.

phenomenon (presented in the next section), as well as three practices driving network dynamics. The developed tools and practices are positioned into this framework to logically structure the presentation of the tools.

Second, we have followed the principles of *design science* to maximize the practical relevance of tools and practices to be developed. Even though our ideas for developing solutions for network management problems derive from theory, we do not strive for scientific validity but rather for practical relevance. To achieve this, all the tools are developed in close interaction with real-life boundary spanners and are laid open to practical judgment by testing them in various network contexts. Actually, we take a critical stance toward the tools developed, and together with the practitioners involved in the development process, we analyze the tools, their usage, and their value for real-life network management.

Third, we approach networking from the boundary spanning perspective. The tools and practices are expected to help boundary spanning managers (e.g. supply chain managers, purchasing managers, or sales managers) overcome the evident cognitive, social, affective, and competition-based boundaries in inter-organizational settings. By adopting the boundary spanning approach, we want to highlight networking as an issue common to network members—not a firm-centered issue typical to supply chain management or customer relationship management. No firm can network alone or impose only its own will. They have to cope jointly with contradicting strategic and operative goals, and in this task the boundary spanners play a critical role. Throughout the research work, we followed a specific "managerial tools" perspective. However, we do not focus on tools as mere "materialized objects", but highlight the *use* of tools (managerial processes) as another important facet of network management. Consequently, with *network-as-practice* we refer to the combination of tools, their use, and the benefits they bring about with the three practices describing fundamental differentiation between organizational intentions. This is in line with the three general steps through which managerial tools are to be understood: tool selection, application, and outcomes (Jarzabkowski and Kaplan 2015).

While we are able to present a collection of 17 novel managerial tools for network management, we do not present them as an exhaustive or even an ideal toolbox, but rather as a set of theoretically grounded tools that have been developed and tested in practice, and which have varying practical value in terms of collaborative advantage for networking firms in different situations and business environments. We believe each tool in this book has significant value. At the very least, a reader will get fresh and theoretically grounded ideas about how to improve inter-organizational interaction by using a deliberate managerial approach.

In the following sections, we explain in more detail the three perspectives that guided the creation of new understanding about network-as-practice and development of relational network management tools.

Network Dynamics: A Systemic and Comprehensive Framework

In order to manage inter-organizational relationships and networks, one has to understand how they work. Therefore, in addition to highlighting the coherency of our development efforts, we defined a unifying conceptual framework that strives to grasp the very essence of network dynamics (Fig. 1.2). A recent meta-analysis of inter-organizational relationships found two basic purposes for their various forms: *co-exploration* and *co-exploitation* (Parmigiani and Rivera-Santos 2011). Co-exploration is defined as a cooperative agreement to create new knowledge, tasks, functions, or activities. In other words, it creates new business potential. Co-exploitation, on the contrary, refers to cooperative activities that deploy existing resources to generate value. While co-exploration focuses on learning and innovation, co-exploitation focuses on expansion and efficiency.

The essence of our framework is three network practices that fall in line with this fundamental differentiation between organizational intentions. The networks-as-knowledge-creating platforms perspective represents the co-explorative purpose of inter-organizational interaction, and the networks-as-value-generating entities perspective represents the exploitative inter-organizational interaction. In addition to these two funda-

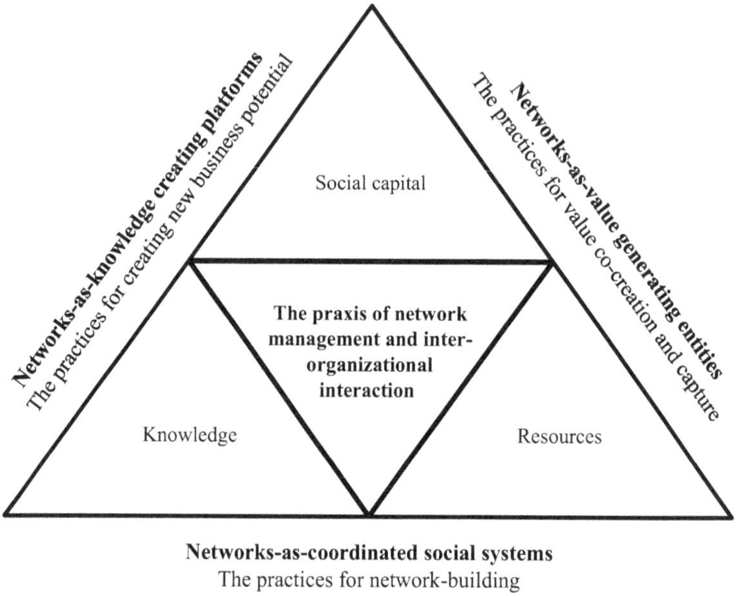

Fig. 1.2 The building blocks of network dynamics and management

mental perspectives, we highlight the importance of a third practice, which serves as an enabler for the two former ones and addresses network-building. These practices are based on the social embeddedness of inter-organizational relationships approaching networks-as-coordinated social systems.

The practices, in turn, rest on three fundamental cornerstones:

- **The resource base**. Firm-specific tangible resources and capabilities in a network available for the network's use, usually firm-specific property, can be shared through legal arrangements
- **Knowledge**. Individual and firm-specific information, knowledge, and skills relevant for business purposes usually possessed by firms, but more easily transferrable and shared than tangible resources
- **Social capital**. The prevailing relational atmosphere in a network in terms of trust, unity, and social norms, typically a product of interpersonal and inter-organizational interaction, not a property of any firm

The framework, illustrated in Fig. 1.2, helps us understand the network dynamics from a systemic perspective and therefore helps form the basis for relational business practices pursuing collaborative and firm-specific competitive advantage through co-exploitation or co-exploration. It is also important to note the managerial point of view concerning the practices as they actually constitute the basis for network management. The managerial activities are at the core of the framework and give networks their goal-oriented and intentional character.

Based on the three cornerstones, we can further elaborate on the three practices:

1. **Networks-as-coordinated social systems**. Social capital does not develop by accident, but has to be developed through deliberate managerial actions; this practice builds interpersonal and inter-organizational relationships. It relates to the fundamental problem of boundary spanning, that is, how to overcome cultural, social, and informational differences as well as competitive pressures to create a benign atmosphere for open and fruitful interaction between network members. However, no single manager is responsible for this kind of *network leadership*, but it is more or less the common activity of all network actors that affects the development of social capital. Network-building efforts are mainly embedded in daily interaction between network members. Various social events and deliberate actions alike are important, but a good network atmosphere is largely based on concrete acts and styles of communication when people interact in inter-organizational contexts.
2. **Networks-as-knowledge-creating platforms**. This practice consists of activities and interactions that enhance inter-organizational learning, knowledge integration, and new knowledge development; it also explores new opportunities and creates new business potential. The question is about inter-organizational learning, which has two facets. First, networks learn as networks, which means that network members develop common practices and therefore learn to act more innovatively and effectively together. Second, networks serve as learning contexts for individual firms. Firms can thus develop firm-specific

knowledge and resources inspired and facilitated by the other network members. Furthermore, firm-specific and individual knowledge becomes available for network-level use if there is enough social capital in a network to interact openly and to co-create new knowledge and innovations. In practice, knowledge creation is about knowledge integration, and the results manifest themselves as improved business potential. Processes where firms involve their customers and suppliers in new product development represent typical network learning in practice. Still, in the current business environment, knowledge creation requires a broader view and involvement of other stakeholders than merely direct customers and suppliers.

3. **Networks-as-value-generating entities**. This is the practice that generates value for stakeholders in and outside the network; it is typically defined as a value stream, value chain, or value network. This practice generates and captures value by exploiting the resources, knowledge, and social capital in a network. It deploys the current resources of network firms by coordinating the inter-organizational value stream. The main task of network management is to coordinate the networks' resources into effective value generation. Both value creation and value capture must be considered. We highlight the term *optimized value creation and capture* to refer to the praxis based on the win–win principle. Getting rid of harmful zero-sum games in a network is a must if a network is aiming for collaborative advantage. Furthermore, the higher the quality of the resource base and the better it is coordinated as a value system, the better the value generation capability.

Design Approach to Maximize Practical Relevance

The research work was built on the principles of design science (Simon 1978). Due to its prescriptive nature, design science is usually contrasted with descriptive science. In mainstream descriptive sciences highlighting the validity of research, quality is judged by other researchers, whereas in design studies highlighting the relevance of research, quality is evaluated against practice and judged by practitioners (Romme 2003; van Aken 2005). Originally, the term *design science* referred to medicine and engineering (and other like disciplines), which share the characteristic of being solution-based. These practice-oriented disciplines are, however, grounded on theories from chemistry and physics, for example. With the help of design science, the common goal in our approaches has been the researcher developing a "means to an end", an artifact to solve a practical problem in network management (Holmström et al. 2009). This resonates well with the practice-based perspective we advocated earlier. Note that practice-theorists differentiate between practice, the institutionalized and more general form of activity-level undertakings, and praxis, the more emergent undertakings at the micro-level, that is, actual activities (Whittington 2006).

To meet the scientific quality, design science has to fulfill the following criteria: (1) the results have to be tested or justified in practice by practitioners; (2) the solution has to be grounded in certain theoretical principles; and (3) the solution has to be generalizable or transferrable into other contexts, too (cf. Romme 2003; van Aken 2004, 2005). Justification is usually realized through a participatory research design, where the solution is developed by researchers in collaboration with practitioners. Justification thus links the created artifacts with practitioner needs in real-life situations. The theoretical grounding of solutions connects a design study to the relevant previous knowledge and reveals the underlying generative mechanisms expected to deliver an anticipated effect. Thus, grounded practical solutions are not merely documented best practices but theoretically linked constructions with a deeper understanding of the premises and mechanisms related to the focal problem.

A design study is generally a solution to a specific problem, guiding practitioners to find the most appropriate way of acting in the situations they face in real-life work settings. A solution shows a context-specific way of acting to achieve anticipated results: in situation *x*, do *y* to achieve *z* (Argyris 1993; van Aken 2005). The instrumentality of design thinking refers both to tools and their use to solve problems or to generate value. Design thinking in general is interested in value generation and the following formula, which represents the design issue in its entirety: what + how = value. *What* represents tools as materialized objects, *how* represents the usage of tools, and *value* represents the perceived value as an outcome of the usage of the tool (Dorst 2011). In managerial practice this would be, for example, the use of the SWOT analysis framework (the tool) in a managerial team meeting; the members first present their own SWOT analysis of a situation (how the tool is used), leading to a rich analytical discussion and the best possible strategic decision in a certain situation (the value). The design task is thus about (1) definition of the value sought; (2) choice or development of a tool to be used; and (3) definition of the process and principles of the chosen tool's usage.

Design scientists talk about ill-defined (or wicked) problems and refer to situations where all the factors in the design task are unknown (see e.g. Buchanan 1992; Romme 2003). It is thus not always certain that the problem or value sought is clear from the very beginning of the design process. In these ambiguous situations, thinking backward is recommended, beginning with the definition of value. In fact, value and managerial interaction (the way the tools are used) form the core of the value-generating process. It is important to understand the generative mechanisms by which certain activities generate specific values. In the above SWOT example, the open interaction among a managerial team enabled the effective use of the tacit knowledge of all the team members. The team possibly succeeded in forming a common understanding of the decision situation and made the best possible strategic choice. An example of the generative mechanism of such a practice can be traced back to Nonaka and Takeuchi's (1995) SECI model, highlighting the mechanisms of the externalization of tacit knowledge. Thus, the main value-creating effect in the SWOT example was the link between value sought and the way the management team approached the task. The tool as such (the SWOT analysis framework) represents a common way to rationalize the impact of internal strengths and weaknesses and external opportunities and threats. The tool also offers the management team a discursive template to approach the issue through a shared framework that gives analysis a clear structure and thus increases the effectiveness of interaction.

Managerial Tools for Spanning Inter-organizational Boundaries

As mentioned earlier in this introduction, management is basically an intra-organizational function that gets its legitimacy from organizational authority. However, many organizational actors in positions of management or expertise have a role in building, organizing, coordinating, and developing networks and business relationships, and they often face challenges what comes to influencing the conduct of the other firms in a network. These people are sometimes called *boundary spanners* and the work they do can be called *boundary spanning*. Boundary spanners use *boundary objects* and *boundary processes* in order to build shared understanding among the members of a network. In management literature, a *boundary* refers mainly to the challenges of knowledge transfer and creation between two different communities of practice (teams, departments, etc.). In organizational contexts, boundaries develop due to differences in language, expert terminology, managerial mindsets, goals, and other important cognitive and affective reasons (Hsiao et al. 2012). A community of practice is thus any constellation of experts who work closely together and share a common interest. Inside a firm, the various departments or teams represent typical communities of practice, where people use certain types of language and share similar views and a common understanding of best practices.

In inter-organizational context when complexity or uncertainty of the situation increases or when the knowledge boundary deepens due to different knowledge bases and dependencies of the cooperating communities of practice, the need for boundary spanning becomes more important. Within these more challenging cooperative contexts, the focus of spanning shifts from mere information sharing to the building of a shared understanding (Carlile 2004). Thus, processes which generate shared meanings (Dougherty 1992) become crucial as a means of dealing with the spanning problem. The need for effective boundary spanning also increases when parties have different interests and those interests collide (Carlile 2004).

Managerial tools represent “technologies of rationality” (March 2006) or “procedural rationality” (Simon 1978) by helping managers to make rational choices in the ambiguous situations they face in managerial reality. On the other hand, they illustrate the practice relevant in a certain network management setting. Managerial tools are, then, supposed to structure strategy-makers’ thinking by offering models of causal structures, providing spaces for collecting data, and establishing decision rules for selection among alternatives (Jarzabkowski and Kaplan 2015). Along with rationalization, managerial tools can be considered “discursive templates” for dialogue (Tsoukas 2009, 947), thus enabling shared sense-making in a group of actors. Leadership is mostly based on high-quality communication, and the key to good communication is a mutual understanding based on language, terminology, analytical frameworks, and cognitive structures. Managerial tools may offer templates for dialogue to improve the actor’s ability to participate in the discussion and thus work toward a common understanding and make the best possible decisions. Managerial tools also have a role in sense-giving when a person in a managerial position tries to “interpret and sell” his or her vision or other strategic goals and means to the members of a network.

Managerial tools can be considered a materialization of managerial praxis, that is, they represent its instrumental aspect. Tools are not self-sufficient, however, but need to be used in order to get results. Although there is no single right way to use a certain managerial tool, there should be a clear understanding among the users of how to use a tool in a managerial process. Research has shown that the practices vary even within the same planning episode, thus indicating that the users’ interpretation of a tool’s inherent logic may be unstable.

Boundary spanners use these managerial tools as boundary objects, which function as a means for information transfer, building of shared meanings, knowledge creation, and alignment of interests (Carlile 2002). Effective boundary objects have to be applicable for various different communities of practice in those situational practices that belong to their daily work. At the same time, a boundary object should also be robust enough to serve as a platform that steers common interest and discussion. An effective boundary object is also tangible, concrete, up to date, and accessible (Levina and Vaast 2005).

The Organization of the Book

In this introduction, we have argued for the need for a book on network management tools, outlined the purpose and basic ideas underpinning it, and presented a novel system framework for understanding network management. The rest of book is organized in line with the systems framework presented above (Fig. 1.2). Thus, in the first part of the book, we present the papers related to *Networks-as-coordinated social systems* practices; in the second part, you will find the papers dealing with the *Networks-as-knowledge-creating platforms* practices; and the third part covers papers addressing the *Networks-as-value-generating entities* practices. A short introduction to each part, further elaborates mechanisms and summarizing the corresponding papers from the framework's point of view, is also provided. The concluding chapter develops the network-as-practice view, outlines some managerial implications, and includes a future research agenda on the topic.

References

Adler, P. S. (2001). Market, hierarchy, and trust: The knowledge economy and the future of capitalism. *Organization Science, 12*(2), 215–234 Retrieved from http://search.ebscohost.com/login.aspx?direct=true&db=bth&AN=5159345&site=ehost-live.

Argyris, C. (1993). *Knowledge for action: A guide to overcoming barriers to organizational change.* San Francisco, CA: Jossey-Bass.

Buchanan, R. (1992). Wicked problems in design thinking. *Wicked Problems in Design Thinking, 8*(2), 5–21.

Carlile, P. R. (2002). A pragmatic view of knowledge and boundaries: Boundary objects in new product development. *Organization Science, 13*(4), 442–455 Retrieved from http://search.ebscohost.com/login.aspx?direct=true&db=bth&AN=6993581&site=ehost-live.

Carlile, P. R. (2004). Transferring, translating, and transforming: An integrative framework for managing knowledge across boundaries. *Organization Science, 15*(5), 555–568. doi:10.1287/orsc.1040.0094.

Chakrabarti, R., Ramos, C., & Henneberg, S. (2013). Network dynamics in the UK pharmaceutical network—A network-as-practice perspective. *Industrial*

Marketing Management, 42(3), 356–371. doi:10.1016/j.indmarman.2012.12.009.

Dorst, K. (2011). The core of "design thinking" and its application. *Design Studies, 32*(6), 521–532. doi:10.1016/j.destud.2011.07.006.

Dougherty, D. (1992). Interpretive barriers to successful product innovation in large firms. *Organization Science, 3*(2), 179–202. doi:10.1287/orsc.3.2.179.

Dyer, J. H., & Singh, H. (1998). The relational view: Cooperative strategy and sources of interorganizational competitive advantage. *Academy of Management Review, 23*(4), 660–679. doi:10.5465/AMR.1998.1255632.

Gulati, R., Puranam, P., & Tushman, M. (2012). Meta-organization design: Rethinking design in interorganizational and community contexts. *Strategic Management Journal, 33*(6), 571–586. doi:10.1002/smj.1975.

Holmström, J., Ketokivi, M., & Hameri, A.-P. (2009). Bridging practice and theory: A design science approach. *Decision Sciences, 40*(1), 65–87. doi:10.1111/j.1540-5915.2008.00221.x.

Hsiao, R.-L., Tsai, D.-H., & Lee, C.-F. (2012). Collaborative knowing: The adaptive nature of cross-boundary spanning. *Journal of Management Studies, 49*(3), 463–491. doi:10.1111/j.1467-6486.2011.01024.x.

Jarzabkowski, P., & Kaplan, S. (2015). Strategy tools-in-use: A framework for understanding "technologies of rationality" in practice. *Strategic Management Journal, 36*(4), 537–558. doi:10.1002/smj.2270.

Levina, N., & Vaast, E. (2005). The emergence of boundary spanning competence in practice: Implications for implementation and use of information systems. *MIS Quarterly, 29*(2), 335–363 Retrieved from http://dl.acm.org/citation.cfm?id=2017254.2017262.

March, J. G. (2006). Rationality, foolishness, and adaptive intelligence. *Strategic Management Journal, 27*(3), 201–214. doi:10.1002/smj.515.

Nonaka, I., & Takeuchi, H. (1995). *The knowledge-creating company how Japanese companies create the dynamics of innovation*. New York: Oxford University Press.

Parmigiani, A., & Rivera-Santos, M. (2011). Clearing a path through the forest: A meta-review of interorganizational relationships. *Journal of Management, 37*(4), 1108–1136. doi:10.1177/0149206311407507.

Powell, W. W. (1990). Neither market nor hierarchy: Network forms of organization. *Research in Organizational Behavior, 12*, 295 .Retrieved from http://search.ebscohost.com/login.aspx?direct=true&db=bth&AN=6815445&site=ehost-live

Romme, A. G. (2003). Making a difference: Organization as design. *Organization Science, 14*(5), 558–573.

Simon, H. (1978). Rationality as process and as product of thought. *American Economic Association Review, 68*(2), 1–16. doi:10.2307/1816653.

Tsoukas, H. (2009). A dialogical approach to the creation of new knowledge in organizations. *Organization Science, 20*(6), 941–957. doi:10.1287/orsc.1090.0435.

van Aken, J. E. (2004). Management research based on the paradigm of the design sciences: The quest for field-tested and grounded technological rules. *Journal of Management Studies, 41*(2), 219–246. doi:10.1111/j.1467-6486.2004.00430.x.

van Aken, J. E. (2005). Management research as a design science: Articulating the research products of mode 2 knowledge production in management. *British Journal of Management, 16*(1), 19–36. doi:10.1111/j.1467-8551.2005.00437.x.

Van de Ven, A. (2007). *Engaged scholarship—A guide for organizational and social research*. Oxford, UK: Oxford University Press.

Whittington, R. (2006). Completing the practice turn in strategy research. *Organization Studies, 27*(5), 613–634. doi:10.1177/0170840606064101.

Part I

Networks-as-Coordinated Social Systems

2

Introduction to Part I—Viewing Networks as Social Systems

Peter Zettinig and Mika Viljanen

In industry settings that are defined by stagnation or diminishing markets, firms often face pressure to rationalize and seek sustainable margins. Three responses are typical. Firms may (a) seek new economies of scale and attempt to increase their overall market size or decrease costs; (b) develop economies of scope and seek new synergies between the different activities the firm is performing so as to distribute overhead and fixed costs across a wider range of products and services, often achieved by measures such as cross-selling; or (c) differentiate through innovation and forge new markets or expand existing ones.

While options (a) and (b) typically entail cost-leadership approaches (e.g., more standardization), increasing productivity (e.g., increasing the output per given resource at the same cost) or cost-saving approaches (e.g., relocating activities to lower cost locations), option (c) is qualitatively quite different. This option requires the firm to develop new products,

P. Zettinig (✉) • M. Viljanen
University of Turku, Turku, Finland

J. Vesalainen et al. (eds.), *Practices for Network Management*,
DOI 10.1007/978-3-319-49649-8_2

services, systems, or business models. While firms typically organize and implement the first two options through traditional planned research and development activities, the third option has components characterized by high complexity and often a degree of uncertainty.

In recent decades, many industrial firms have attempted to implement the third option by developing and launching different solution business models. Solution business models require constant product and business models innovations. However, the biggest challenges often stem from the deep-cutting transformations that such solution business models instigate in value chain constellations, market structures, internal processes, and participant mindsets. The instigating firms must be able to, for example, recraft their product offerings and develop often unprecedented service capabilities, challenge and transform stubborn core assumptions about the firm's role in the value chain, and transform internal mindsets on both the firm's own role and the roles of its partners by redesigning existing, often already firmly established processes, routines, and mindsets.

Despite its vast scope, internal change is often not enough. Solution business refers to the cocreationary and cooperative relationships wherein former "customers", "suppliers", and "contractors" turn into value-creation partners. Thus, the instigator firms must be able to trigger similar transformations across organizational boundaries (see Tuli et al. 2007; Windahl and Lakemond 2006).

Triggering, controlling, and sustaining these internal and external transformation processes is a risky proposition at best. Consequently, solutions business model launches are often complex, uncertain, and unpredictable events fraught with surprises, unexpected difficulties, and even failures, as the ongoing environment is typically stacked against those who seek to disrupt the status quo. Success is typically conditional upon a kind of stubbornness, strong beliefs, and unwavering commitment to a firm's vision, as transformational processes may have plenty of doubters and the excuses not to instigate change can be many. Senior management in instigator firms must foster a can-do attitude, shared across the entire organization. These firms must also cultivate a new sensitive awareness of the probable and improbable changes in the environment and the solution delivery network and be able to interpret these changes in terms of the perspective of their own transformation to solution business. When this internal mindset is in place, the organization is internally set to embark on the new journey.

The business environment is typically stacked against transformation and transformers. What, then, do firms need to do to overcome resistance from outside? Power, many say, is the key to success. Firms need to gain power in their industry and across their value network in order to create new markets. This aspect raises the question of how power forms in an industry and how a firm can use the power it has to control its networks. Some say that a firm has power when others are dependent on it, on either its resources or capabilities, and that firm is in a position to influence how others achieve their own objectives. How much one firm depends on others, on the other hand, will define its degree of power asymmetry or who is more powerful in a given network. In this current narrative, success is dependent on the instigator finding the right position and the efficient levers it can use to force the other actors to submit. While this is a very appreciable economic explanation of power, the explanation has clear limitations in the context of creating new markets or increasing market size because the objects within which power can or should be exercised do not yet exist.

The other possible approach for organizations is having a different understanding of business relationships. Whereas in the power view, business is a bloody fight, a competitive zero-sum game where one actor's gain is another's loss, a co-creating, trust-based accounting stresses the potential gains to all participants from the market structure changes. The instigator does not seek to force action against the will of the competing actors but rather demonstrate and convince those actors that its offering is value-adding for all value chain actors. This approach requires a novel set of capabilities. The instigators have to develop real value-adding service offerings and instruments that demonstrate the value of the offering and how it adds to outside actors, foster trust in its offerings' potential and implement pricing models to allocate that added value legitimately between all the value chain partners. This approach fits the solution business development processes better than the former power narrative. A non-existing market is thus created via a recursive co-creating negotiation process.

Both the power and trust-based approaches will result in long and winding market and network creation processes. After the initial creation phase, solutions business value networks will remain complex social systems. How then can we understand this very abstract process of market creation that redefines industry structures?

We believe it is through action, as actions create structure. Creating new markets requires people who see an empty field as an opportunity to shape their own preferable paths, not see a threat. These pioneers must be neither scared of getting their hands dirty nor fear the absence of structure and take that absence as a negative cue. Instead, the lack of structure must be seen as an opportunity to create a new more desirable structure. It requires these pioneers to have the capacity and the belief in their own abilities to carve the new path, a can-do identity that sees no limitations to using that capacity in full. They must also interpret what is missing in a positive fashion as a way to shape the things still to come.

Actions create structure. In the power narrative, pioneers and the early adopters define the new dependencies, and these dependencies then define the network's power positions. In the co-creation narrative, the pioneers go out on a limb and develop and push their vision of a future where they believe everybody is better off.

What can top management learn from this example? Find the pioneers who can imagine new markets, who are committed to shaping the paths and creating something new. Empower their capacities and make "doing it" a part of organizational identity—the things we do that make us enduringly different—which will generate the movement that will create momentum through early adopters; that momentum will then structure your desirable future and deliver it.

This sub-section of the book is concerned with the approaches that shape network leadership that then develops new ways of being a pioneer in determining the market and structure of an industry. The collection of approaches introduced here can be seen as a sequence that helps connect what we assume to be and what could be when we better understand the challenges and thinking of network partners.

This section begins with the chapter, "Stakeholder Identification, Salience, and Strategic Mindset Analysis", which explains how and why certain members in industrial networks should matter when you strategize or develop new business models. It answers the question of whom we need to collaborate with and why, and it forms the basis for understanding network partners' situational settings and the rationales these partners display when going about their business. It provides a deeper insight into the possible decision-making options they are enabled and/or constrained by. This aspect is to be the starting point for the next four articles in this section, which are concerned with network partners' sense-making.

The second chapter, "Leading Human Values in Complex Environments", focuses on the question of how operational level leadership is based on basic human values and understanding which then furthers the leaders in the network to let them better influence their partners to move in a desirable direction. The third chapter, "Network Picturing As a Sense-making Tool to Envision Network Change", uses an approach that reveals the preferences and requirements of network partners to others to enable focal managers to take the driver's seat and illustrates an approach that uses sense-making of the processes between network partners to develop new ways to span organizational boundaries. All these chapters focus on the social component of understanding network partners, and they relate to the subsequent paper in this part of the book by showing how different approaches to sense-making guide further actions. That chapter, "Functional Contracting for Network Creation and Governance", is an approach for creating and governing industrial solution business networks. The paper conceptualizes the many challenges instigator firms face during the network creation phase as integration problems and puts forth a functional contracting framework to overcome these challenges. The final paper in this part of the book, entitled "Boundary Spanning and The Art of Persuasion", returns to the question of power and trust and how both are established in a social network context. It guides our attention toward individuals and the social contexts within their networks as well as their abilities to influence, shape, and negotiate how organizational boundaries can be spanned by utilizing relational persuasion tactics.

All chapters, we believe, share one common feature. They all consider solution business value as complex social systems. These social systems are networks of multiple actors and must be painstakingly created, coordinated, and managed. The tools used for these processes, however, have to be developed and negotiated by pioneers in each unique network assemblage. Each network will need its own park with unpaved streets where networking-in-practice processes can take abstract tools and fit them successfully into individual contexts.

References

Tuli, K. R., Kohli, A. K., & Bharadwaj, S. G. (2007). Rethinking customer solutions: From product bundles to relational processes. *Journal of Marketing, 71*(3), 1–17.

Windahl, C., & Lakemond, N. (2006). Developing integrated solutions: The importance of relationships within the network. *Industrial Marketing Management, 35*(7), 806–818. doi:10.1016/j.indmarman.2006.05.010.

3

Stakeholder Identification, Salience, and Strategic Mindset Analysis

Danijela Majdenic, Jonathan Van Mumford, Milla Wirén, and Peter Zettinig

Introduction

Stakeholder Theory: Who or What Really Counts?

Operating within a particular network for some years may lead a firm to take for granted the relationships it has with its external stakeholders, the nature of these relationships, and their importance; the truth of the assumptions upon which such judgments are based may go unquestioned in the course of "business as usual." For the most part, a firm may only focus on the relationships it has with its direct customers or suppliers, and may be blind to its position relative to other actors within the greater business ecosystem in which it resides. It is therefore a potentially important and valuable exercise for managers to periodically evaluate who the firm's stakeholders are, how they are important to the firm, how

D. Majdenic (✉) • J. Van Mumford • M. Wirén • P. Zettinig
University of Turku, Turku, Finland

J. Vesalainen et al. (eds.), *Practices for Network Management*,
DOI 10.1007/978-3-319-49649-8_3

the firm is important to them, and most importantly, the reasons why. For conducting such an exercise, a firm's managers must critically evaluate their assumptions, test what they believe they know about their position relative to others, and potentially uncover unexpected information that could open new paths to create value through strategic action. On the other hand, managers who take what they believe they know about their stakeholders for granted do so at their own peril, with unidentified stakeholder interests representing both potential opportunities as well as potential threats.

Firms operating in industries characterized by long and complex value chains are particularly susceptible to either holding false assumptions about or being ignorant of where value is actually created, who it is created by, and for whom. While a company may know what its direct customers demand, they may not know what the needs of their customers' customers are, or who their suppliers' suppliers are, and so on. Such knowledge can be invaluable, and represent unexplored opportunities to implement more farsighted strategies to help cement or improve a firm's network position. The first step for managers who wish to map out their firm's position in the greater network is to *identify* who their stakeholders are, and determine in what way they are *salient*. In the second step, managers must ask themselves "what to do next?"

Strategy: Business Environment, Mindset, and Rationality

There is a classical way of answering the question, "what to do next?" It requires formulating a plan about the desirable outcome and finding ways to reach it. These plans hinge on the existing knowledge of not only the capabilities of the company but also of the business environment in which the company operates. In order to create this roadmap-type strategy, a company must know what to expect along the road, which is increasingly difficult as the business environments of companies become more complex, even threatening. Planning a strategy reliant on the perceived stability and predictability of the environment and disregarding disruptive dynamism of the market can be fatal: if the plan relies on false assumptions of the environment, not only are the chosen ways of pursuing the goal ineffective but also the definition of what a desirable goal is may be flawed.

In addition to the impacts from environmental variation, strategizing is also governed by the mindsets of the people participating in the strategy work. Underlying the roadmap style, strategic planning is a specific understanding of rationality: rational behavior begins with choosing a goal, and continues with seeking the means to achieve it. However, just like the stable market is one of many possible environments, this definition of rationality is one of many possible mindsets driving the behavior of decision-makers. In the contemporary business world, where an increasing amount of the value a company produces is actually co-created in networks, understanding this diversity is vital. Network-level strategic alignment may be difficult to come by when the networking partners each engage in mutual strategy work armed with dramatically different assumptions of the business environment and rationality.

In the following paragraphs, we describe a two-pronged tool for stakeholder identification and mindset analysis and the theories upon which it is grounded, which can be used to systematically classify and compare those stakeholders that are important and influential to a firm's operations. The practical tool defined in this chapter consists of methods that companies can use to assess the following vital but basic assumptions inherent in both their own strategy work and in that of their networking partners: Who are our stakeholders and why are they important to us? What kinds of environments are we doing business in? What do we consider rational behavior? Furthermore, networking partners can employ some possible methods illustrated here in order to establish a common ground upon which they can build value co-creating network-level strategies. Therefore, the tool serves a fourfold purpose:

1. It helps to identify the network surrounding the firm and the firm's position within it.
2. It helps to assess the nature of the environments in which network-level strategies are formed.
3. It aids organizational units in identifying their own underlying strategic mindsets as well as those of their networking partners.

4. It poses relevant questions that illuminate how an organizational unit can bridge the different mindsets identified in network partners under given environmental conditions.

We go on to describe how the tool was utilized by a systems supplier, and how it enabled them to make the transition from being merely a transactional business to being a solutions provider.

Theoretical Background

The Theory of Stakeholder Identification and Salience

According to Mitchell et al. (1997, 854), the theory of stakeholder identification and salience asks a fundamental question in a systematic way: "which groups are stakeholders deserving or requiring management attention, and which are not?" To find the answers to those questions, managers should further inquire: "who (or what) are the stakeholders of the firm?" and "to whom (or what) do managers pay attention?" (Mitchell et al. 1997, 853). The first step for managers is stakeholder identification—managers are asked to logically identify who the firm's stakeholders are; the second step is stakeholder salience—managers are asked to classify the identified stakeholders using three attributes: power, legitimacy, and urgency.

Who are stakeholders? In *Strategic Management: A Stakeholder Approach*, Freeman (2010, 46) defines a stakeholder as "any group or individual who can affect or is affected by the achievement of the organization's objectives." The first part of the tool we present in this chapter involves stakeholder analysis. The first step of stakeholder analysis is to identify those stakeholders who have the ability to influence, in a positive or negative way, the firm's outcomes of strategy, behavior, or success. After identification of the stakeholders, the next step is to classify them according to the number of attributes (power, legitimacy, and urgency) they have, if any (see Fig. 3.1).

According to Mitchell et al. (1997), power, legitimacy, and urgency present the three most important relationship attributes among stake-

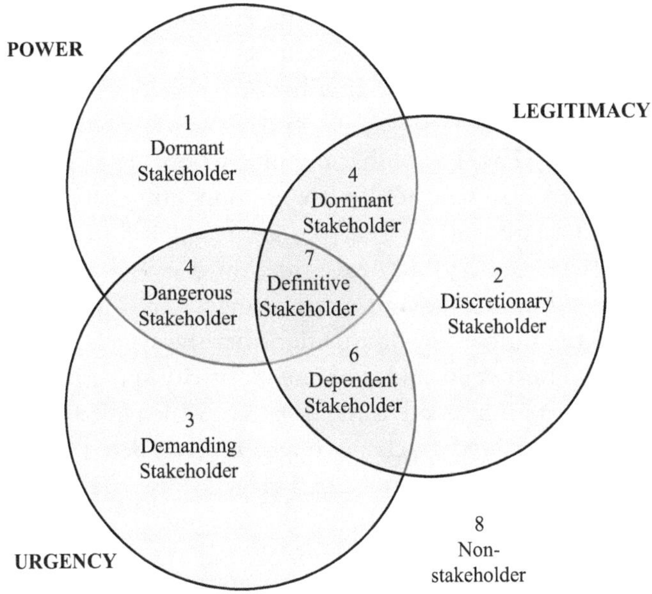

Fig. 3.1 Stakeholder typology (Mitchell et al. 1997, 874)

holders who have independent or interactive roles in the business scenario. It is important to note that all three attributes are transitory; each can be gained or lost over time.

Power is the first attribute proposed by Mitchell et al. (1997) and it suggests that one stakeholder has the ability to influence another stakeholder to do something that otherwise would not have been done. Stakeholders with "high" power possess the ability to influence the firm's survival by controlling the ownership of, and/or access to, various resources which are relevant to the firm. However, some stakeholders might not have power but can still influence the firm's present and future because the claims they have upon the firm are legitimate.

The second attribute, legitimacy, is defined as "a generalized perception or assumption that the actions of an entity are desirable, proper or appropriate within some socially constructed system of norms, values, beliefs and definitions" (Suchman 1995, 574). Here, legitimacy refers to the relationship between the stakeholder and the firm, and to the stakeholder's actions in terms of its expectations of properness, or appropriateness. By seeing legitimacy as desirable, stakeholders' actions within a system of standards, values, beliefs, and definitions can be used on different levels of analysis (i.e., in an individual, organizational, or societal way) (Wood 1991).

Mitchell et al. (1997) state that the interactions with, and dynamics between, the firm and stakeholders are not only influenced by attributes of power and legitimacy. Indeed, powerful and legitimate stakeholders may not have cause to influence the firm due to a lack of urgency. Urgency is the third and final primary attribute and is understood to be a measure of the immediacy of attention that the stakeholder merits. It is based on two further attributes—time sensitivity and criticality. While time sensitivity is understood as the degree to which a managerial delay in attending a stakeholder's claims might be considered unacceptable, criticality refers to the importance of a claim or the relationship to the stakeholder Mitchell et al. (1997).

The theory of stakeholder identification and salience is further complicated by the fact that it is also a dynamic theory, and stakeholders may gain or lose salience to a firm depending on circumstance. Gain or loss can happen for three reasons:

1. Stakeholder attributes are variable, not steady state.
2. Stakeholder attributes are a socially constructed, not objective, reality.
3. Consciousness and willful exercise may or may not be present (Mitchell et al. 1997, 868).

The level and nature of stakeholder salience depends on different combinations of the power, legitimacy, and urgency attributes, and is commonly depicted as a Venn diagram (Fig. 3.1), where the three criteria overlap to create seven stakeholder types. A final "non-stakeholder" group lies outside the diagram, creating eight stakeholder types in total. These stakeholder types and their attributes are summarized in Table 3.1.

As can be seen from the table, stakeholders with one of the three attributes are labeled as latent stakeholders and include dormant, discretionary, and demanding stakeholders. Even though dormant stakeholders possess power to enforce their will, due to lack of legitimacy and urgency,

Table3.1 Stakeholder classification (adapted from Mitchell et al., 1997)

Attributes	Stakeholder subcategory	Stakeholder category	Stakeholder salience
Power	Dormant	Latent	Low
Legitimacy	Discretionary		
Urgency	Demanding		
Power & Legitimacy	Dominant	Expectant	Moderate
Power & Urgency	Dangerous		
Legitimacy & Urgency	Dependent		
Power & Legitimacy & Urgency	Definitive	Definitive	High
None/can gain	Potential or non-stakeholders	N/A	N/A

their power remains dormant. However, there is a high possibility that dormant stakeholders can gain urgency and legitimacy. Examples include stakeholders who could potentially coerce or benefit the firm greatly through contributions of resources (money), or stakeholders who could potentially bring attention to the firm (positive or negative) through the media. Discretionary stakeholders possess legitimacy but are not able to influence the firm due to their lack of power or urgent claims. Examples include voluntary organizations and NGOs. Demanding stakeholders have urgent claims, but without power and legitimacy, those claims cannot be enforced; for example, a lonely picketer.

Stakeholders who possess two of the three attributes are the expectant stakeholders and they include dominant, dangerous, and dependent stakeholders. Dominant stakeholders have power and legitimacy but their demand is not urgent. They have high expectations and the firm should give them a lot of attention. Examples include the boards of directors, employees, HR departments, public relations, and so on. The firm should be able to identify dangerous stakeholders due to their powerful and urgent claims, even though they lack legitimacy. The reason these stakeholders are categorized as dangerous is because they are prone to using violence and resorting to coercion; for example, employee sabotage or coercive/unlawful tactics used by activists. Even though they possess legitimacy and urgency, due to their lack of power, dependent stakeholders, on the other hand, depend on other stakeholders (e.g., dominant stakeholders, who possess power, and therefore, can help the dependent stakeholders to impose their will); for example: bystanders, community members, and so on.

Finally, stakeholders with all three attributes are defined as definitive stakeholders. These stakeholders are considered the most important and influential because they hold power over the firm and present legitimate and urgent claims. For example, stockholders who decide their legitimate interest in the firm is not being met may take drastic action, such as having managers of the firm removed.

Network-Level Strategizing

Many contemporary corporations operate in global industries with business environments defined first and foremost by complexity and uncertainty. In fast-paced markets, it is often not possible to define with any level of certainty the one desired goal guaranteed to still be desirable at the time of its achievement, especially when the time frame is anything other than short-term. Nor is it possible to factor in all the surprising variables that influence the chosen methods of pursuing the goals, even over a relatively short time. Viewing strategy as a plan that incorporates both the goal and the path for reaching it has its merits in some circumstances, but the current international business environment also requires other approaches to strategizing.

In order to understand the requirements different environments pose to strategizing, we first need a method with which we can map environmental diversity. Reeves et al. (2015) inspire three questions that help to position the environment along three continua, creating a firm- or unit-specific pattern:

1. To what degree is the business environment predictable?
2. To what degree can you influence it either alone or with others?
3. To what degree does the environment pose serious threats to survival?

If we consider strategizing in the traditional way, we notice that it requires specific answers to each of these questions. In order to formulate a goal we deem still desirable by the time of its achievement, we need an environment that is predictable enough to allow the creation of such a goal. On the other hand, in traditional strategizing, the environment is a given: it influences us and we need to find the right way of reacting to it—we cannot change it. Also, if we face an imminent threat to our survival, we will most likely not have the luxury of reveling in formulating long-term goals.

These answers begin to reveal the impact of the business environment on the fundamental assumptions driving strategizing processes. How do we answer the question of what to do next if we believe that we can shape the environment, but not predict it? What is a survival strategy? Interestingly, the business environment can also vary within an industry, depending on the position of an actor in the value chain, and even within a firm, depending on how a unit contributes to the value creation process. Considering network-level strategizing, how do we align a traditional roadmap strategy born out of perceiving the environment as predictable, safe, and non-malleable with a survival strategy born out of a heightened notion of perceived threat?

The first assumption that underlies the strategy work is how we perceive the environment in which we act. The second assumption relates to our understanding of rational behavior—our strategic mindset. In his seminal paper on balancing exploration and exploitation activities of the firm, James March (1991) highlights the often perceived dichotomous relationship between activities related to innovation and the firm's attempt to achieve economies in their actions. The exploitation features are often addressed by managerial behavior, whereas exploration requires entrepreneurial qualities of the firm; in this chapter, we present these qualities as something possessed by those who are involved in strategizing, not in an identifiable individual entrepreneur.

This dichotomy is the first clue toward illuminating the underlying mindsets of strategizing. The managerial and entrepreneurial mindsets have been further explored by Saras Sarasvathy and her colleagues, who uncovered two distinct rationalities, *causal* and *effectual.* Causal rationality proceeds in the manner of the strategy process defined at the beginning of this chapter: it begins with goals and continues by procuring the resources necessary to achieve them. Effectual rationality is evidenced in entrepreneurial action: it begins with an assessment of immediately available options creating the goal as an outcome of the chosen activities. The mindsets underlying these two rationalities form the foundation of the mindset identification matrix drafted here.

Just as with assessing the business environment, the evaluation of the mindsets begins with answering specific questions. Wiltbank et al. (2006) managed to identify two questions that reveal a great deal of the underlying mindset of firm decision-making: (1) Do we believe that it is possible and desirable to be able to predict the future? (2) Do we believe that we can change aspects of the environment or are we controlled by them? Even though the questions seem remarkably similar to the questions posed by Reeves et al. (2015), they focus on unveiling a different assumption—revealing how we begin to answer the initial strategizing question, "what to do next?"

Answering the two questions by Wiltbank et al. (2006) provides us with a matrix consisting of four different archetypical mindsets that underlie our possible approaches to strategy work. The traditional mode of strategizing requires us to answer the questions in a specific way: we need to value and believe in the possibility of predicting, and we need to regard the environment as something we cannot control. These features define the managerial approach or the exploitation qualities of the firm. However, wielding entrepreneurial logic, we are prone to answer the questions differently: underlying effectual logic is the notion that we can change our environments and that our actions have an impact. Likewise, as entrepreneurial action begins by utilizing immediately available means, the emphasis on being able to predict is considerably lower—we do what we can and see what happens.

To summarize, the second part of the tool we are about to introduce helps network strategy makers identify two assumptions upon which they and their network partners build their strategy. Answering the three questions about business environments gives a unit- or company-specific pattern of our environmental assumptions. Finding answers to the two mindset questions positions the strategy makers in the rationality matrix. Understanding the diversity of possibilities in both of these assumptions creates a solid foundation for network-level strategizing.

Environmental Assessment Method

As previously mentioned, assessing the business environment begins by posing three questions:

1. How predictable is the business environment? (High-low)
2. How malleable is the business environment? (High-low)
3. How threatening to survival is the business environment? (High-low)

Depending on the industry or circumstances of the firm, the predictability of business can be assessed along two dimensions: the anticipated level of certainty in predictions; and the anticipated duration of time the predictions will span. If the predictability is high, the environment is supportive of goal-oriented, planned strategizing, whereas in an unpredictable environment, the firm should focus its strategic efforts on increasing adaptability and dynamic capabilities.

The market position, technological leadership, or level of networkedness of the firm may have an impact on the ability of the firm to shape its markets and environment. If the firm perceives the environment to be malleable, it has more control over the contingencies, and needs to invest less effort in adapting or predicting the environmental change.

Finally, if the firm is facing an immediate threat to survival, its strategic core must be the revival of its viability. In assessing the level of threat it faces, the firm should also look beyond the immediate financial situation and assess the soundness of its basic business: in the long run, does the revenue exceed the costs by a healthy enough margin? If the answer is no, the level of threat should be reevaluated.

Strategic Mindset Identification Method

Like identifying environmental factors to fit the strategy with the situation at hand, recognizing the assumptions of rational strategic action begins by posing questions: (1) Do we believe that it is possible and important to be able to predict the future? (2) Do we believe that we can change and/or control the environment?

The quadrants in this matrix are *planning*, *adaptive*, *transformative*, and *visionary*. Next, we will take a look at each quadrant to help further identify the inherent mindset of the strategizing company/unit (Fig. 3.2).

Planning mindset. The planning mindset is the one most managers are familiar with. It underlies roadmap-like strategies, and is taught to most business practitioners in business schools. The planning mindset gives weight to predicting the future to a sufficient degree, which provides enough knowledge to formulate a desirable goal and to assess the most efficient methods of reaching it. Environment is viewed as something that happens to us, not something that can be molded by our actions.

Adaptive mindset. This mindset is typical in very fast-paced industries where disruptive innovations are mundane (e.g., technology industries). It shuns the notion of predictability, and instead emphasizes alertness, reaction speed and dynamic capabilities of the company. An adaptive mindset doesn't believe in the possibility of predicting the future to any relevant degree, and strategizing with this mindset tends

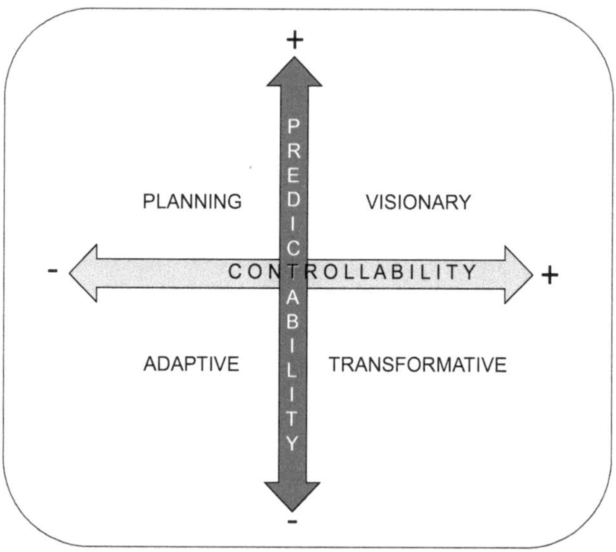

Fig. 3.2 Prediction-control matrix (adapted from Wiltbank et al. 2006)

to highlight the adaptive capabilities of the firm/unit. It is similar to the planning mindset in its view of environment as something given and to be reacted to, not something to be changed by the actions of the company/firm.

Transformative mindset. Unlike the mindsets on the left side of the matrix, it has faith in the firm's ability to actually change its environment and control the market to a degree. Creating a strategy endowed with a transformative mindset doesn't involve attempts of predicting the future, but is instead firmly rooted in its immediately perceived opportunities. If the underlying logic in the planning quadrant states that "We can control what we can predict," the transformative logic inverses the statement into, "What we can control we don't need to predict."

Visionary mindset. Genuine visionaries seem to be a rare breed. Not only does the visionary believe in the possibility of changing the world—or at least the portion of it nearby—but simultaneously believes in predicting and singlehandedly shaping the future. If a company wields a visionary mindset, it is likely a market leader with major first-mover advantages.

Summarizing the Stakeholder Identification and Network Strategy Co-creation Methods

The methods described above can be applied on many levels. At the individual level, they help the people responsible for strategizing to better understand their own perspectives and assumptions. At the team and unit levels, they provide fertile ground for uncovering the collective understandings of the perceptions and mindsets driving the collective action. They provide valuable input at the firm level that supports market analyses and other methods of gaining sufficient knowledge and understanding that is used as the foundation of the major strategic decisions of the company.

However, our interest lies in the ability of these methods to create a common ground for strategizing on the network level. In practice, we suggest a method where all the network partners first answer the two sets of questions independently, then hold a workshop or series of workshops where the different initial assumptions can be identified, discussed, and negotiated to a degree that facilitates creating a common ground for network-level strategizing.

Case: Transforming from Transactional Business to Solution Business

The development of this tool was driven by the needs of a real case in the context of a globally operating systems supplier in the ship-building industry. Due to the stagnant market growth in certain types of ships, a business concept innovation project was launched. The objective was to find new ways to redefine the markets of the case firm and, as result, create a new business model. The core idea of the project was to transform the business from selling products and systems to base business on the provision of solutions.

Solutions business follows a particular logic: it decouples the *transactional value* (the price a customer pays) from the *value-in-use*. This means that ultimately the value doesn't reside in the product/system as the object of sales, but is defined as the value generated by the use of the object. In our case, it meant shifting the emphasis from supplying maritime systems to developing a wider perspective of the value a merchant ship produces over its lifetime for the user(s) of the ship.

Essentially, this required broadening our understanding of who the customers are, what affects their balance sheets, and how the systems supplier can support the long-term performance of diverse customer and user groups in terms of both costs and revenues. To achieve this, it was vital to understand customer groups better: their market situations, how they operate, what drives their business, and how they perceive the world they operate in. The tool drafted here was created and used to help in this process.

First, we carried out a stakeholder analysis that identified the key stakeholders. We used the stakeholder identification and salience tool to help the managers of the systems supplier to identify those stakeholders that are important to the firm's activities and business. The tool allowed industry participants to estimate the relative strength and importance of the identified stakeholders. In many cases, industry participants may only have an incomplete picture of who the most important stakeholders are for their activities. This tool brings a much needed systematic approach to the identification and categorization of stakeholders and their relative importance.

The stakeholder identification and salience tool was implemented in a workshop attended by managers. Using the tool, the participants were able to identify those stakeholders that "really matter" to their firm. According to the aforementioned themes, the managers identified these stakeholders as: shipyards, system suppliers, financiers, designers, the International Maritime Organization (IMO), classification societies, ship owners, non-operative owners, cargo owners, port operators, alliances, and government (Table 3.2).

Applying the typology allowed managers to determine what approaches and responses are appropriate for different stakeholders, and which stakeholders warrant greater attention as they have strategic implications.

We implemented this tool in two stages. In the first stage, participating managers from the system supplier were requested to nominate stakeholders to be included in the analysis by deciding who and what counts for their firm. We asked the firm's managers to conduct a brainstorm-

Table3.2 Identification of a system supplier's stakeholders based on Mitchell et al. (1997)

Stakeholder	Power	Urgency	Legitimacy
Shipyards	1	X	X
System suppliers			
Financiers	X		
Designers	X	X	
IMO			X
Classification societies		X	X
Ship owners	2	X	/indirect
Non-operative owners	X	X	/indirect
Cargo owners			
Port operators			
Alliances	x		
Government	varies		x

ing session in order to list people/groups/institutions that are related to the firm. We asked them to focus on these themes: Who are the stakeholders that have a fundamental impact on the firm's performance? Who exercises influence over other stakeholders? Does the firm's management know exactly what it wants from the stakeholder? Would the firm be able to exist without the stakeholder or can the stakeholder be easily replaced? In the next stage, the identified stakeholders were categorized based on the judgment of the managers according to their power, legitimacy, and urgency attributes. Once categorized, the stakeholders could then be situated in the Venn diagram typology and their salience to the firm could be analyzed.

The utility of the tool does not end with the simple categorization described above. The exercise also made explicit the assumptions that the managers held in regard as to why they thought each stakeholder possessed the attributes they did. These would later be tested and verified or disproven in the field by meeting with the relevant stakeholders and hearing first-hand what they had to say. Using the analysis produced, in combination with the mindset analysis we discuss below, the managers could then ask themselves what can be done differently. By manipulating the attributes of the various stakeholders, they were able to construct a number of different scenarios and could imagine what effect these would have on the firm's core business. One of the most important and valuable outcomes of the stakeholder identification and salience exercise was that it helped the firm's managers to identify that shipyards, their traditional direct customers, consist of different stakeholders groups within. This was an important insight made explicit because it is vital to generate value-in-use for other identified key stakeholder groups (direct customers' customers = ship owners, and subsequently their customers = ship operators). As it turned out, each stakeholder group with their differentiated claims operates under a variety of logics that need to be considered and served when trying to construct a network level strategy.

Once stakeholder identification and salience was established, we used the strategic mindset analysis tool in a series of intensive workshops consisting of managers with different expertise and experience from several functional departments of the division. After that, we analyzed the current market development of the identified key stakeholders, from their own perspective, against the three environmental aspects: how predictable is their business environment, which aspects of it do the stakeholders try to control, and what poses threats to them? The findings of this analysis were further tested by the managers of our case company through direct communication with individuals in the stakeholder organizations, and it soon became clear that many of the assumptions about what the stakeholders know and how they perceive their business environments needed reconsideration. As a result, after these series of assessments, we began to better understand how the business environment shapes the playing field of different stakeholders and how that matches the perceptions of the business environment of our case company.

In the next phase, we initiated another round of workshops with the same group of managers to discover the strategic mindsets of the different interest groups (corporate level, division level, and project team level) within the case company. It was soon evident that the corporation level, represented by the top management, subscribed to the planning mindset, the exploitation of knowledge in formulating medium-term roadmap-style strategies. However, the division level was more adaptive to the changes unfolding, and the project team identified with a transformative mindset, emphasizing what can be controlled in its own partner network.

This mindset identification exercise was repeated with the stakeholders to identify the partners who were the most responsive to building network-level strategies, and who were the most receptive to the notion of a solutions-oriented business approach. As a result, we developed a deeper understanding of how to drive a network to develop common strategizing efforts to implement a business model driven by value-in-use. We also understood that the better insights one has about the business logic of the stakeholders, the more power one holds to drive the network-level strategizing. Subsequently, these insights into the mindsets and business environments of the stakeholders have been used to develop better means to influence the engagement of network-level strategizing.

The result of the analysis conducted by the managers in the workshops and their subsequent footwork out in the field was that they developed a more comprehensive understanding of the industry and network in which they were operating. It is worth noting that the company did not previously have any formal discussion on stakeholders other than about their direct customers, but now they constantly monitor what is happening in the ecosystem and analyze how these changes influence their immediate stakeholders and the company itself. The company's ability to see the big picture—understanding the needs and logic of stakeholders beyond the immediate customers and suppliers—allows it to reimagine the firm's value proposition and establish itself as a solutions business rather than a simple transactional business. By understanding who or what is important, how they are important, and why, a firm can ensure that their own role in a network of stakeholders is a vital one.

Conclusions

In the course of doing business as usual, it is sometimes easy to lose sight of, or take for granted, the position of one's own firm in the broader ecosystem in which it operates. Managers who remain ignorant of the nuances of their stakeholder network too long run the risk of their firm's losing relevance in an ever-changing business environment. We strongly advocate for the systematic identification and analysis of stakeholders for any business. The stakeholder identification and salience tool we have described provides a better understanding of the priority and level of attention that needs to be given to any particular stakeholder. Furthermore, the tool helps managers choose the proper communication approach for each stakeholder group. It also classifies stakeholders according to their salience toward the firm based upon the attributes of power, legitimacy, and urgency. Managers are then better able to distinguish more important—or salient—stakeholders and prioritize them as well as actively communicate with them.

Analyzing an organization's business networks is also insightful in terms of knowing each key partner's perceptions about the business environment and the respective strategic mindsets that drive their actions; analysis enables an organization to take the driver's seat for network-level strategizing. Understanding each key stakeholder's environment and strategic response propensity is equally as valuable. It allows for strategizing based on forming shared meanings, which are often not given when interacting partners have substantially different baseline assumptions about the nature of the environment and the options on how to react to them.

We hope we have tangibly illustrated here the importance and utility of stakeholder identification and salience, and strategic mindset analysis. With today's ever-complex value chains and dynamic business environments, the ability to see the forest for the trees is not only necessary for continued survival but is also a valuable source of new opportunities. We affirm that to know how and why others are important to you enables you to ensure that you are valuable to them. The practical tool we described in this chapter, however, should not be seen as a normative tool. It allows for sketching out different tactics that subsequently serve to build better interactions and conversations in the pursuit of co-creating strategies and value at the inter-firm level.

References

Freeman, R. E. (2010). *Strategic management: A stakeholder approach*. Cambridge: Cambridge University Press.

March, J. G. (1991). Exploration and exploitation in organizational learning. *Organization Science, 2*(1), 71–87.

Mitchell, R. K., Agle, B. R., & Wood, D. J. (1997). Toward a theory of stakeholder identification and salience: Defining the principle of who and what really counts. *Academy ofManagement Review, 22*(4), 853–886.

Reeves, M., Haanaes, K., & Sinha, J. (2015). Navigating the dozens of different strategy options. *Harvard Business Review*, 93(6), 1–17.

Sarasvathy, S. D. (2001). Causation and effectuation: Toward a theoretical shift from economic inevitability to entrepreneurial contingency. *Academy of Management Review, 26*(2), 243–263.

Suchman, M. C. (1995). Managing legitimacy: Strategic and institutional approaches. *Academy of Management Review, 20*(3), 571–610.

Wiltbank, R., Dew, N., Read, S., & Sarasvathy, S. D. (2006). What to do next? The case for non-predictive strategy. *Strategic Management Journal, 27*, 981–998.

Wood, D. J. (1991). Corporate social performance revisited. *Academy of Management Review, 16*(4), 691–718.

4

Leading Human Values in Complex Environments

Johnny Långstedt, Robin Wikström, and Magnus Hellström

Going Beyond the Planning-Monitoring-Reporting Axis

When engineering projects are procured, the contractor is required to assemble a temporary organization that consists of several actors, for example, sub-contractors and suppliers; this is referred to as a project network (Powell 1990). The contractor may or may not be familiar with the actors and has limited time to achieve the required integration and commitment. The project becomes a network that the contractor is required to coordinate and maintain in order to complete the project. The project network may include adversarial actors with divergent interests that may decrease project performance (Hellström et al. 2013). If it is a global project, which the projects that were involved in the development of this tool are, there are also several legitimate organizational and cultural norms and assumptions that may impact performance (Orr and Scott 2008).

J. Långstedt (✉) • R. Wikström • M. Hellström
Åbo Akademi University, Turku, Finland

J. Vesalainen et al. (eds.), *Practices for Network Management*,
DOI 10.1007/978-3-319-49649-8_4

According to the Project Management Institute (PMI) "Project managers accomplish work through the project team and other stakeholders" (Project Management Institute 2013, 17). This is consistent with research that shows that high levels of emotional competence correlates with project success (Müller and Turner 2010). Lately, project management as a research field has become increasingly interested in stakeholder management (Pollack and Adler 2015). Additionally, as technical competences grow in non-western countries, western countries cannot compete merely by technical know-how, nor do they have similar possibilities to compete with price. Hence, customer satisfaction has grown to become an important part of construction project management, that is, the requirements of "soft skills" have increased.

Still it seems that "soft skills" is a relatively novel topic in project management (Pant and Baroudi 2008). Research in project management has focused mainly on planning techniques and developing various incentive mechanisms and organizations. These are still crucial elements of project management and our purpose is not to diminish them. However, there is a clear lack of understanding "people skills" and what these comprise in a project context. Here, people skills refer to the project managers' ability to coordinate actors within the project network to act according to the project requirements while ensuring the highest possible level of satisfaction. Research that offers concrete methods for coordinating the project network with soft means is scarce. Let us refer to soft means as leadership: the means to influence someone's behavior by rhetoric and action. A project manager is faced with various projects, none of which are identical (Lundin and Söderholm 1995). Therefore, project managers cannot rely on a single, universal, leadership style but are rather required to adapt their leadership according to their operational context, that is, their stakeholders and the environment in which they perform their tasks.

Project Leadership

Many conventional leadership theories have been applied in project management; however, many of them are constrained by the characteristics of projects, namely, temporality, uniqueness, boundary-spanning and dynamism (Lundin and Söderholm 1995; Tyssen et al. 2013). These characteristics separate the project domain from traditional organizations. A major challenge for establishing constructive relationships in projects is the temporary nature of the projects. Contrary to functional organizations, project relationships are discontinuous and the development of authority is restricted by the duration of the project. In order to lead the project, managers need to identify their project leadership style early on in the project. However, as projects rarely comprise the same constellation of stakeholders, project managers are required to modify their leadership style to correspond with the requirements of the project (Müller and Turner 2007). Beyond that, project managers are required to approach each stakeholder in a suitable way that may vary greatly within a project. A universally applicable leadership style is therefore unlikely to be found even within a project, and hence project managers are required to adapt their style according to each stakeholder. This is true particularly when the success of projects relies on the cooperation of various stakeholders. Under such circumstances, managers have to engage in "boundary-spanning" activities, that is, project managers have to influence stakeholders beyond their own organizational boundaries (Brion et al. 2012). It is especially important as project success relies on the joint performance of various stakeholders. Hence, cooperation between each stakeholder within the project network is crucial.

Moving from Transactional to Relational Practices

Developing "soft skills" is linked to relational practices as the satisfaction of external parties becomes important in order to create long-term relationships and reap their benefits (Dyer and Singh 1998). Project companies have traditionally focused on product quality, costs and the time it takes to complete specified tasks or products. The focus has been on one-off business cases where short-term gains have dominated and services that add value to the customers have received less attention (Savolainen and Ahonen 2014). The benefits of repeat and long-term business have been emphasized recently as strategically advantageous (Johnsen and Lacoste 2016). Dyer and Singh (1998) advocate a relational turn in mainstream transactional business. Relational business practices are expected to accumulate wealth through increased collaboration and "sharing" of resources. Whereas a transactional approach emphasizes maximization of profits from transaction, more or less at the expense of the other party, a relational approach focuses on long-term gains that sustain the collaboration between the parties and increases the efficiency of the trade through formal and informal integration. In a world dominated by transactional practices, convincing other organizations of one's good intention may be a challenging task; additionally, such relationships can be expected to be quite delicate. Therefore, it is important that managers are able to understand their potential partners at a personal level, and how they should manage the relationship.

Conventional methods for managing complexities and uncertainties in projects include a number of strategies: increasing and improving leadership, which seems to be assumed to be a universal solution (Blom and Alvesson 2015); matching each project with an appropriate leadership style (Munns and Bjeirmi 1996; Müller and Turner 2007), which assumes a project manager with suitable traits would always be available; increasing monitoring (Turner and Simister 2001), which limits agility and increases expenses by resource allocation; increasing planning and information collection (Maylor 2001), which is both expensive and time consuming with varying results; and devising various forms of incentives (Badenfelt 2011; Laan and Dewulf 2011), which may or may not be sufficient in order to regulate behavior in the desired way and may ruin relationships in the worst case. These methods are resource-intensive in terms of money, people and time, yet often fail to mitigate the risks. Despite the highlighted importance of various forms of collaboration in project management, current stakeholder management tools do not offer solutions to what interests or motivates stakeholders (Jepsen and Eskerod 2009) nor does the current project leadership literature provide practical methods for project managers. In order to close this gap, we developed a tool that creates a framework for analyzing stakeholders and provides the user with suggestions on how to manage the stakeholder.

The Theoretical Foundation of the Project Leadership Tool

Due to the nature of projects, the tool is required to be both dynamic and universal. In other words, the tool needs to be based on a theory that has a globally proven validity; second, it has to be able to be updated during the project as new stakeholders are introduced. In order to ensure that the tool is as universally applicable as possible, we turned to Schwartz (1992) theory of basic human values. The framework is especially applicable as it identifies ten universal factors that motivate people. Therefore it offers a relevant framework for bridging the gap that Jepsen and Eskerod (2009) identified.

Schwartz built his theory on Rokeach's (1973) early theory of human values. Schwartz's theory has been tested in 32 countries, with later extension to over 50 countries. The initial studies showed remarkable strength in the theoretical structure of the thesis, and the data clearly illustrated ten value theorized "domains" (see Fig. 4.1). These domains, called motivational types, represent the social and psychological needs that values, core beliefs, are based on. The motivational types were later (Schwartz et al. 2012) refined into 19 motivational types, adding subcategories to universalism, power and security values, as well as adding humility and face values.

The motivational types on different sides of Fig. 4.1 are opposites; for example, if one seeks power or recognition, he is expected to value equality and the well-being of others less (Schwartz 1992). Similarly, if one reveres traditions one is likely to enjoy variation (stimulation value) less than continuity (tradition) (for a complete overview of values see Schwartz (2012). Values are a prominent feature of human life; however, their relative importance varies (Schwartz 1992). The variance in the importance of values is referred to as a value structure. A value structure is the basis for how individuals evaluate actions and situations (Bardi and Schwartz 2003), and this structure is expressed in attitudes (Rokeach 1973), that is, a person who regards security as important will have a "negative attitude" toward risky endeavors. Identifying the stakeholders' value structure is, therefore, a relevant point of departure when a proj-

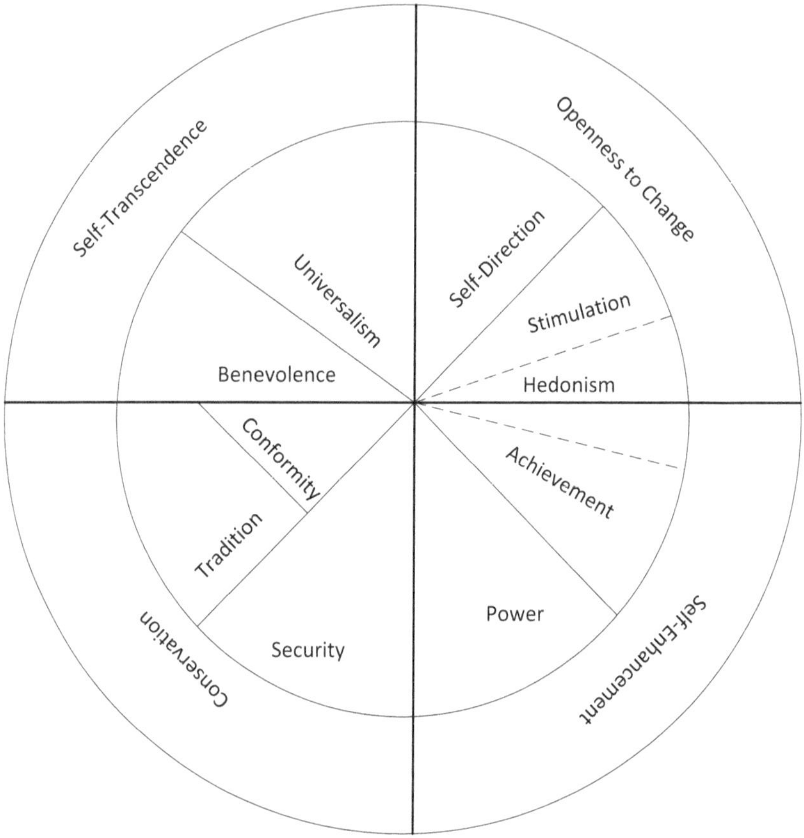

Fig. 4.1 Schwartz's (1992) ten motivational types

ect manager needs to influence his stakeholders, especially beyond formal arrangements. The value structures can be utilized in constructing a favorable frame for actions and events that the manager wants to advance in a project. Project managers' influence on stakeholders becomes a question of them framing their proposition in a manner that fulfills their counterpart's needs (Schwartz's motivational types). This should not be restricted to mere rhetoric, but comprise the symbolism that is inherent in actions. Therefore, the project manager should not merely understand what should be communicated to stakeholders, but how it should be communicated and what actions communicate it.

Description of the Tool

Overall, the tool is aimed at enabling project managers to influence stakeholders and lead projects efficiently. More specifically, the purpose is to provide tactical advantage in negotiations or, in layman's terms, to identify what buttons to push. The tool offers an intuitive and user-friendly interface that enables users to analyze various stakeholders within the framework of the theory of basic human values. The tool consists of three phases as summarized in Fig. 4.2: (1) an evaluation matrix where the tool presents a set of questions to determine the values and needs of a stakeholder; (2) a response matrix, which provides advice on how the stakeholder should be lead and managed; and (3) a profile component that provides an overview of the project stakeholders. The fourth step, the leadership style, is a result of following steps 1–3. However, it is likely that project managers need to reconfigure their leadership style during the project, in an iterative fashion. Therefore, the process is described as circular rather than linear.

The mechanics are simple and intuitive. In the first step (see Fig. 4.3), the user chooses the statements that describe the given stakeholder by answering the main questions listed in Table 4.1. These questions represent contextualized versions of Schwartz's (1992) ten motivational types. As the user chooses a statement that describes his stakeholder, a pop-up with further sub-questions appears (see Table 4.2). The pop-up contains a three-color scale of green-yellow-red: "I can handle it"; "Need additional resources"; and "Potential disaster." The evaluation of the stakeholder shows in the matrix as the chosen color on the scale; therefore, it is easy for the user to get an overview of the project at a glance.

Fig. 4.2 The stakeholder analysis process

Step 1. Questionaire.

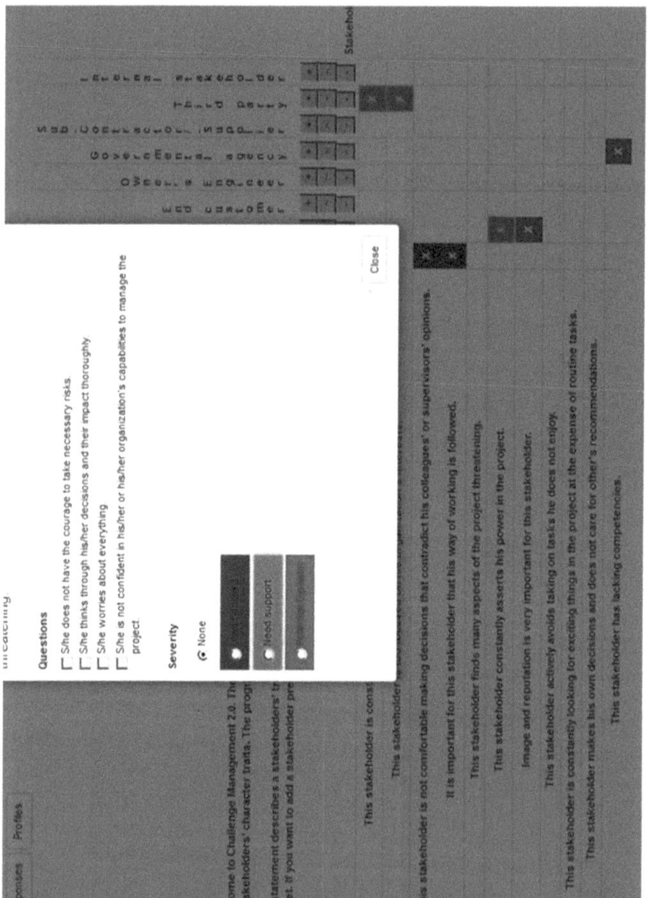

Fig. 4.3 The graphical interface of the leadership tool

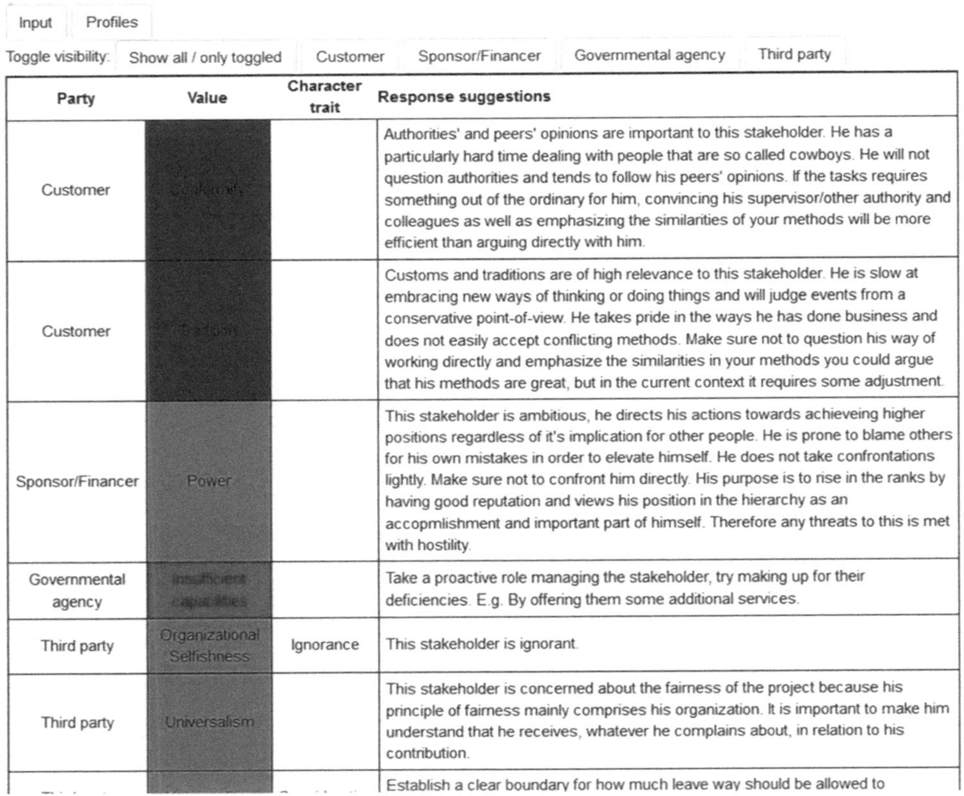

Input | Profiles

Toggle visibility: Show all / only toggled | Customer | Sponsor/Financer | Governmental agency | Third party

Party	Value	Character trait	Response suggestions
Customer	Conformity		Authorities' and peers' opinions are important to this stakeholder. He has a particularly hard time dealing with people that are so called cowboys. He will not question authorities and tends to follow his peers' opinions. If the tasks requires something out of the ordinary for him, convincing his supervisor/other authority and colleagues as well as emphasizing the similarities of your methods will be more efficient than arguing directly with him.
Customer	Tradition		Customs and traditions are of high relevance to this stakeholder. He is slow at embracing new ways of thinking or doing things and will judge events from a conservative point-of-view. He takes pride in the ways he has done business and does not easily accept conflicting methods. Make sure not to question his way of working directly and emphasize the similarities in your methods you could argue that his methods are great, but in the current context it requires some adjustment.
Sponsor/Financer	Power		This stakeholder is ambitious, he directs his actions towards achieveing higher positions regardless of it's implication for other people. He is prone to blame others for his own mistakes in order to elevate himself. He does not take confrontations lightly. Make sure not to confront him directly. His purpose is to rise in the ranks by having good reputation and views his position in the hierarchy as an accopmlishment and important part of himself. Therefore any threats to this is met with hostility.
Governmental agency	Insufficient capabilities		Take a proactive role managing the stakeholder, try making up for their deficiencies. E.g. By offering them some additional services.
Third party	Organizational Selfishness	Ignorance	This stakeholder is ignorant.
Third party	Universalism		This stakeholder is concerned about the fairness of the project because his principle of fairness mainly comprises his organization. It is important to make him understand that he receives, whatever he complains about, in relation to his contribution.
[illegible]		[illegible]	Establish a clear boundary for how much leave way should be allowed to

Step 2. Triggered responses

Fig. 4.3 (continued)

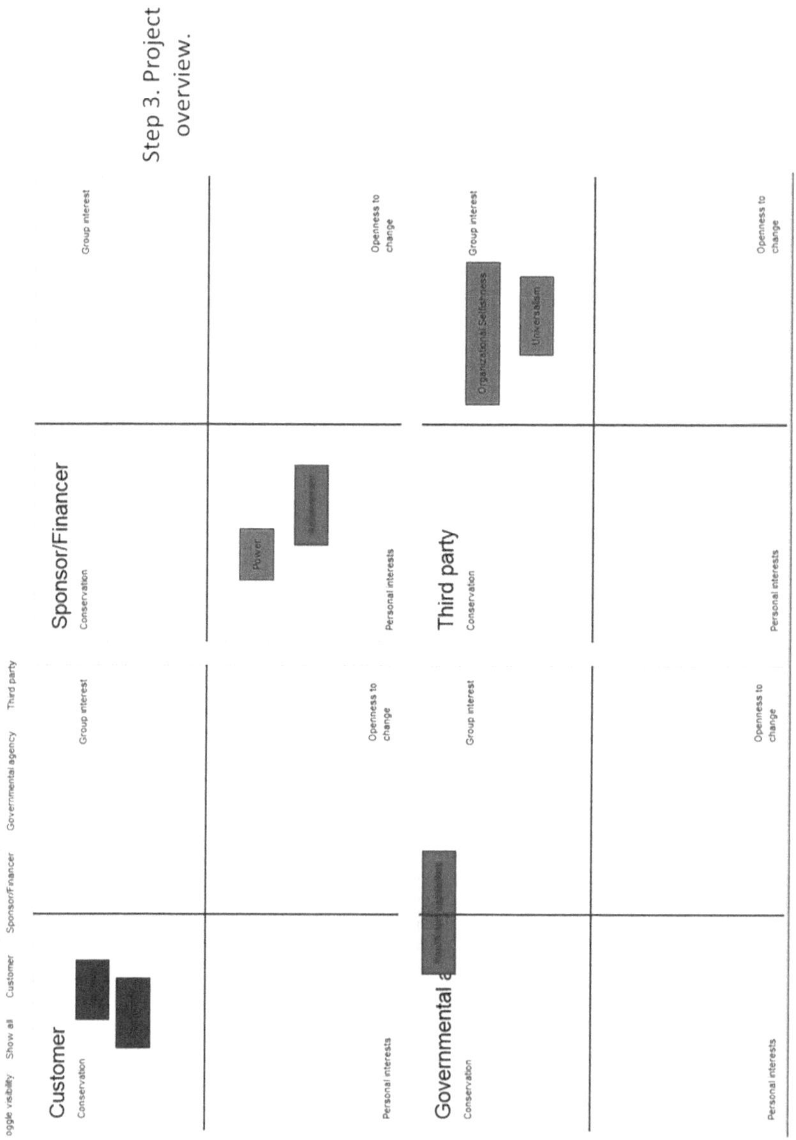

Fig. 4.3 *(continued)*

Table 4.1 The main questions that represent the ten motivational types

Values	Main questions
Universalism	This stakeholder is constantly worried about fairness and equality in the project.
Benevolence	This stakeholder is too focused on his organization's interests.
Conformity	This stakeholder is not comfortable making decisions that contradict his colleagues' or supervisors' opinions.
Tradition	It is important for this stakeholder that his way of working is followed.
Security	This stakeholder finds many aspects of the project threatening.
Power	This stakeholder constantly asserts his power in the project.
Achievement	Image and reputation is very important for this stakeholder.
Hedonism	This stakeholder actively avoids taking on tasks he does not enjoy.
Stimulation	This stakeholder is constantly looking for exciting things in the project at the expense of routine tasks.
Self-direction	This stakeholder makes his own decisions and does not care for other's recommendations.
Competencies	This stakeholder has lacking competencies.

Table 4.2 An example of sub-questions (the sub-questions are from the power category)

Power value sub-questions
S/he is convinced his/her organization knows everything better than others.
S/he gets annoyed easily.
S/he does not possess the knowledge needed for the project and does not care for advice.
S/he is easily offended when flaws in her work are pointed out.
S/he is ignorant.
S/he makes all the decisions.
If s/he has a goal s/he will pursue it regardless of its impact on others.

The second step is a list of responses as shown in Fig. 4.3. The responses are triggered by several factors. If, for example, the evaluation matrix signals that the stakeholder is motivated by security and power values, a different response will be triggered than if the evaluation matrix signals that the stakeholder is motivated by security and achievement. Similarly, combinations of sub-questions trigger different responses. Step 3 is a profile picture based on how the user has answered the questions in step 1 and offers the user an overview of project stakeholders. The identified motivational types are ordered according to the order of the original theory. The profile picture offers the project manager the information in a visually attractive form and provides him with an overview of the stakeholder's values. It contains the responses in pop-ups that are rendered on the basis of the user's evaluation.

The tool was tested with a workshop format where the main author assisted the project managers in interpreting and using the tool in practice. The projects ($n = 13$) were followed with approximately four months' intervals and the strategies were updated according to the stakeholder changes in the projects. This step is extremely important as the projects are quite dynamic and the stakeholders may change quite suddenly. Whenever a stakeholder enters the project, the project manager needs to assess him/her in a systematic fashion and make sure his/her leadership style matches the stakeholder's values.

User Comments

The leadership tool is aimed at practitioners that operate in complex and dynamic environments. The tool has been tested in 13 projects around the world with 10 different project managers. Here are some comments after and during workshops:

After testing the tool on his turnkey project in the middle-east a seasoned project manager remarked:

> *It's incredible how accurate responses it produces by so few questions.*

Project managers are often flustered by planning the technical aspects of projects and do not have sufficiently time to analyze the stakeholders adequately. A senior project manager facing a potential addition of seven simultaneous projects concluded:

> *This is really good we don't always have time to think who we are dealing with.*

One of the project managers involved in piloting the tool was confronted with a tricky situation. He had to convince his stakeholder of a solution that was not completely in accordance with their agreements, but which would enable a more efficient execution of the project. Regardless of the benefits, the customer did not want to accept it. As he had identified that the key motivators for the stakeholder were security and achievement, he used this knowledge to his advantage when he was debating with his stakeholder:

> *This is really interesting, otherwise I would not be involved. I got the chance to try this during negotiations in one of my projects and it worked really well.*

The PM increased the use of the tool from one to three projects during piloting.

Conclusions

The complexity, temporariness and interdependencies of projects make them an ideal context to develop a leadership tool. As businesses become more dependent on other stakeholders, they will benefit from similar tools. The strength in the tool lies in the utilization of Schwartz (1992) theory of human values, which is currently the most refined tool for investigating individual values and needs. The tool itself arose from the increased interdependencies with stakeholders and is designed to offer project managers support in aligning and framing their propositions with stakeholder needs and values. The tool supports business relationship maintenance and leadership and managers' transition from transactional planning-monitoring methods to relational practices. What we argue is that in order to become a leader, a manager is required to understand his stakeholders' core beliefs, that is, their motivations. Framing and aligning propositions and actions with stakeholder core beliefs and motivations makes tasks more attractive to stakeholders.

We have preliminary proof that as managers become capable of reflecting in a structured manner on *how* to frame their arguments to their stakeholders, they will experience an increase in stakeholder satisfaction. However, the benefits are not merely restricted to stakeholder satisfaction but will decrease petty disputes and, consequently, make the project manager's day-to-day work easier. As project managers are able to formulate themselves in a compelling manner, their valuable time will not be wasted on prolonged disputes about matters of questionable relevance. Projects may flow more smoothly and repeat orders may become more commonplace due to increased stakeholder satisfaction.

Although decision-support systems is an established research field, additional research is required to understand how decision-making systems, such as the one described here, affect the leadership proficiencies in organizations. As the tool is used, it may become an integral part of how its users interpret their environment; however, these effects should be further investigated. Additionally, our method is based on one case company. In order to ensure its applicability in other contexts, it should be tested in several companies, and preferably from different industries. With the rapidly developing technological working environment, the possibilities to develop and implement different decision-support systems dealing with qualitative values increases. This offers an alternative to mainstream leadership courses for managers who want to improve their leadership skills without consuming too much time and energy. We believe that the research community will experience a boom in developing tools addressing leadership challenges in the near future (Gudauskas et al. 2015).

Acknowledgements We are very grateful for the collaborative disposition of our case company and for the cooperation with members of their staff: this constituted the core of our research. Furthermore, we would like to acknowledge Dr. Magnus Gustafsson for providing valuable insights. Finally, this would not have been possible without our programmers, Mr. Mikael Sand and Mr. Robert Syring, who are gratefully acknowledged.

References

Badenfelt, U. (2011). Fixing the contract after the contract is fixed: A study of incomplete contracts in IT and construction projects. *International Journal of Project Management, 29*(5), 568–576.

Bardi, A., & Schwartz, S. (2003). Values and behavior: Strength and structure of relations. *Personlity and Social Psychology Bulletin, 29*(10), 1207–1220.

Blom, M., & Alvesson, M. (2015). All-inclusive and all good: The hegemonic ambiguity of leadership. *Scandinavian Journal of Management, 31*(4), 480–492.

Brion, S., Chauvet, V., Chollet, B., & Mothe, C. (2012). Project leaders as boundary spanners: Relational antecedents and performance outcomes. *International Journal of Project Management, 30*(6), 708–722.

Davis, P., & Love, P. (2011). Alliance contracting: Adding value through relationship development. *Engineering, Construction and Architectural Management, 18*(5), 444–461.

Dyer, J. H., & Singh, H. (1998). The relational view: Cooperative strategy and sources of interorganizational competitive advantage. *The Academy of Management Review, 23*(4), 660–679.

Gudauskas, R., Jokubauskiene, S., Zavadskas, E. K., Kaklauskas, A., Binkyte, A., Peciure, L., et al. (2015). Intelligent decision support system for leadership analysis. *Procedia Engineering, 122*(Orsdce), 172–180.

Hellström, M., Ruuska, I., Wikström, K., & Jåfs, D. (2013). Project governance and path creation in the early stages of Finnish nuclear power projects. *International Journal of Project Management, 31*(5), 712–723.

Jepsen, A. L., & Eskerod, P. (2009). Stakeholder analysis in projects: Challenges in using current guidelines in the real world. *International Journal of Project Management, 27*(4), 335–343.

Johnsen, R. E., & Lacoste, S. (2016). An exploration of the "dark side" associations of conflict, power and dependence in customer–supplier relationships. *Industrial Marketing Management, 59*, 76–95.

Laan, H. V., & Dewulf, G. (2011). Reducing opportunistic behaviour through a project alliance. *International Journal of Managing Projects in Business, 4*(4), 660–679.

Lundin, R. A., & Söderholm, A. (1995). A theory of the temporary organization. *Scandinavian Journal of Management, 11*(4), 437–455.

Maylor, H. (2001). Beyond the Gantt chart: Project management moving on. *European Management Journal, 19*(1), 92–100.

Meng, X. (2012). The effect of relationship management on project performance in construction. *International Journal of Project Management, 30*(2), 188–198.

Müller, R., & Turner, J. R. (2007). Matching the project manager's leadership style to project type. *International Journal of Project Management, 25*(1), 21–32.

Müller, R., & Turner, R. (2010). Leadership competency profiles of successful project managers. *International Journal of Project Management, 28*(5), 437–448.

Munns, A. K., & Bjeirmi, B. F. (1996). The role of project management in achieving project success. *International Journal of Project Management, 14*(2), 81–87.

Orr, R. J., & Scott, W. R. (2008). Institutional exceptions on global projects: A process model. *Journal of International Business Studies, 39*(4), 562–588.

Pant, I., & Baroudi, B. (2008). Project management education: The human skills imperative. *International Journal of Project Management, 26*(2), 124–128.

Pollack, J., & Adler, D. (2015). Emergent trends and passing fads in project management research: A scientometric analysis of changes in the field. *International Journal of Project Management, 33*(1), 236–248.

Powell, W. W. (1990). Neither market nor hierarchy: Network forms of organization. *Research in Organizational Behavior, 12*, 295–336.

Project Management Institute. (2013). *PMBOK guide* (5th ed.). Newtow Square, PA: Project Management Institute.

Rokeach, M. (1973). *The nature of human values*. New York: Free Press.

Savolainen, P., & Ahonen, J. J. (2014). Knowledge lost: Challenges in changing project manager between sales and implementation in software projects. *International Journal of Project Management, 33*(1), 92–102.

Schwartz, S. (1992). Universals in the content and structure of values: Theoretical advances and empirical tests in 20 countries. *Advances in Experimental Psychology, 25*, 1–65.

Schwartz, S. (2012). An overview of the Schwartz theory of basic values. *Online Readings in Psychology and Culture, 2*(1).

Schwartz, S. H., Cieciuch, J., Vecchione, M., Davidov, E., Fischer, R., Beierlein, C., et al. (2012). Refining the theory of basic individual values. *Journal of Personality and Social Psychology, 103*(4), 663–688.

Turner, J. R., & Simister, S. J. (2001). Project contract management and a theory of organization. *International Journal of Project Management, 19*(8), 457–464.

Tyssen, A. k., Wald, A., & Spieth, P. (2013). Leadership in temporary organizations: A review of leadership theories and a research agenda. *Project Management Journal, 44*(6), 52–67.

5

Making Sense of Network Dynamics through Network Picturing

Tiina Valjakka, Valtteri Kaartemo, and Katri Valkokari

Introduction of the Problem

Constant change is often seen as the main challenge facing firms in today's economy, and therefore research interest has also focused on the types of networks that enable dynamics (e.g., agility, renewal, and even exploration of new business opportunities). When approaching networks as systems including several sub-systems, as described in the introduction of this book, it can be understood how the future structure and paths of dynamic business network development are fundamentally unknowable. It is because they are co-produced through interactions within the sub-systems and not traceable in any simple way to the individual actions

T. Valjakka (✉) • K. Valkokari
VTT Technical Research Center of Finland, Tampere, Finland

V. Kaartemo
University of Turku, Turku, Finland

J. Vesalainen et al. (eds.), *Practices for Network Management*,
DOI 10.1007/978-3-319-49649-8_5

of the participants. The managerial challenge is to guide the development within a business network over the boundaries of organizations. Thus, practical tools are needed to better understand how actors' network strategies actually come into being in continuous interaction between the organizations. In line with earlier studies of strategy-as-practice research, this chapter reflects utilization of strategy tools and how they facilitate the work of strategists (e.g., Kaplan 2011; Jarzabkowski et al. 2013).

The network-picturing tool extends our understanding of strategic management in dynamic business networks. We explicate this through two cases. In the first case study, we showcase how network picturing helps in recognizing alternative network trajectories and to develop value propositions that are beneficial to the network, to the dominant actors, to the ones serving the dominant actors, and to those who are challenging the status quo. The second case study focuses on the downstream (demand) dimension of business networks, including from the perspectives of sales, distribution, after-sales, and service networks. In the context of a business network, each of these actors has its own perception of the network and its position within it. In a way, network pictures are the actor's network theory, its individual beliefs (theories in use) of what the relevant business network looks like and how it "works." In practice, this is one of the reasons why attempts to manage a network often fail or create no response while actors have not considered the interests of other parties. Therefore, drawing from the management point of view, the network-picturing tool aims to support managers in making sense: how can they picture and combine the different network perspectives in order to better manage the network?

Background of Network Pictures as a Sense-Making Tool

Networks are multilevel systems. According to Moliterno and Mahony (2010), network theory of the organization should therefore be multilevel in its scope, considering how networks at one level of the organizational system influence networks at higher and/or lower levels. In order to manage actors and their activities within the network-system level, managers need to understand the perceptions and interests the other actors have (Valkokari 2015). In addition to joint business activities and strategic intents, managers should make sense of the evolving and dynamic nature of networks. Thus, the network dynamics consist of a complex pattern of activities, both intentional and emerging. Emerging from these activities and interactions between the business network actors are the network-system level dynamics that we can observe as changes in the network's characteristics (i.e., in structures, relationships, actors, and roles of actors) (Valkokari 2015).

In the IMP (Industrial Marketing and Purchasing) literature, *network pictures* have been defined as business actors' subjective mental representations (or frameworks) of their surroundings, and thus as sense-making tools that underlie decision-making in networks (Mattsson 2002; Ford et al. 2003). They have also been used as a tool by either researchers or practitioners to grasp the actors' understanding of their surrounding business network (Henneberg et al. 2009; Ramos and Ford 2010). Furthermore, Laari-Salmela et al. (2015) state how an interesting topic for research includes opening up the relationship between network pictures and the sense-making taking place between organizations. In such cases, network pictures can be utilized as *boundary-spanning mechanisms* (Hawkins and Rezazade 2012), which serve as an interface between different organizations (Koskinen and Mäkinen 2009). Network pictures are particularly useful in revealing both multilevel structures as well as processual realm, thus enabling sense-making of a changing network (Kaartemo et al. 2015).

The network actors build a shared understanding about the network's strategic intent through formal business negotiations as well as informal interactions (Valkokari 2015). Thus, the managers' understanding of perceptions across boundaries is a key to firm's success in complex business environments, where knowledge and resources are dispersed and value co-creation for customers requires integration of resources. In other words, network management requires understanding of networks as a system and furthermore getting a clear picture of the different mechanisms within this system.

Network-Picturing Tool

The network-picturing tool builds on the assumption that through understanding relationships, activities, and interactions between network members, the development path of networks can be managed and guided by influencing other network actors. As mentioned in the introduction (Chap. 1), this kind of boundary-spanning *network leadership* is the common activity of all network actors that affects the development of social capital, that is, *networks-as-co-ordinated social systems*. Thus, a careful review of a firm's own position among the networks as well as different networking directions offers managers new *theories in use*, how their business networks will currently operate, or how they should look in the future. In other words, network pictures are strategic sense-making tools that can be utilized in shaping stability and change in business networks. Firms are simultaneously acting in various networks in different roles as illustrated in Fig. 5.1.

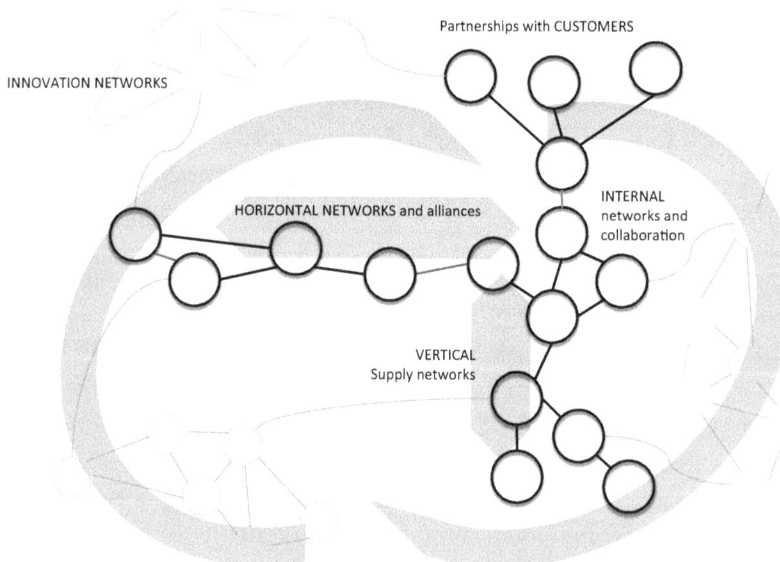

Fig. 5.1 Network-picturing tool

Often, companies anchor themselves to a single vision of their customer needs and network structures, which may preclude considering the viewpoints of other network actors. Many businesses have a complex nature, and *network picturing makes* **it possible to see beyond the most obvious and traditionally proximate actors.** In other words, missing links between the actors and structural holes are also considered within network picturing. Managers who understand the different forms of inter-organizational relationships are also able to manage their dynamics and consequential uncertainty better while they are more aware of the choices and decisions of others and their influence to the game as a whole.

The focus of **vertical customer–supplier networks** and relationships is, by definition, typically to supply present products. Joint operations are usually managed in direct business relationships and through formal governance mechanisms like agreements. Naturally, customers are important sources of knowledge about needs, requirements, wants, and ideas that are crucial for developing new offerings that meet market demand. On the other hand, in addition to direct supply in the form of products or resources, there is a range of intangible knowledge such as reputation, network connections, and experiences which are important to business development. In customer–supplier collaboration, the vertical relationship often guides the actors toward a one-track mindset of action, where the customer is a major player and the supplier an object of the action. In such relationships, the feedback loops and bi-directional interaction are often missing. For smaller supplier companies especially, the claim for and protection of their rights in relationships with larger customers is typically inconvenient.

Horizontal development networks and alliances cover different direct and indirect relationships with other companies, consultants, and regional development agencies. The focus is, for instance, on development learning, benchmarking, or joint activities in limited areas like research, marketing, or export. Thus, horizontal relationships may counterpoint equality between the actors and thereby overlook the need for vision and mechanisms for decision-making and management of the operations. Universities, research centers, innovation intermediators, and funding agencies act as important sources of knowledge about information, technology, and finance for the innovation process within **innovation networks.** In such co-operation settings, the similarity between knowledge bases as well as network positions has a significant influence on the possibilities and willingness to share or transfer knowledge.

In practice, network management is typically disturbed in different operational units within one firm, and the focus of network management differs in each dimension. Thus, there are two basic purposes for the various forms of inter-organizational relationships, that is, co-exploration and co-exploitation (Parmigiani and Rivera-Santos 2011). In line with that our framework distinguished (see Chap. 1) network practices, networks-as-knowledge-creating platforms (co-exploration), and networks-as-value-generating entities (co-exploitation). The exploration of new ideas for innovation and the exploitation of present knowledge to develop their offerings require firms to integrate different knowledge sources and network actors into their dynamic business development. On the other hand, the exploitation requires co-ordination of the networks' resources into effective joint value generation. It is important to note that besides formal observable business relationships, there are less noticeable informal relationships between the actors—and these social networks and interconnections may be an even more efficient way to find new solutions and fill structural holes within network operations.

Network dynamics and timing pose challenges to management; network actors can have different perceptions of how the network should work, what its interests should be, and why they are participating. For instance, one of the network actors might consider the objective to be the exploration of new knowledge and future business opportunities, while others operate within the present business model and expect that the benefits will materialize faster. The role and network position of the firm are critical factors in the selection of suitable methods for network development and management. The choices and decisions of network actors can be perceived only when managers have an understanding about their development agenda and strategic targets.

Furthermore, it is important to evaluate the network pictures (i.e., actors, their targets, and relationships between them) regularly. While firms are sold and bought and the strategies change, this causes changes at the network-system level. The scenarios of different value propositions can help to foresee the development paths of networks. In the following section, we present two cases which showcase how network picturing may be used for envisioning and driving changes in networks.

Network Picturing as a Tool to Envision Network Change by a Multinational Company

The first case company is a large multinational company (MNC) that designs and supplies cargo systems for global container shipping industry. The main customers are Asian shipyards. The company has decades of history in serving container shipyards. The case company gave up manufacturing already in the early 1990s and has since then delivered cargo handling systems manufactured by their suppliers. In the aftermath of the financial crisis in 2008, the market for new container ships diminished drastically. In order to survive in the challenging market condition, the case company created new solutions team which questioned the reliance on shipyards as customers and started portraying its network from a novel angle.

In the following paragraphs, we present how network picturing was employed to help developing value propositions for multiple actors under alternative scenarios, which were identified in workshops with the case company managers. There is an extensive amount of literature on and around scenario workshops (Miesing and Van Ness 2007), and therefore we do not go into detail on running the workshops here. Instead, we focus on the unique part of the process, namely the development of value propositions for multiple actors under alternative network scenarios (Fig. 5.2).

First, in our two workshops, we envisioned multiple network scenarios about how the future might evolve for global container shipping, and we discussed the potential role of the focal company under each scenario. We ended up describing alternative scenarios in terms of the dominance of different actors (A, B, and D) and spent some time imagining what kinds of network practices might be characteristic to these scenarios.

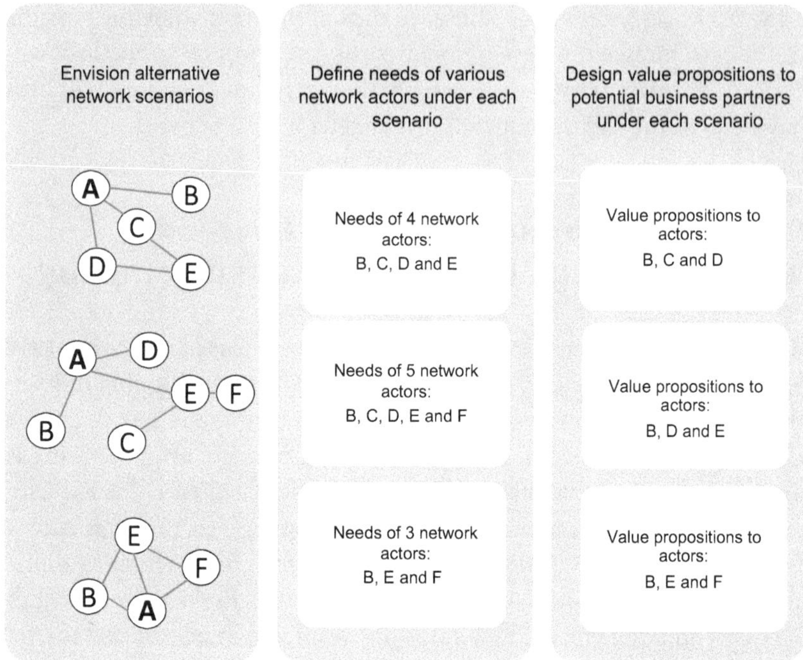

Fig. 5.2 The process of developing value propositions to multiple actors under alternative network scenarios

Second, in order to define the needs of various actors under each scenario, we ran another workshop. Starting with pre-defined scenarios and related network practices, we asked case company managers about the basic network principles: (1) What is needed by the dominant actor in the given scenario? (2) What is the position of the other actors? As a result, we were able to identify not only the needs of the dominant actor but also the needs of those serving the dominant actors and those willing to challenge the dominant actor under each network scenario. Based on the discussion in the workshop, the researchers drew network pictures that visualized the roles of each actor under each scenario.

Third, we initiated a discussion on what kind of value the focal company could propose to each actor under each scenario. This gives guidance to the focal company in determining what kinds of capabilities are needed in-house in the future. In addition, drafted value propositions should also initiate internal processes in the R&D department to launch research and development that enables the proposition of value to various actors in the future. Thus, the exercise helps the company tackle the changes in the network.

In our workshop, the consensus was that our focal company would prefer two scenarios over one, and therefore it was deemed necessary to drive the network toward desired future. In addition to designing value propositions that may be attractive a decade from now, the method also facilitated discussion about potential activities that the focal company could perform in order to guide the network development toward a preferable future. Thus, it is also useful for deciding upon more short-term development projects.

The discussion further highlighted the importance of understanding customer problems and providing solutions for them. Employing the method not only enabled the focal company to focus on one solution approach to one customer segment but also broadened the horizon for long-term value proposition development for multiple actors. Moreover, the network-picturing workshops initiated discussion on how the focal company could communicate its network proposition (i.e., what the focal company does to improve the viability of the ecosystem, proposing value that is beneficial for multiple actors). Furthermore, the method is useful not only for imagining different situations but also for considering early on what kind of value could be proposed to network actors when actual events indicate that one scenario is becoming more likely than the others.

Network Picturing as a Tool to Drive Network Change by an SME

The second case company is an SME (Small and medium-sized enterprise) that develops and manufactures machines for construction, multipurpose machines, and utility machines for demanding applications. The main market area of the company is the Nordic region, where the typical customer is a privately owned SME or an entrepreneur. The company has a strong history in development and manufacturing; previously, sales and service functions were responsibilities of a specialized partner company. Due to changes in the market, the case company started to build its own sales and service organization and downstream network seven years ago.

In our second case study, we utilized network picturing as a tool for strategic management in the case company. We first drew two focal company perspectives, factory (Fig. 5.3 upper left) and sales (Fig. 5.3 upper right), identified their most important connections, and described the roles and content of interaction with these first-level partners.

The managing director and the main owner of the company is responsible for strategic-level issues, but the operations are run by the factory director, so they are the key actors whose network pictures are considered. Sales representatives are responsible for sales and customer relationships

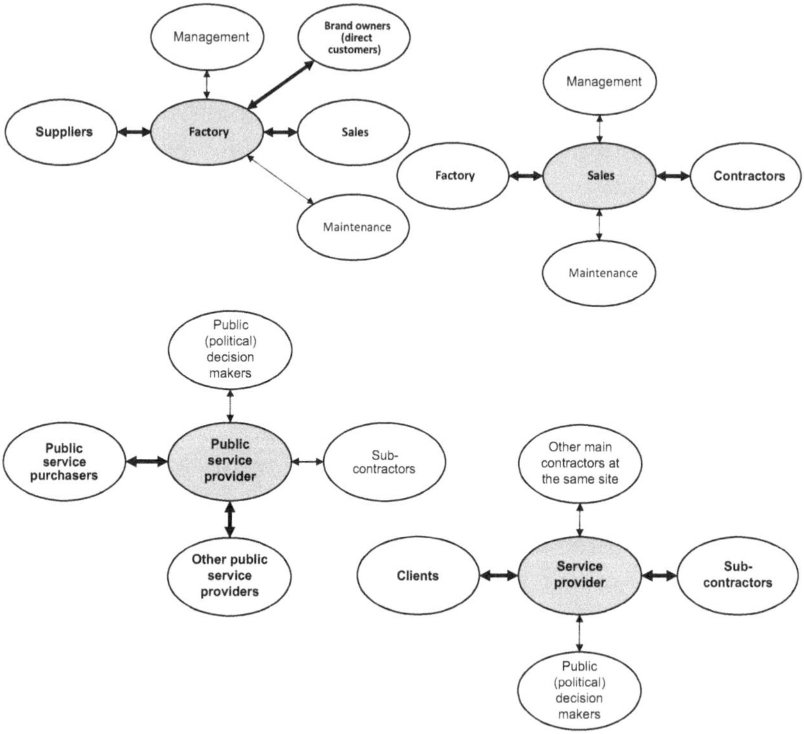

Fig. 5.3 Network from factory and sales perspectives (upper half), and, Networks from different customers' perspectives (lower half)

in certain geographical areas. Most of them have a long history and experience in the industry, thus knowing their traditional customer base, competitors, and the machines they sell. There are loyal customers in each area that ideate new solutions and applications for the machinery in order to enhance their businesses. The machines are customized, and dealing with the versatile customer requirements and requests is the motivation of the regular communication between the sales and the product development and production. Also, the tenders and order-to-delivery process require co-operation. The company has built a maintenance network in the field, but the sales representative is often the first contact concerning repair or maintenance.

The broader network perspectives of the two "end-customers" were sought in application areas where the machines of the case company are used (Fig. 5.3 lower left and lower right). These network pictures, snapshots from different network actors' perspectives, were then utilized to draw the network management perspective. The first end-customer is a public service provider operating in one large city. The other end-customer perspective is from a private sector service provider specializing in power network services (e.g., designing and building wind farms). The main collaboration partners of both end-customers were their own customers and the parallel actors (i.e., other public service providers for the first and other large contractors in joint projects for the second). The end-customer views of the network and their own non-existent role in those pictures were eye-opening for the case company.

Network picturing resulted in the identification of new relevant network actors and the needs for building connections to them (Fig. 5.4). *The strategic aim of the case company management is to act as a driver of change to guide the industry in the direction they believe is profitable to them and also to the other relevant network actors (e.g., service purchasers, service providers, and contractors).* Their vision is that the mobile multipurpose machinery they offer is more productive and environmentally friendly than other solutions. Traditional methods and approaches still dominate at work sites and sub-optimization is common. The current focus of sales is to their direct customers, the contractors. This is a slow bottom-up approach for change: the contractors work and market their versatile machines to service providers. Thus, our case study suggests that different

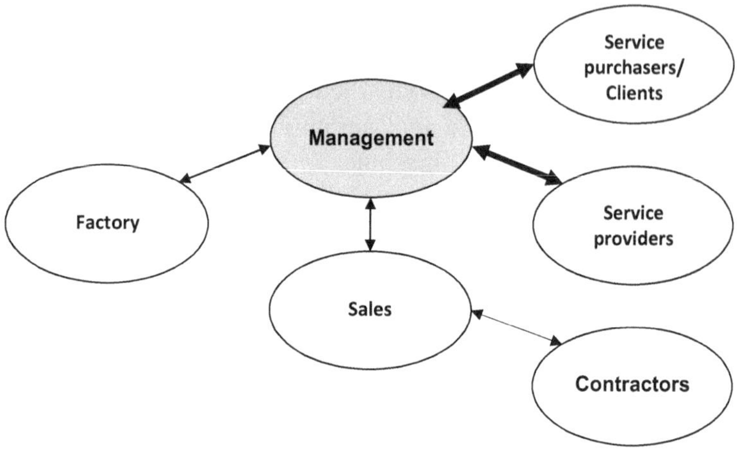

Fig. 5.4 Network from SME management perspective

network-picturing tools can be utilized as a means of transformation in companies seeking growth in new markets and internationalization.

Conclusions

Although no firms are in such a position that they could manage the whole network system, every firm, MNC or SME, is able to manage its own position and role within their networked environment. This requires systematic and strategic analyses of the network environment, its actors, and their targets. In this chapter, we showcase how network picturing may be utilized in sense-making network dynamics and associated needs of various network actors. Based on these analyses, firms are able to make more conscious decisions, take calculated risks, and leap at emerging opportunities by making explicit the potentially beneficial value propositions that would otherwise remain hidden. Thus, we explicate that network picturing is particularly beneficial in envisioning and driving change in business networks. Naturally, the strategic analyses of networked business environments are challenging and time-consuming, thereby requiring more open dialogue between different units of the firm as well as with network actors. Visualization of networks through simple pictures can anyhow provide a helpful tool for such discussion and support managers in sharing their own *network theories in use*. To sum up, the workshop process included the following key questions: (1) Where are we now and in the future (strategic positioning)? (2) What are our targets and where do we want to go (vision)? and (3) With whom and how do we get there (strategic change and required network relationships)?

This chapter contributes to the emerging *network-as-practice* research by describing the sense-making tool and the relevant workshop process. Originally Jarzabkowski and Seidl (2008) had discussed the role of meetings in the social practice theory and defined three critical aspects of those strategic episodes in meetings: initiation, conduct, and termination. The workshops facilitated utilization of network picturing as a strategy tool and supported the interaction of strategists in dynamic business network setting. Strategic discussion in the workshop meetings socially validated the current order and served as a place for participants' sense-making (Weick 1995). On the other hand, through network picturing, the strategists explored and generated change in their shared strategic orientations over boundaries of a company or its units. Our cases brought out three workshop praxis that can support critical aspects of the strategic meetings: initiation, conduct, and termination. First, for initiation, it is important to have quite open and informal agenda, in order to allow organizational members to step out of their daily routines, to reflect on them and, based on that, to propose variations to the existing strategic orientations. Second, for conduct, researchers' active role in guiding the workshop supported open discussion and joint problem-solving. Third, for termination, visualization of network picture enabled to recouple the workshop results, that is, the abstract network theories in use, to the outside processes in the daily routines of workshop participants.

In a dynamic environment it is necessary to constantly reflect one's value propositions against the development of the network. This is the only way to ensure that value propositions are appealing to those in power and that they serve the dominant players or alternatively that they help the challengers to break the status quo. Here, it is important that a company identifies certain events that are needed for the scenario to actualize. Therefore, as a managerial implication we suggest companies to run network-picturing workshops on a regular basis.

References

Ford, D., Gadde, L.-E., Håkansson, H., & Snehota, I. (2003). *Managing business relationships* (2nd ed.). Chichester: John Wiley and Sons.

Hawkins, M. A., & Rezazade, M. M. H. (2012). Knowledge boundary spanning process: Synthesizing four spanning mechanisms. *Management Decision, 50*(10), 1800–1815.

Henneberg, S., Naudé, P., & Mouzas, S. (2009). Sense-making and management in business networks—Some observations, considerations, and a research agenda. *Industrial Marketing Management, 39*(3), 355–360.

Jarzabkowski, P., & Seidl, D. (2008). The role of meetings in the social practice of strategy. *Organization Studies, 29*(11), 1391–1426.

Jarzabkowski, P., Spee, P., & Smets, M. (2013). Material artifacts: Practices for doing strategy with 'stuff'. *European Management Journal, 31*(1), 41–54.

Kaartemo, V., Makkonen, H., & Olkkonen, R. (2015). The potential of network pictures for international alliance and network research. In J. Larimo, N. Nummela, & T. Mainela (Eds.), *Handbook on international alliance and network research* (pp. 229–242). Cheltenham, UK: Edward Elgar.

Kaplan, S. (2011). Strategy and PowerPoint: An inquiry into the epistemic culture and machinery of strategy-making. *Organization Science, 22*(2), 320–346.

Koskinen, K. U., & Mäkinen, S. (2009). Role of boundary objects in negotiations of project contracts. *International Journal of Project Management, 27*, 31–38.

Laari-Salmela, S., Mainela, T., & Puhakka, V. (2015). Beyond network pictures: Situational strategizing in network context. *Industrial Marketing Management, 45*, 117–127.

Mattsson, L. G. (2002). *Dynamics of markets: How 'Actor-Network Theory' and 'Markets-as-Networks' can learn from each other.* Paper presented at the Nordic Workshop on Interorganizational Studies, Kolding, August 2002.

Miesing, P., & Van Ness, R. K. (2007). Exercise: Scenario planning. *Organization Management Journal, 4*(2), 148–167.

Moliterno, T. P., & Mahony, D. M. (2010). Network theory of organization: A multilevel approach. *Journal of Management, 37*(2), 443–467.

Parmigiani, A., & Rivera-Santos, M. (2011). Clearing a path through the forest: A meta-review of interorganizational relationships. *Journal of Management, 37*(4), 1108–1136.

Ramos, C., & Ford, I. D. (2010). Network pictures as a research device: Developing a tool to capture actors' perceptions in organizational networks. *Industrial Marketing Management, 40*(3), 447–464.

Valkokari, K. (2015). Describing network dynamics in three different business nets. *Scandinavian Journal of Management, 31*(2), 219–231. Weick, K. E. (1995) *Sensemaking in organizations*. Thousand Oaks, CA: Sage.

Weick, K. E. (1995). *Sensemaking in organizations*. Thousand Oaks, CA: Sage.

6

Functional Contracting for Network Creation and Governance

Mika Viljanen, Anna Hurmerinta, Johanna Liinamaa, Maria Ivanova-Gongne, Hanna Luotola, and Magnus Gustafsson

Contracts: The Missing Dimension in Inter-organizational Integration?

Creating and sustaining solutions business networks pose considerable challenges to network leader firms. These challenges, in our contention, often stem from inadequate integration. To achieve integration—"a unity of effort"—among the solutions business network participants, managers deploy a wide variety of integration mechanisms, ranging from technical integration (Davies and Hobday 2005; Iansiti 1995; Martinez and Jarillo 1989; McCord and Eppinger 1993) and formal integration to relational

M. Viljanen (✉) • A. Hurmerinta
University of Turku, Turku, Finland

J. Liinamaa • M. Ivanova-Gongne • H. Luotola • M. Gustafsson
Åbo Akademi University, Turku, Finland

J. Vesalainen et al. (eds.), *Practices for Network Management*,
DOI 10.1007/978-3-319-49649-8_6

(or social) integration (Barki and Pinsonneault 2005; Barnard 1968; Galbraith 2002; Henderson and Clark 1990; Hobday et al. 2005).

Even if the different types of integration mechanisms are not mutually exclusive but are constantly overlapping and interacting (Liinamaa and Wikström 2009), mainstream accounts tend to stress the importance of technical and relational integrations. Creating and sustaining a network require considerable amounts of relational work in building boundary objects to transfer and synchronize technical knowledge, to build common understandings across organizational boundaries, and to ensure persistent alignment of values and objectives.

We argue, though, that the stress put on technical and relational integrations leads to the relative neglect and underutilization of what are typically understood as formal integration techniques. Our contention, in particular, is that innovative contracting techniques have untapped potential in business network creation and governance. On a more abstract level, we argue, in line with Poppo and Zenger (2002), that formal contracts may have relational uses and can, thus, supplement or outright replace some relational integration efforts.

A Case Study of Functional Contracting

Our conclusions are based on an explorative action research case study on deploying an innovative contractual structure as a value-adding network creation and governance tool. To demonstrate and test the potential a set of non-standard contracting techniques might have in the creation and governance of a dyadic solution delivery network, we contributed to the development of a new solution business model and its concomitant sales process within a division of a global logistical equipment firm, Gamma (see in detail Liinamaa et al. 2016).

The case firm had made a decision to transform from a traditional equipment manufacturer to a solution seller. As a part of its migration efforts, the company planned to abandon its traditional technical sales orientation and cost-plus-pricing approach, and replace the two with a value-based selling methodology (Storbacka 2011; Terho et al. 2012; Töytäri et al. 2015) backed up by a value-based pricing scheme (Töytäri and Rajala 2015; Töytäri et al. 2015; Liinamaa et al. 2016).

Successful implementation of value-based selling and pricing requires companies to overcome a number of barriers (Töytäri and Rajala 2015; Töytäri et al. 2015; Liinamaa et al. 2016). The barriers encountered in introducing a value-based pricing approach typically derive from two intertwined sources.

First, the value-based pricing approach unsettles a dominant incumbent business practice: the cost-plus-pricing pattern. This is risky as the majority of market participants will likely perceive the incumbent practices as fair and will be unreceptive to the change. Network participants' reluctance stems from the fundamentality of the concomitant transformation. Value-based selling and pricing recast the relationships within the delivery network. The cost-plus approach enacts and performs the network within a transactional setting. The parties' value-creation processes are discrete and unentangled. An outside product or service enters the parties' value-creation processes as a discrete factor of production. Value-based pricing, however, unravels the frame and reforges the relationships into co-creationary partnerships. This shifts the expectations that govern value-sharing. A partnership is a single value-creation entity, where multiple network participants have claims to the value the individual firms generate. Studies suggest that the resistance can only be overcome by concerted, well-designed marketing efforts that are implemented consistently. Even then, successful implementation may be possible only if the seller has an extremely strong market position and no feasible, traditionally priced alternatives for the seller's offering exist (Töytäri et al. 2015).

Second, drafting and devising a value-based pricing model entail serious legal-technical difficulties, in part stemming from the complexity of the network value function. In our case study, the value function contained a bewildering array of variables, including (1) the mechanical performance of the solution platform; (2) its usability; (3) market conditions; (4) idiosyncrasies in the network participants' value capture and pricing models; (5) the particular uses the end users chose to deploy the platform; (6) the network actors' operational capabilities; and (7) pure luck. Complexity forces highly complicated contracts. In Gamma's case, the pricing mechanism had to build on an extensive simulation-based infrastructure. The infrastructure was expensive to build and run. Moreover, the pricing model had to be tailored to each individual solution network in a co-creationary process. Our research suggests that contracting in such an environment requires considerable resources and efforts.

In order to overcome the challenges, Gamma not only had to convince the network participants of the benefits of its technological offering but also had to induce the other parties to accept the contractual model implementing it. The company, however, had no established tools to market the new network business model and its concomitant contracts. To meet this need, the project team, which comprised researchers and Gamma personnel, designed new sales and contracting processes. The contracting process was designed using *a functional-contracting approach* as a theoretical template.

Theoretical Background of the Functional-Contracting Process

As discussed earlier in this chapter, our contention is that many of the previously mentioned challenges are, in fact, integration problems stemming from inadequate alignment of the network participant organizations. Thus, integration theory is the first cornerstone of our tool.

Integration is key to successful pursuit of solutions business, as solutions providers aim to initiate co-creationary relationships with their customers and often their customer's customers. The network, be it a dyad or consisting of more than two participants, must be able to function as a co-ordinated whole to facilitate complex co-dependent performances and make the solutions business models feasible.

Multiple possible integration mechanisms have been proposed for use in achieving the "unity of effort" complex performances require. *Technical integration* refers to techniques and mechanisms firms use to align their technological offerings to complement and co-function with one another (Davies and Hobday 2005; Iansiti 1995; Martinez and Jarillo 1989; McCord and Eppinger 1993). *Formal* and *relational* (or *social*) *integration mechanisms* ensure that the organizations are interoperable and capable of functional co-operation (Barki and Pinsonneault 2005; Barnard 1968; Galbraith 2002; Henderson and Clark 1990; Hobday et al. 2005). The literature further suggests that different types of integration mechanisms are not mutually exclusive but constantly overlapping and interacting (Liinamaa and Wikström 2009). For example, managers employ greater levels of relational integration mechanisms when contracts are customized. Similarly, they are more likely to increase contractual complexity as they develop greater levels of relational governance (Poppo and Zenger 2002).

Functional-contracting theory is the second cornerstone of the tool as it views contracts as active management tools crucial to business success (Barringer and Harrison 2000; Saxena 2008). In this paradigm, the contracting focus moves from *safeguarding* and *codifying* a deal to active *co-ordination* and *adaptation* of a co-creationary process (Schepker et al. 2014; Eigen 2012).

When in the traditional safeguarding and codifying mode, firms typically perform contracts as devices that allow them to lock in certain futures. The contract, as an artifact, documents and ossifies what the parties are to do, when and how to achieve the future. After the contract is signed and closed, the document loses its significance as anything but a to-do checklist—until a dispute arises. Then the contract becomes relevant again as parties fight over who is liable for failing to bring about the locked-in future (see e.g., MacNeil 1978).

When contracts are used to serve the co-ordination and adaptation functions, the picture changes. To illustrate, imagine a greenfield delivery contract for power generation plant construction. If in the safeguarding mode, the parties will draft an exhaustive, unambiguous contract which spells out an immutable list of performance requirements detailing what the parties must do, how they must do it, and when. However, if the parties' contracts are designed for co-ordination and adaptation purposes, the contracts will look different. In addition to outlining the scope and extent of each party's performance obligations, the parties will agree, for example, upon (1) the procedures to be used for managing the inevitable revisions to performance requirements the unforeseen changes will trigger and (2) the processes and methods used to facilitate concrete co-ordination and co-operation during project implementation. The processes and methods may include forging appropriate organizational interfaces (integration of legal departments, escalation procedures) for communication and problem-solving, and incentive structures to align organizational and staff interests.

The innovation in our tool is to combine integration and functional contracting by transporting contractual integration to the precontractual phase. We argue that contractual techniques can be used to govern sales processes. In fact, our findings suggest that an appropriate *precontractual integration model* may be an important success factor that determines whether lead firms can introduce and entrench value-based pricing models. In practice, the integration model refers to a collection of integration mechanisms that allows the network lead firms and other network participants to align their sales and purchasing processes, synchronize their value perceptions, and become convinced of the beneficiality of the proposed new value-sharing arrangements. A functional-contracting process, thus, may be crucial in facilitating the alignment of parties' value-quantification tools, communication methods, decision-making sequences, and even negotiation ethics.

Outline of the Functional-Contracting Process

The functional-contracting process (Fig. 6.1) deploys functional, adaptive, and co-ordinative contracting tools and builds on the idea that contractual techniques can be used as point intervention devices to co-ordinate interactions between the network participants during the precontractual negotiation phase.

The tool was designed to function in an environment where the lead firm had already decided to implement a value-based selling approach and seeking to introduce a value-based pricing model. The background assumption was that the lead firm was likely to encounter resistance from other network participants who viewed the pricing model with suspicion and were unwilling to share a portion of the value the lead firm's offering would generate. Initially, the tool was designed to help the lead firm to effect changes in the network participants' organizations in order to induce them to adopt the offered value-based pricing model. During the process, as new challenges emerged, the tool developed into a full-blown precontractual integration model.

Technically, the tool consists of four memoranda of understanding (MoUs). The MoUs are contract-like instruments that utilize contractual impact pathways even if their exact legal-technical nature is, by design,

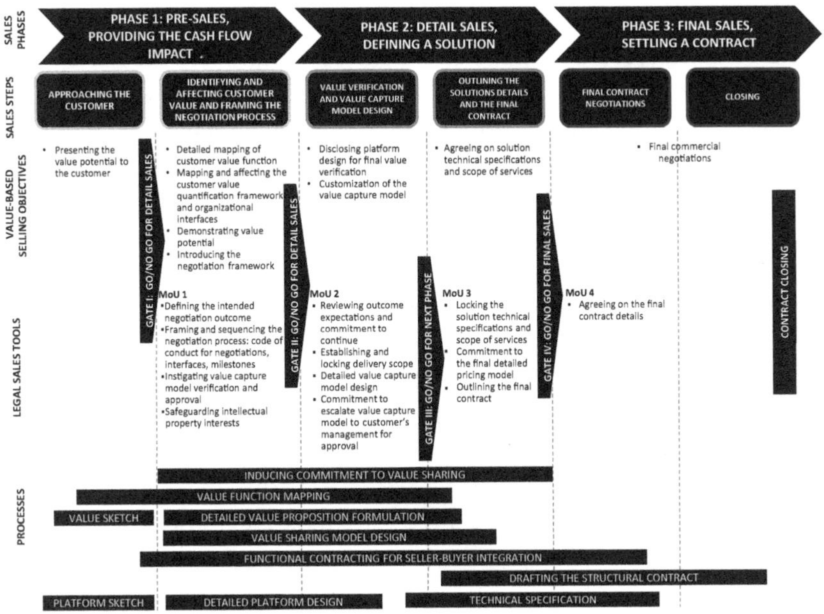

Fig. 6.1 Functional-contracting process

ambiguous. The key objectives of the MoUs are to align the organizations to facilitate successful negotiations. The MoUs are sequential, where each MoU is customized to match and address the specific challenges the parties are expected to confront during the negotiations.

MoU 1 is designed to frame the negotiation process. Consequently, the document (1) sets forth the basic outline of the contracting process, (2) offers a preliminary "marketing" description of the value-based pricing model and its related contracts, (3) outlines the principles for information exchange during negotiations, and (4) establishes obligations to negotiate in good faith and to terminate the negotiations if it becomes clear that either party will not conclude the final contract. MoU 1 also contains important non-utilization and non-disclosure terms.

MoU 1 serves several purposes. First, it formulates a clear structure for the negotiation process. The MoU establishes a gate (milestone) structure for the participants to track the progress toward the final contracts. Second, it communicates the terms on which the lead firm is willing to negotiate with the other participants. As such, MoU 1 is also an internal commitment device for the lead firm: the gates are integrated as key performance indicators into its management system. Third, the MoU—the good faith negotiation and prompt termination obligations as well as the non-utilization and non-disclosure terms, in particular—attempts to mitigate the risk that the parties engage in opportunistic behavior by binding them to an explicit negotiation ethics and establishing penalties for unauthorized use of the other parties' information or designs. Fourth, the memorandum serves as a strategic business intelligence tool. If a prospective participant is not willing to sign the MoU, which only weakly binds the parties, the lead firm gains important information about the party's motivation and interests. Fifth, MoU 1 engages in legal sales by introducing the structure of the final contract and informing the gatekeepers of its crucial features.

MoU 2 is designed to govern the pricing model co-creation process. As indicated previously, value-based pricing models are often complex and have to be adjusted to the particular business models and monetization methods each participant employs. MoU 2 contains a blueprint for this co-creationary process and sets up a pricing model co-creation organization that consists of both lead firm's and other firms' employees.

MoU 3 is designed to address a specific problem the lead firm expected to encounter. While the other firms' frontline employees may become convinced of the functionality of the lead firm offering, the pricing model might not be acceptable for the actual decision-makers. This problem will likely result in sales resource misallocation and, possibly, other adverse consequences. MoU 3 attempts to force the other firms to escalate the pricing model to their board for agreement-in-principle relatively early in the contracting process. If and once the firms agree to the pricing model, it is locked-in; adopting parties are committed to the value-based pricing logic.

MoU 4 is signed after all network participants have made their investment decisions and commit to the pricing model. MoU 4 includes the final solution delivery scope and pricing model, the final details for the performance measures, and the model for sharing value within the network. It also documents the remaining contractual issues the firms agree to before closing the final agreement.

Conclusions and Managerial Implications

Migrating toward the value-based selling with value-based pricing model in industrial solution business is an illustrative example of a situation where complex multi-layer intra- and inter-organizational transformations must take place. Our contention is that a functional-contracting process may be an effective tool for achieving these transformations and may thus have great potential as managerial tool. Moreover, functional-contracting process has both formal and relational uses and can, thus, supplement other relational governance efforts.

Although our study concerned the precontractual sales phase integration efforts, functional contracting as a heuristic for contract use carries promise outside the ambit within which it was tested. Similar contractual solutions could be used and are used to govern, in particular, long-term co-creationary processes which are situated in the gray area between Williamson's two governance extremes: the market and the hierarchy.

The process opens up new mechanisms that may be used to influence market structures, and create and govern business networks, adding a new significant impact pathway to the management repertoire. Although our study primarily concerned dyadic seller–customer relationships and did not produce quantitative data on the effects of the process on success rates, the process demonstrated potential on a conceptual level. Functional contracting may enable boundary spanners to co-ordinate and affect expectations along the value chain, prompt the co-creation of new added value allocation patterns, and initiate and guide the development of appropriate organizational interfaces. These techniques may buttress the boundary spanner's relational integration efforts, increase trust between networks participants, create credible commitment, and, thus, contribute to the social capital on which the co-creationary business networks are dependent. For example, MoU 1 was designed to entrench the new sales and contracting process within Gamma and affect parties' behavior during negotiations, creating an honest negotiation space; MoU 3 attempted to force a new interface in network participants by requiring them to commit to escalate the pricing model to their board for approval before the negotiations proceed.

A more general-level lesson is that the creation of a new business network may require not only the development of a contractual governance model for the network but also serious legal marketing and sales efforts. Should a firm try to disrupt incumbent business practices, it will likely face, among other challenges, the legal entrenchment effect: existing contract structures and patterns have inertia of their own and are, consequently, hard to change.

The underlying causes of this effect are speculative. On the one hand, an intuitively appealing explanation is lawyers' professional identity, predicated upon risk identification and uncertainty reduction (Penland 2006). On the other hand, our research in Gamma suggests that value-based pricing and its concomitant contracts sit awkwardly with the underlying traditional contract law structures, which stress unambiguity, completeness, and certainty (Macneil 1978, 862–865). The same goes for contractual governance models for networks in general. Drafting a network governance contract that satisfies the lawyers' yearning for risk reduction and certainty will be difficult as will be demonstrating the other network participants that the contracts are functional and reliable. Thus, contracts, like value, have to be marketed. The target audience, legal experts and executives with the power to ratify fundamental business model changes, is typically not addressed in sales processes, has different expectations than the traditional business audience, and resides in organizational silos that are inaccessible to traditional sales processes and guarded by gatekeepers. Traditional integration tools will likely fail to open up access and convince this audience. We think the functional-contracting process is an effective methodology under these circumstances.

However, our experience with Gamma and its partners suggest that implementing the functional-contracting approach requires considerable conceptual dexterity. The contracts and contractual techniques we refer to here are not the deal codifications, namely the final contracts, but much smaller-scale objects, point intervention devices deployed to serve particular limited functions and address specific process governance and integration issues. They might not even live up to the conventional legal standards on what binding contracts are.

The required change in our perception of contracts will pose a considerable challenge to both business executives and legal experts. Agile functional contracting requires not only inter-organizational but also deep proactive intra-organizational integration of all business functions, including, for example, legal, sales, procurement, execution, and business and product development departments. Further, the adoption of functional contracting will require deep mindset changes. First, it requires lawyers to proactively engage in business and product development processes and serve a forward-looking role in developing creative legal governance structures for emerging business models. Second, business functions have to recognize that lawyers may contribute substantively to value-adding innovations during business development.

References

Barki, H., & Pinsonneault, A. (2005). A model of organizational integration, implementation effort and performance. *Organization Science, 16*(2), 165–179.

Barnard, C. I. (1968). *The functions of the executive*. Cambridge, MA: Harvard University Press.

Barringer, B. R., & Harrison, J. S. (2000). Walking a tightrope: Creating value through interorganizational relationships. *Journal of Management, 26*, 367–403.

Davies, A., & Hobday, M. (2005). *The business of projects: Managing innovation in complex products and systems*. Cambridge, UK: Cambridge University Press.

Eigen, Z. J. (2012). Empirical studies of contract. *Annual Review of Law and Social Science, 8*, 291–306.

Galbraith, J. R. (2002). Organizing to deliver solutions. *Organizational Dynamics, 31*(2), 194–207.

Henderson, R. M., & Clark, K. B. (1990). Architectural innovation: The reconfiguration of existing product technologies and the failure of established firms. *Administrative Science Quarterly, 35*(1), 9–30.

Hobday, M., Davies, A., & Prencipe, A. (2005). Systems integration: A core capability of the modern corporation. *Industrial and Corporate Change, 14*(6), 1109–1143.

Iansiti, M. (1995). Technology integration: Managing technological evolution in a complex environment. *Research Policy, 24*(4), 521–542.

Liinamaa, J., Viljanen, M., Hurmerinta, A., Ivanova-Gongne, M., Luotola, H., & Gustafsson, M. (2016). Performance-based and functional contracting in value-based solution selling. *Industrial Marketing Management, 59*, 37-49.

Liinamaa, J., & Wikström, K. (2009). Integration in project business: Mechanisms for knowledge integration. *International Journal of Knowledge Management Studies, 3*(3/4), 331–350.

MacNeil, I. R. (1978). Contracts: Adjustment of long-term economic relations under classical, neoclassical, and relational contract law. *Northwestern University Law Review, 72*(6), 854–905.

Martinez, J. I., & Jarillo, J. C. (1989). The evolution of research on coordination mechanisms in multinational corporations. *Journal of International Business Studies, 20*(3), 489–514.

McCord, K. R., & Eppinger, S. D. (1993). *Managing the integration problem in concurrent engineering*. Working Paper No. 3594, M.I.T. Sloan School of Management.

Penland, L. (2006). The hypothetical lawyer: Warrior, wiseman, or hybrid? *Appalachian Journal of Law, 6*(73), 73–100.

Poppo, L., & Zenger, T. (2002). Do formal contracts and relational governance function as substitutes or complements? *Strategic Management Journal, 23*(8), 707–725.

Saxena, A. (2008). *Enterprise contract management*. Fort Lauderdale: J. Ross Publishing.

Schepker, D. J., Oh, W. Y., Martynov, A., & Poppo, L. (2014). The many futures of contracts: Moving beyond structure and safeguarding to coordination and adaptation. *Journal of Management, 40*(1), 193–225.

Storbacka, K. (2011). A solution business model: Capabilities and management practices for integrated solutions. *Industrial Marketing Management, 40*(5), 699–711.

Terho, H., Haas, A., Eggert, A., & Ulaga, W. (2012). It's almost like taking the sales out of selling—Towards a conceptualization of value-based selling in business markets. *Industrial Marketing Management, 41*(1), 174–185.

Töytäri, P., & Rajala, R. (2015). Value-based selling: An organizational capability perspective. *Industrial Marketing Management, 45*, 101–112.

Töytäri, P., Rajala, R., & Alejandro, T. B. (2015). Organizational and institutional barriers to value-based pricing in industrial relationships. *Industrial Marketing Management, 47*, 53–64.

7

Boundary Spanning and the Art of Persuasion

Jukka Vesalainen, Anni Rajala, and Joakim Wincent

The Challenge of Managing in Relationships

Networks differ from organizations in basically two ways. First, they do not have an owner, and second, they cannot be managed on the basis of hierarchical positions held by managers. In other words, people with boundary roles do not have any authority over others in the network. Firms and boundary-role persons (BRPs) can, however, exercise power over each other through their relative positions in the market and in the network. Typically, the market mechanism functions as the legitimizing source for the use of power because it is socially acceptable for firms to choose the partners they aim to do business with. It is not only the bargaining of certain transactions or business deals that is important

J. Vesalainen (✉) • A. Rajala
University of Vaasa, Vaasa, Finland

J. Wincent
Luleå University of Technology, Luleå, Sweden

J. Vesalainen et al. (eds.), *Practices for Network Management*,
DOI 10.1007/978-3-319-49649-8_7

but also the threat of competition that is a relevant means for exercising power over business partners. The exercise of power manifests itself in inter-firm communication, and parties of a business relationship may refer to competition or market situations in order to strengthen their own firm's position. Suppliers, for example, blame customers for using the "China card" in negotiations or other interaction episodes which they refer to as the customers' urge to highlight "another alternative" from a low-cost country. Power asymmetry may also manifest itself in the form of a hierarchical position taken by one party of the relationship. The most usual source of asymmetry in business relationships is the size of the firm. Bigger firms tend to have certain types of power over the smaller ones. Representatives of more powerful firms may easily take a hierarchical position which manifests in their communication as utterances highlighting, for example, their own firm's position as a customer or their better know-how on how things should be done. Business partners can also be influenced by using a relational tone during interaction. Relational interaction is based on trust, commitment, and unity between the parties, and the win–win principle is often highlighted as the basis for partnerships. Research on networks and business relationships leans strongly on the firms' and BRPs' relational orientation and collaborative capabilities as the foundation for collaborative advantage.

In our project, we observed that firms are generally not aware of their boundary-spanning behavior orientation. At least they do not use various persuasion tactics as deliberate means to manage in networks. In some extreme cases, firms run into boundary-spanning behavior issues as in the example of our partner firm, which found one of its buyers to have an extremely hierarchical and competitive attitude during interactions with his suppliers' representatives. His behavior raised bad blood among the suppliers, and finally, the buyer was moved to another position. The point of departure in this tool development process was the notion that boundary-spanning behavior may vary, but is not usually controlled as a strategic principle or a code of conduct that has to be followed in inter-organizational interaction. A firm may have a relationally oriented sourcing strategy, but it does not fit with the buyers' interaction styles. Implementation, thus, does not follow intention.

The developed tool and managerial processes using the gathered information are expected to enhance network building. By making boundary-spanning behavior explicit, we aim to raise new important issues to be discussed in business relationships. It may be possible to define a relationship or network-specific code of conduct, which outlines what kind of behavior is preferable in the focal network. The information about one's own boundary-spanning behavior at least serves as a valuable point of departure when single firms analyze and develop their collaborative capabilities.

In the following sections, we present the results of an experimental project where boundary-spanning behavior was cross-analyzed in a supply network. We begin with a review on the theoretical foundations of boundary-spanning behavior, followed by a short section explaining the tool development process and the presentation of the analysis tool itself. We continue by describing the pilot project and showing the results of the cross-firm boundary-spanning behavior evaluation in four supply networks. The chapter ends with a discussion of the managerial value this kind of tool and related managerial practices may create.

Theoretical Foundation for Boundary-Spanning Behavior

Rhetoric—The Art of Persuasion

We define boundary-spanning behavior as *rhetoric* by which BRPs try to influence the conduct of the representatives of partner firms while pursuing their task-oriented goals. Rhetoric concerns the persuasion-oriented part of discourse (Heracleous and Marshak 2004). Cheney et al. (2004), for example, define rhetoric as "the conscious, deliberate and efficient use of persuasion to bring about attitudinal or behavioral change." Rhetoric has a persuasive role in situations where a credible source, clear evidence, or background in logical support is missing. Referring to Aristotelian rhetoric, broadly defined as the art of persuasion (Rapp 2010), a task-oriented goal in a conversation between a buyer and seller can be boosted by emotional or other utterances in the discussion. A BRP's persuasion tactics rely on psychological influence to convince or compel a partner firm's representative to assent to his/her position and act accordingly. In Aristotelian terms, ethos, pathos, and logos are the elements of persuasive communication. Ethos refers to the charisma of the speaker; pathos is the tone of speech that appeals to the audience; and logos describes how the speaker appeals to the intellect or to reason (Rapp 2010). Moreover, the *organizational rhetoric* perspective emphasizes that discourse is produced by organizations, not individuals (Crable 1990), and that individuals interact with an organizational voice (Boyd and Waymer 2011). In our context, BRPs use organizational rhetoric in order to implement organization-level purchasing strategies into practice through relationship governance modes. Thus, boundary-spanning behavior is also based on multiple governance theory.

Persuasion Tactics in Cross-Border Communication

Boundary-spanning behavior, as we define it here, is derived from the multidimensional governance theory, which defines governance as market-oriented, hierarchical, and relational. These ideal-typical modes of organizing appear in varying proportions in different institutions: "inter-firm relations in real markets embody and rely on varying degrees of trust and hierarchical authority, even if their primary mechanism is price" (Adler 2001, 216).

We expect these governance principles to manifest themselves as embedded in the communication of BRPs. As pointed out above, communication and discourses in general have two parts: the task-oriented part and the persuasion-oriented part. For its persuasion-oriented part, we assume boundary-spanning behavior to be colored by the three abovementioned persuasive arguments. Consider the following examples of communication where a buyer firm's representative discusses the supplier's quality problems:

(a) You have recently had serious quality problems in your deliveries. This low level of quality is hard to tolerate because there are plenty of qualified suppliers in the market and we are seriously considering opening negotiations with one of those.

(b) You have recently had serious quality problems in your deliveries. As a customer we cannot tolerate this low level of performance from any supplier and we expect you to tackle this issue as soon as possible.
(c) You have recently had serious quality problems in your deliveries. Would it be possible to look at the problem together with our specialists?

The task-oriented issue in each of these examples deals with supplier's quality problems, but the rhetoric by which the message is expressed varies. In example (a), the speaker uses a competitive tone; in example (b), a hierarchical tone; and in example (c), a relational tone. Boundary-spanning behavior thus refers to a particular type of rhetoric, which indicates how an issue is communicated.

We expect each BRP to have the propensity to use a certain kind of persuasive style. The style is a product of personality, the position held by the person, a firm's culture and strategy, and various situational factors, such as the type of operations the focal BRP is working with. A firm's boundary-spanning behavior is the sum of the individual BRPs' styles, which is the reason why it is so difficult to manage.

Examining boundary-spanning behavior as a multidimensional phenomenon also means that all of the modes of persuasion can "score low" simultaneously. This makes the presence of a laissez-faire (or neutral) boundary-spanning behavior possible for BRPs. In this respect, our theorizing and empirical exercise communicates to classic managerial models (Lewin et al. 1939), which introduced laissez-faire managerial behavior, where neither the autocratic nor the democratic style clearly dominates. We assume this view is also relevant for investigating BRPs' boundary-spanning behaviors.

Competitive Persuasion Tactics

From a market governance perspective, a BRP prefers to use *competitive tactics* (Walker and Weber 1984), which means offsetting investments in other relationships to signal the existence of market forces. Through the use of competitive tactics, the industrial purchasers' goal is to optimize price. Arm's-length relationships are typical in industrial business, and a buying firm usually applies the competitive force of the market by requesting competitive bids from multiple suppliers (Dyer and Ouchi 1993). Along with the bargaining itself, the market-driven behavior of a BRP is based on the threat of using alternative partners implicitly by signaling such a possibility or by highlighting the existence of competition by referring to the other firms.

Hierarchical Persuasion Tactics

In the inter-organizational context, *hierarchical tactics* exist when the parties in a relationship try to exercise power over each other by referring to their own superiority or position. Power can be defined as the ability of the BRP to influence the intentions and actions of the other party (Maloni and Benton 2000). The literature identifies five bases of inter-firm power: *reward, coercion, expert, referent*, and *legitimate* power. Exercising power through reward presumes that the BRP has the ability to mediate incentive for the target firm (e.g., when the customer can offer additional business to a supplier). Coercion power refers to the BRP as an actor to mediate punishment for the target firm. For example, the customer can reduce the volume of business with a supplier or cease to do business with it altogether. When the BRP and the source firm have access to knowledge and skills that the target firm desires, they may use expert power. Referent power refers to a situation in which the target firm wants to be identified with the firm a BRP represents. Legitimate power can be used when the target firm believes that the partner has the right to request and expect things to be done according to its requirements as part of the relationship (Maloni and Benton 2000). The amount of power and its direction are determined by the dependencies in a relationship. The higher and more asymmetric the dependency, the more potential there is for authoritarian behavior in a relationship (Ritter 2007). We expect that the abovementioned sources of power all represent potential content for the rhetoric used to persuade the partner firm.

Relational Persuasion Tactics

Relational tactics leverage social capital and relational orientation to maintain relationships in contrast to using the threat of termination (hierarchical enforcement) or maintaining competition (market governance) (Heide 1994). Instead of continuously looking for new partners, firms develop joint values and expectations about "proper and acceptable behavior" (Macneil 1980, 38). Drawing on Macneil's work, scholars of marketing management have defined ten norms as a basis for relational behavior. Through *long-term orientation*, the use of relational tactics refers to the desirability and benefit of a supplier or buyer having a long-term relationship with a specific exchange partner, and thus the relevance of BRPs to think and act from such a perspective (Ivens 2004). Using *role integrity*, BRPs signal that they will behave properly and care for the relationship in all circumstances (Blois and Ivens 2007). Moreover, relational tactics imply using *relational planning* to emphasize proactive and bilateral goal setting for future joint actions. This is thought to be central in the use of relational tactics among BRPs that want to signal the importance of a long-term relationship with *mutuality*, the belief that a party owes its success to the mutual benefits of a partnership. Relational tactics also imply that BRPs should show *solidarity*, particularly in situations in which one partner is having difficulties, because relational tactics include the expectation that joint rather than individual outcomes are highly valued (Ivens 2004). Moreover, relational tactics imply a readiness to *adapt an existing agreement* to new environmental conditions and changing needs in the buyer–supplier relationship (Cannon and Homburg 2001). This includes the willingness of the parties to proactively provide all information that could be useful in information exchange (Ivens 2004). Through *conflict resolution*, BRPs are expected to use informal and personal mechanisms to resolve conflicts. Finally, the expectation that actors will not apply their legitimate power to the detriment of their partners is classified as the norm of *restraint in using power*. We expect these norms to represent the sources for relational persuasion tactics.

Monitoring Boundary-Spanning Behavior in Networks

In order to make the boundary-spanning behavior explicit, the partner firm in this project found it relevant to experimentally conduct an evaluation of their boundary-spanning behavior style. The evaluation was conducted in 24 supplier relationships so that the representatives of the suppliers evaluated the boundary-spanning behavior of the customer firm by using the developed scale.[1] Along with the evaluation conducted in the focal network, we invited three other supplier networks to join the evaluation in order to get comparative data. The boundary-spanning behavior data used in this chapter thus consists of four supplier networks and 65 supplier–customer relationships. In the following section, we take the focal network's (Network Delta) and the focal customer firm's (Delta) perspectives to analyze the current situation in terms of the customer's boundary-spanning behavior.

Boundary-Spanning Behavior at the Network Level

Delta's boundary-spanning behavior profile was found relatively balanced as none of the styles score extremely high (Fig. 7.1). In comparison to the other customer firms' profiles, Delta seems to behave more hierarchically than the others (especially Alpha and Gamma). Delta (along with Beta) also uses strong competitive rhetoric in its interaction with suppliers. The customers Alpha and Gamma quite clearly behave in a less competitive way, at least when it comes to the competitive rhetoric they use in supplier relationships. The level of Delta's relational rhetoric is a bit lower than that of Beta and Gamma. Only Alpha seems to stand out as a strong relational actor. In sum, the boundary-spanning behavior profile of Delta (along with Beta) at the general level corresponds with the *competitive/hierarchical style* found in the pilot research. Network-specific profiles seem to vary when boundary-spanning behavior is reviewed at

[1] On the development and validation of the tool, see Vesalainen et al. (2016); the boundary-spanning behavior scale was found statistically to differentiate between the three persuasion tactics.

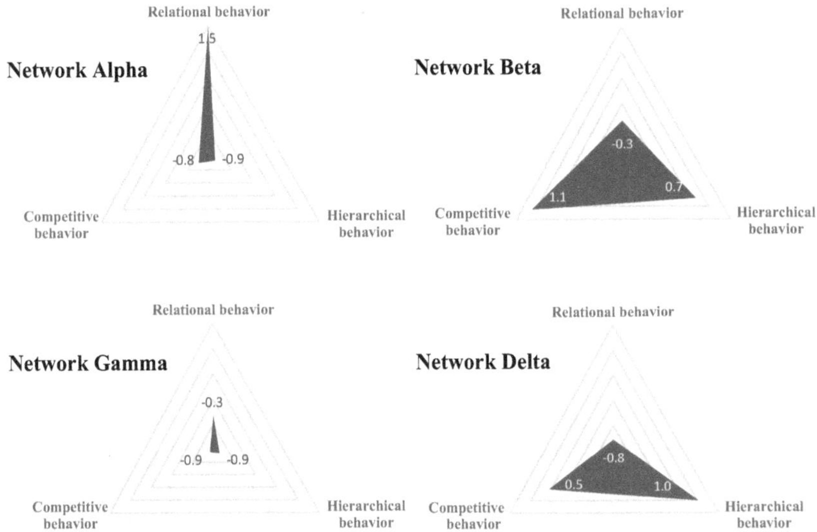

Fig. 7.1 Customer firms' boundary-spanning behavior profiles in four supplier networks (standardized values)

the network level; in the network Alpha, the customer has clearly adopted the *relational style*, and in the network Gamma, the customer has the *laissez-faire style*.

The network-level comparison enables Delta to critically scrutinize its boundary-spanning behavior against the comparative data. Does the result of evaluation and comparison to other networks correspond to the firm's overall understanding of its interaction with suppliers? One can also ask if the result is in line with the supply chain management strategy chosen by Delta.

Boundary-Spanning Behavior at the Supplier Category Level

Supplier relationships are—and should be—different. From the customer firm's perspective, it is not necessary to build close relationships with all the suppliers, but it should differentiate relationships into categories according to various reasons and practice differentiated relationship management in each category. This differentiation also concerns boundary-spanning behavior with different persuasion tactics and rhetorical emphasis. In the network Delta, the customer firm divides suppliers into three categories: strategic suppliers (delivering sub-systems and technology designed and owned by the supplier), contract manufacturers (delivering parts and sub-assemblies designed by the customer), and standard suppliers (delivering standard parts). We continued the analysis with a comparative setting where Delta's boundary-spanning behavior is compared in the three supplier categories (Fig. 7.2).

Delta's boundary-spanning behavior seems to be quite competitive in interaction with the strategic suppliers. This is understandable because suppliers in this category generate a great deal of purchasing costs, which make the customer very interested in using the market to bargain for lower prices. Concerning the contract manufacturing relationships, the competitive rhetoric of Delta seems to be quite low. These suppliers are mainly local actors, and Delta has put quite a lot of effort to help them develop manufacturing and logistical operations. These business relationships are basically cooperative and the governance mechanism in general relies on means other than competition and market mechanism.

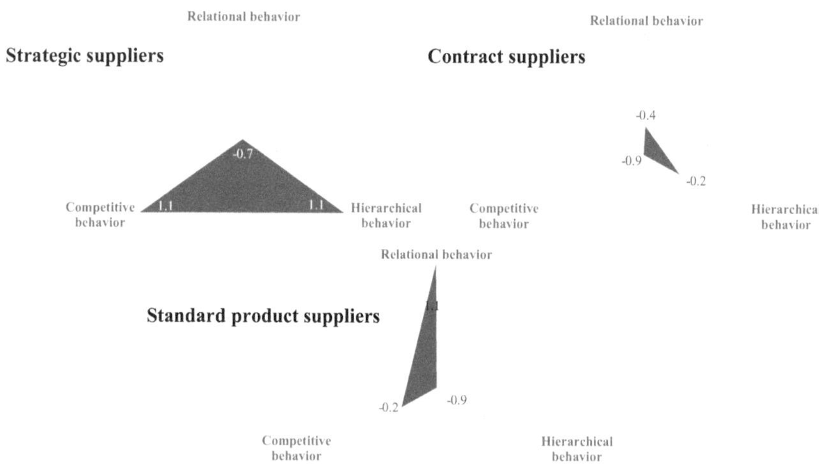

Fig. 7.2 Delta's boundary-spanning behavior in three different supplier categories

Against that background, it is surprising that relational and hierarchical boundary-spanning behaviors do not manifest themselves at a higher level. Furthermore, it is also surprising that Delta seems to use relational rhetoric, especially in relationships with standard product suppliers. Is it possible that relational boundary-spanning behavior is a question of personal chemistry rather than a deliberate managerial means?

The above analysis, taking a specified look into boundary-spanning behavior data, is, of course, only one analytical setup. It would be useful to conduct analyses by differentiating between supplier types such as local versus international suppliers, small versus large firms, or ownership structures and nationality. This kind of analysis would more accurately expose the focal firm's behavioral orientation in its supplier network. The analysis is important to extend even to single relationships in order to find out whether there is something that does not fit in the picture. In Delta's network there is, for example, a strategic supplier who perceives Delta's boundary-spanning behavior as extremely competitive. Is this in line with what the purpose was, or is there some kind of misunderstanding on the supplier's part or a harmful overkill that happened in the supplier–customer interaction?

Managerial Practices and Value Related to Boundary-Spanning Behavior Analysis

From the managerial point of view, the crucial question is: does the evaluation procedure have any use in network management, and how can these possible gains be achieved? From a researcher's point of view, the first valuable aspect of using this kind of tool is the fact that it makes boundary-spanning behavior with various persuasion tactics and rhetorical means visible. When BRPs acknowledge the importance of alternative communication styles, they can evaluate if this aspect of network management is useful for them or not.

From a customer firm's (like Delta) perspective, boundary-spanning behavior analysis is valuable only if it is used in connection with supply chain management. If supplier relationships are an important part of a firm's supply chain strategy, then managerial consideration directed to boundary-spanning behavior and its related issues become relevant. We see boundary-spanning behavior with various persuasion tactics as an important means to influence other firms' BRPs. The ultimate goal is to deliberately define a firm's boundary-spanning behavior tactics on a general level, particularly in different supplier categories where the effects of different persuasion tactics may vary. It may also be useful to fine-tune persuasion tactics even at the relationship level because firms and BRPs differ from each other in so many ways.

Boundary-spanning behavior is basically a firm-specific feature. From the managerial perspective, it can be linked to networking as a firm-specific capability. This means that a firm like Delta benefits if its business partners give feedback on the boundary-spanning behavior of its BRPs. However, Delta may not want to involve suppliers in the discussions dealing with their persuasion tactics. It is a firm's internal issue.

Networking is about coopetition (competition + cooperation). The fact is that firms do not lean on relational interaction as the only behavioral orientation. Boundary-spanning behavior as a comprehensive concept makes it possible to address relational behavior as one dimension of a firm's persuasive arsenal. Relational persuasion tactics are thus embedded in competitive and hierarchical orientations, and these three together constitute the firm's basic orientation.

Boundary-spanning behavior belongs to concepts that are basically subjective and thus hard to measure. The boundary-spanning behavior measure used here fulfills the scientific criteria in terms of validity and reliability. Still, its relevance for managerial purposes is questionable if evaluation procedure does not enable comparisons. Comparative data thus adds the value of evaluation because it offers a calibrated yardstick telling what is a lot and what is a little.

References

Adler, P. S. (2001). Market, hierarchy, and trust: The knowledge economy and the future of capitalism. *Organization Science, 12*(2), 215–234.

Blois, K. J., & Ivens, B. S. (2007). Method issues in the measurement of relational norms. *Journal of Business Research, 60*(6), 556–565.

Boyd, J., & Waymer, D. (2011). Organizational rhetoric: A subject of interest(s). *Management Communication Quarterly, 25*(3), 474–493.

Cannon, J. P., & Homburg, C. (2001). Buyer-supplier relationships and customer firm costs. *Journal of Marketing, 65*(1), 29–43.

Cheney, G., Christensen, L., Charles, C., & Lair, D. J. (2004). Corporate rhetoric in organizational discourse. In G. David, C. Hardy, C. Oswick, & L. Putnam (Eds.), *Handbook of organizational discourse* (pp. 79–103). London: Sage Publishing.

Crable, R. E. (1990). "Organizational rhetoric" as the fourth great system: Theoretical, critical, and pragmatic implications. *Journal of Applied Communication Research, 18*(2), 115–128.

Dyer, J., & Ouchi, W. (1993). Japanese-style partnerships: Giving companies a competitive edge. *Sloan Management Review, 35*(1), 51–63.

Heide, J. B. (1994). Interorganizational governance in marketing channels. *Journal of Marketing, 58*(1), 71–85.

Heracleous, L., & Marshak, R. J. (2004). Conceptualizing organizational discourse as situated symbolic action. *Human Relations, 57*(10), 1285–1312.

Ivens, B. S. (2004). How relevant are different forms of relational behavior? An empirical test based on Macneil's exchange framework. *Journal of Business & Industrial Marketing, 19*(5), 300–309.

Lewin, K., Lippitt, R., & White, R. K. (1939). Patterns of aggressive behavior in experimentally created 'social climates'. *The Journal of Social Psychology, 10*(2), 269–299.

Macneil, I. R. (1980). Power, contract, and the economic model. *Journal of Economic Issues, 14*(4), 909–923.

Maloni, M., & Benton, W. (2000). Power influences in the supply chain. *Journal of Business Logistics, 21*(1), 49–74.

Rapp, C. (2010). Aristotle's rhetoric. In E. N. Zalta (Ed.), *The Stanford encyclopedia of philosophy*. Retrieved from http://plato.stanford.edu/archives/spr2010/entries/aristotle-rhetoric

Ritter, T. (2007). A framework for analyzing relationship governance. *Journal of Business & Industrial Marketing, 22*(3), 196–201.

Vesalainen, J., Rajala, A., & Wincent, J. (2016). Measuring industrial purchaser boundary spanning behavior in supplier relationships. *Nordic Journal of Business, 65*(2), 66–72.

Walker, G., & Weber, D. (1984). A transaction cost approach to make-or-buy decisions. *Administrative Science Quarterly, 29*(3), 373–391.

Part II

Networks-as-Knowledge-Creating Platforms

8

Introduction to Part II—Knowledge Integration in Networks

Rainer Breite

In order to achieve the needed competence and knowledge in the business world, companies more and more today need and indeed must depend on their external knowledge sources. In this section of the book, we examine networks as external knowledge sources, from a focal company's and network node's point of view. Knowledge integration in this context means learning the processes, in other words, the needed knowledge collected from network parties that is performed for a specific purpose to accumulate existing knowledge of the organization. Our examination is based on *epistemological assumptions*. We understand that knowledge sharing and utilization of a company's external knowledge are not self-evident processes. They are both strongly related to individual learning; that is, different forms of knowledge (tacit or explicit) are needed for different learning or knowledge acquisition methods that in turn lead to different ways of examination. Further, according to cognitivist epistemology,

R. Breite (✉)
Tampere University of Technology, Tampere, Finland

J. Vesalainen et al. (eds.), *Practices for Network Management*,
DOI 10.1007/978-3-319-49649-8_8

when an individual gathers information from an external environment (from his/her own organization or a network partner's organization), the person stores and interprets the received information based on his or her own existing experiences. On the other hand, connectionist epistemology emphasizes the large number of integrating units (e.g., network) more than the individuals. According to this epistemology, units have the possibility to affect one another using stimulus connections. Both epistemological assumptions do examine information processing as the basic activity of the system. However, the connectionist assumption emphasizes the system itself, and then relationships and communication become the most important issues of cognition.

This assumption is close to our viewpoint of network practice. In our context, a network node is like a system that forms a knowledge entity, or entities, that then facilitates the knowledge of all its members and continually transforms itself. We suggest that a network node or focal company is like a learning organization, that is, an organization that learns via its individual members where the learning process is different at both the individual and node levels. This focus implies that individuals' *cognitive activities* play an important role in the acquisition of knowledge, that is, when individual has already acquired knowledge and then utilizes own memory for specific purpose, or individual will acquire new knowledge for the specific purpose and accumulates this new knowledge into his or her memory. Thus, a node can be seen as *a cognitive system* that is autonomous with respect to knowledge, the creation of knowledge, and the application of knowledge distinctions and its norms. It can thus be suggested that learning occurs within a node when an individual gains new knowledge, behavior, skills, values, preferences, or understanding.

Each network node or focal company is also an autonomous node. In this context, the concept of the autonomous node means it has its own knowledge and it makes knowledge decisions motivated by self-organization at the local level. Although a node may exist independently of particular individuals, it is necessary to recognize that people working for a company need to acquire that sufficient knowledge in the execution of their tasks. The five tools presented in this section represent practices of knowledge sharing that are more related to the connectionist epistemology point of view. Then the tools are presented and used more for the focal company (integrating units) than on individual levels.

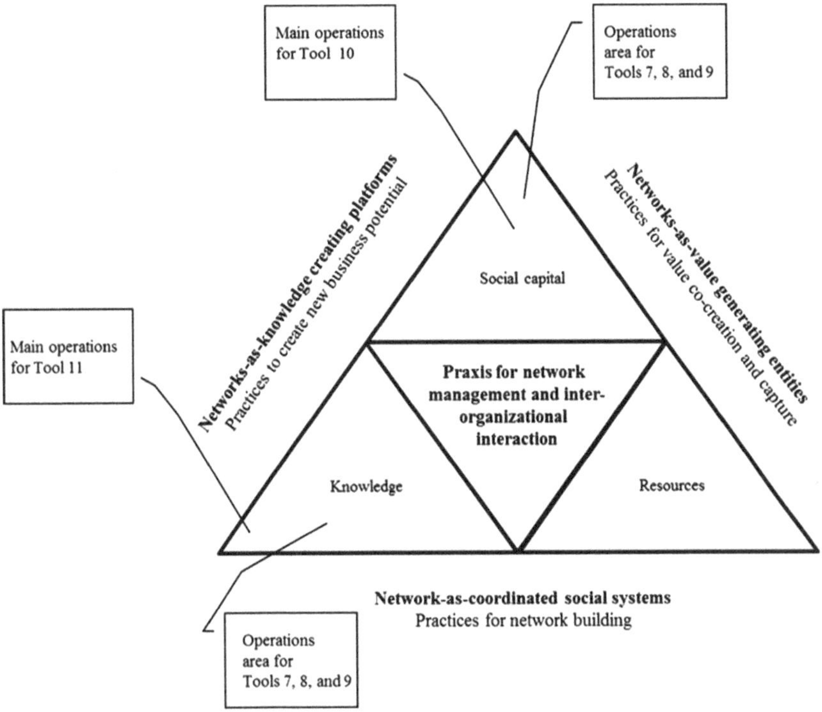

Fig. 8.1 The influence areas for the suitable tools (adapted from Fig. 1.2)

According to this design thinking (see Chap. 1), the abovementioned new knowledge, behavior, skills, values, preferences, or understanding of learning "outcomes" represent value as the key outcomes of the use of those tools. In line with our framework in Fig. 8.1, these tools focus on capabilities for enhanced system-level knowledge creation and on a knowledge-sharing mechanism that moves toward a common or an organizational goal. The tools that are mainly used in areas of *networks-as-knowledge-creating platform* also partially reflect the area of *networks-as-value-generating entities.*

As mentioned above, knowledge sharing and learning are not self-evident processes. Knowledge and information sharing are contextualized and in turn relate to the receiver or user's background that will set the challenges for knowledge sharing. Therefore, efficient and effective knowledge sharing in networks recognizes the cognitive, relational, and structural-based confines of knowledge sharing. For this purpose, "third-party-controlled benchmarking" (Chap. 10) and "knowledge integration system" (Chap. 9) tools have been developed. Both of these tools also reflect *networks-as-value-generating entities*, which mean that the ultimate purpose of knowledge sharing is new knowledge and organization learning that creates greater value for the network node and its customers. Tools like "Value Proposition Co-development" (Chap. 11) and "Relational Factors as Part of Network Relationship Evaluation" (Chap. 12) also represent method, and with its help network partners can strive for greater mutual value, both in forming and knowledge sharing. The tool "Increasing Supplier–Buyer Fit in Global Project Business" (Chap. 13) offers a different facet to use for the *knowledge-creating platform*.

In the "Expert Knowledge Integration—A Systematic Approach for Multi-Stakeholder Innovation" (Chap. 9), the focal company can, in a systematic way, create new knowledge with its network partners. This tool integrates separate knowledge sources according to the pre-set goal. It helps to collect the necessary network resources and their knowledge and harnesses them to create new knowledge, for example, for R&D or investment projects, where the stakeholders are network partners. This tool also takes into account the social capital aspects, especially the relational point of view, the resource aspect, and the knowledge point of view (see the top triangle and the bottom left triangle in Fig. 8.1). With this tool, knowledge management activities are centered around the focal company's internal functions and also the capabilities of the company's network partners (see Table 8.1).

Correspondingly, the main idea of the "Third-Party-Supported Benchmarking for Reciprocal Learning" (Chap. 10) tool is to collect and recognize the information needed for successful benchmarking in a company network. With the help of this tool, it is possible to share and receive knowledge with network parties. It also helps an organization recognize its capability need and then structure the organization's knowledge need. The tool takes into account the social capital aspect (the top triangle in Fig. 8.1) and considers knowledge as an external and separate source (the bottom left triangle in Fig. 8.1). With the help of this tool, existing knowledge can be efficiently shared with all network parties. From a management point of view and the purpose of knowledge integration activities, this tool can help focus on the operations of both the focal company's and its partners' internal functions (see Table 8.1).

Table 8.1 Sum of the tool descriptions and management situations, where the tools can be utilized (P = Problem, S = Solution)

Tool	Description	Management situation and activities
Third-party-controlled benchmarking	P: How to benchmark complex practices in a network S: The tool structures practices into manageable elements	Knowledge integration between focal company and its partner company to be further utilized in focal company's network
Knowledge integration system	P: How to integrate knowledge in a multi-stakeholder environment S: It integrates knowledge from different sources according to a pre-set goal	Knowledge integration between multi-stakeholders, especially, focal company's internal functions and company's network partner
Relational evaluation of service outsourcing value potential	P: How service providers and customer companies could systematically evaluate potential outsourcing value S: It forms an effective boundary object that facilitates knowledge sharing, knowledge integration, and joint sense making	Drawbacks and advantages of outsourcing should be estimated, and potential service providers should be evaluated
Supplier integration system with relational factor	P: How to ensure relational fit between network partners S: The tool scans relational factors and their consistency	Knowledge integration between focal company's network partners
Increased cognitive ergonomics in operative supplier selection in a global context	P: How to avoid inappropriate supplier selection in a global supply network S: The tool scans suitable factors for global supply and sourcing management	Knowledge integration between focal company's internal functions

The tool for "Value Proposition Co-development" (Chap. 11) helps companies find and estimate a suitable network partner as outsourcing activities are thought through fully. The tool highlights co-creation value and presents both a practice and a method for evaluating the potential of an outsourcing value (see Chap. 11). The concept is based on utilizing the relational factors that, in turn, then form an effective boundary object that facilitates a common endeavor to share and integrate knowledge. The tool highlights the social capital aspects, especially the relational point of view, and the knowledge aspects of knowledge sharing, knowledge integration, and mutual understanding (see the top triangle and the bottom left triangle in Fig. 8.1). Knowledge management activities are then centered on both creating value and positive outsourcing between all the network partners (see Table 8.1).

Correspondingly, the "Relational Factors as Part of Network Relationship Evaluation" (Chap. 12) tool was developed to estimate the pre-conditions for successful co-operation and knowledge sharing between network partners. It also helps estimate relationship quality and offers steps for an estimation route for boundary spanning. It can be well utilized when relationships are being improved between a focal company and its network partners. The tool utilizes the theory of social capital (see Chap. 12), and especially relational factors (such as power, trust, collaboration, and commitment), and their role as boundary spanners are a focus (see the top triangle in Fig. 8.1). With this tool, managers of knowledge integration endeavor stay in focus, as the focal company co-operates with network partners (see Table 8.1).

The four tools mentioned above focus mainly on contributing knowledge sharing to all the network nodes. The fifth tool, "Increasing Supplier–Buyer Fit in Global Project Business" (Chap. 13), collects the necessary information about the current and new potential suppliers from a global supply network point of view. It emphasizes the company's internal development activities of the network by delivering background information on the circumstances related to the supply environment. With the help of this tool (Chap. 13), it is possible to collect necessary information about options for both global sourcing and supply chain activities. The tool scans and increases a new potential supplier in a holistic way as it expands a company's supplier network and increases that company's understanding of its suppliers' capabilities and weaknesses (see Chap. 13). Therefore, the tool affects the bottom left triangle in Fig. 8.1. The objectives of these knowledge integration activities also emphasize the focal company's internal functions (see Table 8.1).

9

Expert Knowledge Integration—A Systematic Approach for Multi-stakeholder Innovation

Anu Suominen, Sari Mäenpää, and Rainer Breite

Introduction

Global competition set demands on rapid knowledge exchange throughout industrial networks. For example, transferring product changes into the manufacturing network in a more agile way is a necessity, whether they were initiated by internal operations, such as R&D or production, or external stakeholders, such as customers. Therefore, it is important that all internal operations understand the big picture, that is, the broader network-level needs. Thus, tools are needed for industrial networks to be able to rapidly react—and to act collaboratively on change demands from various parts of the network, such as R&D or the customer.

When companies are developing their products or production, they often face complex problems that demand networked, system-level, boundary-spanning innovations, often calling for diverse expertise that

A. Suominen (✉) • S. Mäenpää • R. Breite
Tampere University of Technology, Tampere, Finland

J. Vesalainen et al. (eds.), *Practices for Network Management*,
DOI 10.1007/978-3-319-49649-8_9

does not exist within one company or even in its immediate network. Therefore, networks can function as knowledge-creating platforms, in which with the help of practices, the diverse expertise of various network stakeholders can be exploited. These practices may consist of activities and interactions enhancing inter-organizational learning, knowledge integration, and new knowledge development. Therefore, since innovation, especially networked innovation, requires expert knowledge integration (Grant 1996), the applied activities and interactions should focus on supporting the integration. Specifically, in the case of cross-learning type of knowledge integration, the applied activities and interactions should focus on communication and extensive knowledge sharing (Enberg 2012).

According to Tiwari (2015, 13),

> Knowledge integration refers to the ability of the project network to transform knowledge into action.

Furthermore, due to the complexity of the problems in cross-learning knowledge integration, transformation into action should be carried out in simultaneous collaboration (i.e., in the presence of multiple stakeholders). However, besides common knowledge and understanding (Grant 1986) in such an inter-organizational setting, knowledge integration requires overcoming organizational boundaries (Carlile 2004) with the help of concrete (Star and Griesemer 1989; Star 2010) and metaphoric (Koskinen 2005) boundary objects. Management tools give means to the participants to engage in various organizational processes (Jarzabkowski and Kaplan 2015), such as innovation. Therefore, companies need a tool or method that allows them to carry out these complex innovation projects, which require the integration of multi-stakeholder expert knowledge in a systematic manner.

Knowledge integration system (KIS) tool is a method for transforming expert knowledge into action in a systematical manner. The KIS tool combines the two categories of knowledge management practices of networked innovation, transaction, and co-creation networks. Applying to some extent the transaction network viewpoint, KIS includes three systematic stages of knowledge integration: knowledge identification, knowledge acquisition, and knowledge utilization in co-ordination (Tiwari 2015). Additionally, to those three stages, also new knowledge creation is supported in co-creation processes, where interaction and connections between actors are enabled with the participatory method of workshop, which creates space for social interactions. The main goal of the KIS tool is to transform expert knowledge into action. It focuses particularly on identifying knowledge from different sources and integrating it—through co-ordination and collaboration—to be usable for innovation efforts in a multi-stakeholder environment (Enberg et al. 2010; Koskinen 2012; Tiwari 2015). The tool utilizes the participatory method of workshops or series of workshops due to their inherent communication and knowledge-sharing characteristics. Furthermore, when experts from various fields and organizations communicate and share knowledge, themes, operations, or organizational boundaries may occur. Therefore, boundary objects were also included in the method, as the multi-stakeholder environment requires the spanning of different boundaries. With the help of boundary objects, knowledge integration can become understandable for everyone, and therefore, efficient and effective.

In a piloted case in a project network, the overall objective was to integrate the various types of expert knowledge in a process aiming to accomplish functional solutions that would benefit not only the focal company but the entire network. In that pilot, the KIS tool was useful in supporting expert knowledge integration, which is carried out by communicating and sharing knowledge collaboratively in a multi-stakeholder environment, to create both new solutions for products and production systems.

Characteristics of Knowledge Integration and Knowledge Integration Tools in Project Networks

Prior research on management tools via practice lens has highlighted that tools people utilize in organizations require a few characteristics, such as aid in building a common language, creation of space for social interactions, and flexible content and structure. A common language should be created across hierarchical, functional, and geographic boundaries; that is, tools should have boundary-spanning interpretive parts for the participants to focus and make sense of the problem at hand. The space for social interactions signifies possibilities to negotiate and legitimate the solutions the participants are working on. Flexible content and structure denote tools' possibilities for improvisational use and its adaptation for various types of, for example, innovation endeavors. Additionally, the success of tools should be evaluated from various viewpoints and in multiple levels such as in organization level with their level of adaptation and part of organization's routines, and in actor level with, for example, the ways the tool provokes new explorations and enables interim decisions moving the project or organization to go forward (Jarzabkowski and Kaplan 2015).

Innovation is a process of idea transformation into new, value-adding, tangible or intangible outcome (Merx-Chermin and Nijhof 2005, 137; Martins and Terblanche 2003). Innovation can also occur across firm boundaries by sharing ideas, knowledge, expertise, and opportunities; thus, the outputs are called collaborative innovations (Ketchen et al. 2008). In networked innovation, interdependent but independent network actors co-produce the innovation outcome (Valkokari et al. 2012).

> Networked innovation occurs through relationships that are negotiated in an ongoing communicative process, and which relies on neither market nor hierarchical mechanisms of control (Swan and Scarbrough 2005, 916).

Networked innovation has the following characteristics: (1) the collaboration of multiple actors is seldom open to everyone, (2) collaboration has always a particular purpose, and (3) the collaboration models deal with both the knowledge transfer and co-creation functions between actors (Valkokari et al. 2012). Organizational and networked innovation requires combining different expertise (i.e., the technical, procedural, and intellectual knowledge of individuals) (Amabile 1998). Yet sometimes, yielding innovation requires organizations to cross organizational borders for ideas (Amabile et al. 1996) and knowledge (Enberg 2012), and also maximizing the benefits of their own resources and capabilities call for co-operation (Arora and Gambardella 1990; Cassiman and Veugelers 2002).

Distinctive particularly for project networks is their temporal nature, the co-operation of various organizations (none of which have a completely dominating role), and an aspiration toward precise and specified objectives (Tiwari 2015). Therefore, knowledge integration introduced by Grant (1996), according to Enberg (2012, 772), is a

> goal-oriented process with the purpose of taking advantage of knowledge complementarities which exist between individuals with differentiated knowledge bases

and needed when knowledge is specialized and dispersed among individuals. Knowledge integration can be enabled by the use of different integration mechanisms. Some mechanisms emphasize frequent communication and extensive knowledge sharing, also called the cross-learning approach (Enberg 2012), which our view is also based on.

Knowledge integration has three stages aiming at their seamless connection: knowledge identification, knowledge acquisition, and knowledge utilization. Particularly in a multi-stakeholder environment, an important intermediate process is also knowledge co-ordination, which presupposes collaboration (Tiwari 2015). However, in project networks the essence of knowledge integration is the *ability to transform knowledge into action* (Tiwari 2015, 13), meaning that identifying needs and acquiring knowledge are not enough; the knowledge has to be altered, or utilized, in operations.

Knowledge integration in inter-organizational environment demands common knowledge and comprehension (Grant 1986), thus crossing knowledge boundaries between organizations (Carlile 2004). Boundary objects are concrete or abstract *bridges* (e.g., maps, repositories, and standardized forms) that enable contribution to a broader overall target between groups with various views and goals (Star and Griesemer 1989; Star 2010). Additionally, to concrete and abstract, there are also metaphoric boundary objects, which may be particularly helpful when tacit knowledge and comprehension is shared between people (Koskinen

2005). Therefore, boundary objects should be taken into account while designing tools for knowledge integration.

Knowledge Integration System

The KIS, or KIS tool, was developed and piloted according to the design-science approach. KIS tool development for use in the multi-stakeholder innovation process focused on the method or artifact design. Peffers et al. (2006) define this type of design-science approach, which occurs after the problem and objectives have already been acknowledged, as the design and development centered approach. In practice, this means that the lack of knowledge integration methods for communication and knowledge sharing with multiple stakeholders had been acknowledged prior to the design. Therefore, the objective of the solution was to enhance communication and knowledge sharing by putting the knowledge into action. Thus, in the research's entry point, design and development, the designed artifact or tool is a method for knowledge integration that includes boundary objects to create a common language and ensure boundary spanning (c.f. Jarzabkowski and Kaplan 2015) in a multi-stakeholder collaboration. *Demonstration* is an essential part of the design-science approach, and therefore, in the pilot, the designed artifact has been used to solve an existing problem within a real-life organizational case.

Designed Artifact: A KIS Tool with Boundary Objects

The designed artifact is a process-type method for knowledge integration, KIS tool. The tool focuses on expert knowledge sharing and communication in collaboration. Additionally, complex problem-solving requires learning from all stakeholders during the process via active participation and involvement. Thus, a workshop has many benefits of interactive learning, as well as its typical facilitation of problem-solving and decision-making, communication skills, and *thinking on your feet* (Steinert 2010). Therefore, workshops as participatory methods, which create a space for social interactions (c.f. Jarzabkowski and Kaplan 2015), were chosen as part of the tool, as they provide a collaborative environment where the same information, in the same form, utilizing the same boundary objects, is conveyed to all participants simultaneously, allowing for further concurrent communication. Thus, workshops increase the potential for the creation of collective understanding.

Pilot Case Description

KIS tool was piloted according to the design-science approach in the context of a temporary R&D and innovation project in an industrial organization's network. The networked organization contemplated a major manufacturing investment that would alter their production process, and early on, they noticed that they did not have all the internal capabilities needed to come up with decisions required by the investment. In a process aiming to accomplish a functional solution for a production system, which later expanded to include new product solutions, the goal of the pilot case was to integrate the various types of expert knowledge that would benefit not only the focal company but also the entire network. Figure 9.1 illustrates the connections of the many stakeholders in this

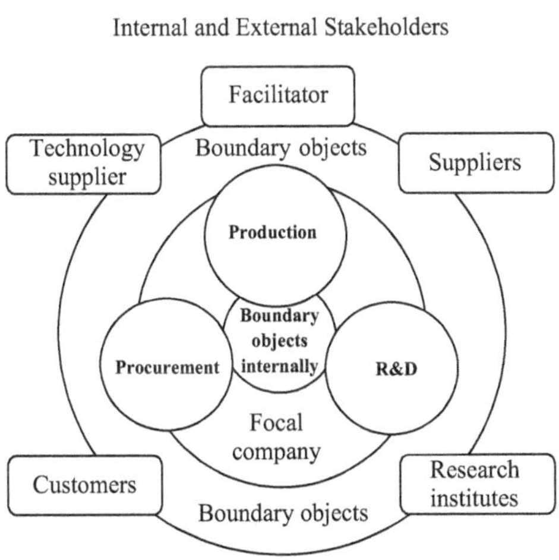

Fig. 9.1 Pilot context in a temporary R&D and innovation project

pilot. The process involved the operations of various focal companies (i.e., internal stakeholders such as R&D, procurement, and production). As external stakeholders operated the customers, suppliers, technology suppliers, and research institutes, the facilitator co-ordinated the knowledge integration process with the multiple stakeholders. The boundary objects expedited knowledge sharing among both the internal (i.e., operations) and the external stakeholders.

The temporary R&D and innovation project was initially concerned with the production process development. In the end, the project required the introduction of a new production method for the focal company.

KIS Tool Description and Observations from the Pilot

In practice, the KIS tool combines a set of workshops planned according to three knowledge integration process phases with usable boundary objects for boundary-spanning communication and knowledge sharing. The knowledge integration process phases are (1) knowledge identification, (2) knowledge acquisition, and (3) knowledge utilization (see Fig. 9.2). The boundary objects can be either concrete or metaphoric. As a result, the tool starts with the two phases of knowledge identification, followed by co-ordinated knowledge acquisition and three phases of co-ordinated knowledge utilization. At the end come conclusions and proposals, followed by the final phase, actions.

1. **Knowledge Identification**

    a. *Internal Knowledge Identification: First, the organization discovers a problem that needs to be solved and recognizes that they do not have the capabilities to solve it internally.*
    In the pilot, the internal knowledge identification lasted for two months. And early on, the preparation team in the focal company recognized that it did not have the required knowledge or capabilities to implement the production method nor the insight into the potential change or problems that might interfere with its production. The focal company turned to the facilitator for assistance in

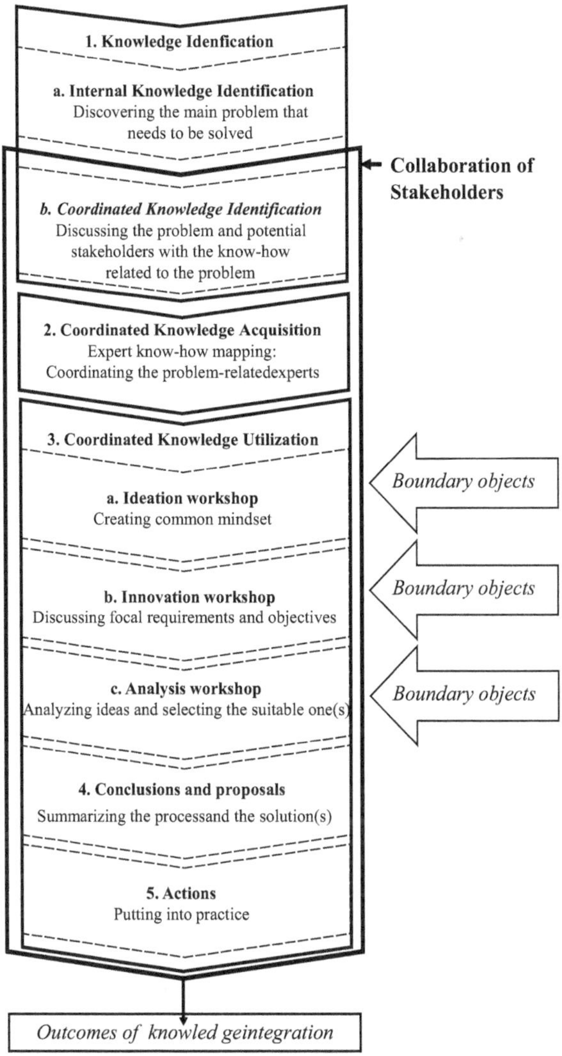

Fig. 9.2 KIS tool phases with collaborative workshops and boundary objects (adapted from Tiwari 2015, 14)

expert knowledge integration. Internal knowledge identification started the process.

b. *Co-ordinated Knowledge Identification: The organization and the facilitator discuss the problem and potential internal and external stakeholders that might contribute to the solution.*
   In the pilot, in the external knowledge identification phase, the focal company and facilitator discussed potential technologies and concluded that the complexity of the project would benefit from a multi-stakeholder approach. This approach required experts to fill the knowledge gap and inquire about their availability and willingness to collaborate with this production process development.

2. **Co-ordinated Knowledge Acquisition**: *The facilitator contacts the various stakeholders and maps the expert know-how and potential experts available for collaboration.*
   In the pilot, the facilitator mapped the needed expertise, contacted its experts, and set up the first workshop, and this phase lasted for one month.

3. **Co-ordinated Knowledge Utilization**

   a. *Ideation workshop: Together, the facilitator and internal and external stakeholders have the first ideation workshop. In it, the problem is discussed in more detail with various experts about potential solutions to the problem. Various concrete boundary objects can be used, such as expert presentations, blueprints, and so on. Some of the experts might realize that they do not have the expertise needed to resolve the issue and may withdraw from the project. On the other hand, the group of stakeholders might be lacking in some area of expertise and will seek it as soon as possible. However, the final solution is more in the sketching phase and is not yet drawn. At this point, the problem might be either limited to a smaller entity or enlarged, depending on the case.*
   In the pilot, in a first half-day multi-stakeholder workshop, a fairly large number of various internal and external experts gathered together. They gave presentations and had group discussions about different aspects of the problem, and contemplated introducing new production technology. The experts noticed that this new pro-

duction method might require deployment of a new technology and thus changes to the product design as well. Therefore, the project expanded from production process development to include a product development process. Consequently, the new product design had implications to the production processes of the suppliers too.

- To share knowledge, boundary objects included presentations and a memo that were written and distributed to all participants.

b. *Innovation workshop: In this workshop, the problem is discussed in collaboration with various internal and external stakeholders, and two to three potential solutions are drawn up to be analyzed in the third collaborative workshop. This phase allows for the use of various boundary objects, both concrete, such as presentations, blueprints, sketches, photographs, and metaphoric (e.g., hourglass or plank).*

   In the pilot, in this second half-day multi-stakeholder workshop, the technology provider as well as the customer worked with experts from suppliers, research institutes, and the focal company. The stakeholders contemplated potential problems in using the new production solutions and the required changes for the product.

   - To share knowledge, boundary objects included presentations, blueprints, pictures, and a memo that was written and distributed to all participants. Also, at this stage, the stakeholders started using two metaphors: one for the old product structure and one for the new one.

c. *Analysis workshop: The third collaborative workshop aims to choose one of the two to three potential solutions drawn in the innovation workshop. Various experts can give their input on rating the solution that they feel should be selected. Various boundary objects can also be used in this phase.*

   In the pilot, in this third half-day workshop, the required product changes were discussed, and a new product structure was designed at the basic level.

– To share knowledge, boundary objects included a tour of the production facilities in the factory, presentations, blueprints, pictures, and also a memo that was written and distributed to all participants. Also, two metaphors (e.g., *round* and *cubicle*, not used in this case) were utilized to convey needed changes to the product structure.

4. *Conclusions and proposals: The organization and the facilitator analyze the whole process and the proposed solution. They may consider revisiting some of the previous steps if the solution is not operable for one reason or another.*

   In the pilot, this phase lasted altogether five months. The facilitator and the focal company gathered together to discuss the process and its outcomes. The company was satisfied with both the process as well as its result and will utilize this multi-stakeholder knowledge integration tool with other internal and external knowledge integration cases.

5. *Action: The organization with the problem puts the solution into practice and collaborates with one or all of the experts if needed.*

   In the pilot case, the focal company will put the new production method into practice within one year, along with other stakeholders, and the changes to the product structure are currently being fine-tuned.
   In the pilot, there were altogether six utilized boundary objects within the three multi-stakeholder workshops. The four concrete boundary objects were workshop memos, pictures and blueprints, presentations, and a factory tour (third workshop); there was one metaphoric boundary object for the new structure and one for the former structure.

Pilot Process Outcome: The Manifestation of the KIS Knowledge Integration Tool on a Practical Level

On a practical level, the manifestation (outcomes) of the knowledge integration process shows in the form of new relations, new business opportunities, and new technical solutions and operating models. The main outcomes of the piloted knowledge integration process are as follows:

1. A focus on new structure as its most critical part in relation to automation
    a. enables cost savings with benefits such as reduced production times and improved quality,
    b. requires a focus on assembly, and
    c. relocates component production to subcontractors (more subcontractors are needed).
2. Possibilities for research tasks, for which the universities will offer specific research packages for the focal company.
3. New business cases between suppliers as well as between universities and suppliers.
4. New concept/model (i.e., knowledge integration/sharing platform) for multi-actor collaboration to be used in other cases as well.

KIS was also found useful in supporting expert knowledge integration while communicating and sharing knowledge in a multi-stakeholder environment and collaborating to create solutions for both new products and production systems. Viewed from actor level, the tool provoked new explorations and enabled interim decisions which moved the project forward. From organization level, the focal company indicated that the tool will be adopted more widely within the organization and its network, and made as part of the organization's routines. Therefore, the tool may be evaluated as a success from various viewpoints and in multiple levels (c.f. Jarzabkowski and Kaplan 2015).

Conclusions

Networked innovations are essential for the success of companies in the current business environment. Networked innovations require the co-production of outcome by the interdependent but independent network actors. The innovation outcome calls for expert knowledge integration of those network actors. With its practices including systematic activities and interaction, KIS tool helps the network to function as knowledge-creating platform. KIS combines the needed knowledge transfer and co-creation functions for the systematic cross-learning type of expert knowledge integration and new knowledge development. KIS brings it about by emphasizing frequent communication and extensive knowledge sharing in its activities and interaction.

In practice, the piloted KIS tool employs a multi-stakeholder approach by utilizing a participatory method of workshops or series of workshops to integrate required expert knowledge through communication and knowledge sharing. The KIS method includes boundary objects to assist experts in various fields in crossing organizational, operational, and subject boundaries. With the help of boundary objects, knowledge integration is understandable to everyone and is, therefore, efficient and effective. Thus, combining workshops and the use of boundary objects, KIS both aids common language creation and boundary spanning, required in successful management tools (c.f. Jarzabkowski and Kaplan 2015).

In the pilot case, neither the focal company nor its suppliers were familiar with the newly selected production technology, so both product and production changes required the acquisition of technical expertise from new external stakeholders, such as technology suppliers and university researchers. Thus, the chain of requirements led to a collaborative development process with multiple inter-organizational stakeholders, necessitating knowledge integration that relied on communication and knowledge sharing.

The use of KIS encourages its application to other network development projects. We suggest that this tool is applied to cases where the complexity of expertise and knowledge presupposes the utilization of boundary objects, and the possibilities of boundary spanning have to be estimated. The phases used in our case may have to be tailored on a case-by-case basis, but most of them are general enough to be used for other cases. Cases can be at the network level (i.e., multi-lateral relationships) or in purely dyadic relationships where different organization functions co-operate for common purposes. Therefore, both the content and the structure of the KIS tool are flexible, providing possibilities for improvisational use and its adaptation for various types of, for example, innovation endeavors, which are requisitions for successful management tools (c.f. Jarzabkowski and Kaplan 2015).

References

Amabile, T. M. (1998). How to kill creativity. *Harvard Business Review, 76*(5), 76–87. doi:10.4135/9781446213704.

Amabile, T. M., Conti, R., Coon, H., Lazenby, J., & Herron, M. (1996). Assessing the work environment for creativity. *Academy of Management Journal, 39*(5), 1154–1184. doi:10.2307/256995.

Arora, A., & Gambardella, A. (1990). Complementarity and external linkages: The strategies of the large firms in biotechnology. *Research Policy, XXXVIII*(4), 361–380.

Carlile, P. R. (2004). Transferring, translating, and transforming: An integrative framework for managing knowledge across boundaries. *Organization Science, 15*(5), 555–568. doi:10.1287/orsc.

Cassiman, B., & Veugelers, R. (2002). R & D cooperation and spillovers: Some empirical evidence. *The American Economic Review, 92*(4), 1169–1184. doi:10.1257/00028280260344704.

Enberg, C. (2012). Enabling knowledge integration in coopetitive R&D projects—The management of conflicting logics. *International Journal of Project Management, 30*(7), 771–780. doi:10.1016/j.ijproman.2012.01.003.

Enberg, C., Lindkvist, L., & Tell, F. (2010). Knowledge integration at the edge of technology: On teamwork and complexity in new turbine development. *International Journal of Project Management, 28*(8), 756–765. doi:10.1016/j.ijproman.2010.05.003.

Grant, R. M. (1986). Toward a knowledge-based theory of the firm. *Strategic Management Journal Winter, 17*(109), 109–122. doi:10.2307/2486994.

Grant, R. M. (1996). Prospering as in dynamically-competitive environments: Organizational capability as knowledge integration. *Organization Science, 7*(4), 375–387. doi:10.1287/orsc.7.4.375.

Jarzabkowski, P., & Kaplan, S. (2015). Strategy tools-in-use: A framework for understanding "technologies of rationality" in practice. *Strategic Management Journal, 36*(4), 537–558. doi:10.1002/smj.2270.

Ketchen, D. J., Ireland, R. D., & Snow, C. C. (2008). Strategic entrepreneurship, collaborative innovation, and wealth creation. *Strategic Entrepreneurship Journal, 1*(2007), 371–385. doi:10.1002/sej.

Koskinen, K. U. (2005). Metaphoric boundary objects as co-ordinating mechanisms in the knowledge sharing of innovation processes. *European Journal of Innovation Management, 8*(3), 323–335. doi:10.1108/14601060510610180.

Koskinen, K. U. (2012). Knowledge integration in systems integrator type project-based companies: A systemic view. *International Journal of Managing Projects in Business, 5*(2), 285–299. doi:10.1108/17538371211214950.

Martins, E. C., & Terblanche, F. (2003). Building organisational culture that stimulates creativity and innovation. *European Journal of Innovation Management, 6*(1), 64–74. doi:10.1108/14601060310456337.

Merx-Chermin, M., & Nijhof, W. J. (2005). Factors influencing knowledge creation and innovation in an organisation. *Journal of European Industrial Training, 29*, 135–147. doi:10.1108/03090590510585091.

Peffers, K., Tuunanen, T., Gengler, C. E., Rossi, M., Hui, W., Virtanen, V., et al. (2006). The design science research process: A model for producing and presenting information systems research. *The Proceedings of Design Research in Information Systems and Technology DESRIST'06, 24*, 83–106. doi:10.2753/MIS0742-1222240302.

Star, S. L. (2010). This is not a boundary object: Reflections on the origin of a concept. *Science, Technology & Human Values, 35*(5), 601–617. doi:10.1177/0162243910377624.

Star, S. L., & Griesemer, J. R. (1989). Institutional ecology, 'Translations' and boundary objects: Amateurs and professionals in Berkeley's Museum of Vertebrate Zoology, 1907–39. *Social Studies of Science, 19*(3), 387–420. doi:10.1177/030631289019003001.

Steinert, Y. (2010). How to design and conduct effective workshops. In K. Skeff & G. Stratos (Eds.), *Methods for teaching medicine* (pp. 89–115). Philadelphia: ACP Press.

Swan, J., & Scarbrough, H. (2005). The politics of networked innovation. *Human Relations, 58*(7), 913–943. doi:10.1177/0018726705057811.

Tiwari, S. R. (2015). Knowledge integration in government-industry project network. *Knowledge and Process Management, 22*(1), 11–21. doi:10.1002/kpm.1460.

Valkokari, K., Paasi, J., & Rantala, T. (2012). Managing knowledge within networked innovation. *Knowledge Management Research & Practice, 10*(1), 27–40. doi:10.1057/kmrp.2011.39.

10

Third-Party-Supported Benchmarking for Reciprocal Learning

Sari Mäenpää, Anu Suominen, and Rainer Breite

Introduction of the Problem

Benchmarking is a widely known and used method for companies to learn from each other (Reider 2000). However, applying a relational and practical approach, that is, managing a benchmarking process in a manner that both parties would gain or that it would actually solve practical problems, is not an easy target. Furthermore, the organization may not have capabilities or resources to learn the process of benchmarking and possible tools and techniques to handle the gathered information, let alone to train the whole team to do it. Therefore, a third-party involvement is in many cases beneficial, along with a systematic proceeding process for the benchmarking.

The developed third-party-supported benchmarking (3P BM) is a systematic process type of benchmarking tool. It includes a five-step

S. Mäenpää (✉) • A. Suominen • R. Breite
Tampere University of Technology, Tampere, Finland

J. Vesalainen et al. (eds.), *Practices for Network Management*,
DOI 10.1007/978-3-319-49649-8_10

procedure: definition, team forming, selecting the target, comparison and implementation. The 3P BM focuses on knowledge sharing and learning both on intra- and inter-organizational levels and therefore includes boundary objects also. Additionally, process coordination and support implemented by a third party is in a focal role. The goal of the tool is to provide the needed guidelines with focus on essential themes and steps for successful benchmarking, that is, collecting data, comparing, reciprocal learning and gaining support for particular views (Jarzabkowski and Kaplan 2015). The 3P BM is applicable in any kind or a mixture of several benchmarking types.

In the piloted case, the practical problem the focal company wanted to improve was its R&D processes, that is, to evaluate the operability of its existing R&D-related operations and to plan for improvements. The overall objective was to integrate the focal company's design and manufacturing (i.e. steel structure). The method for this was comparing the differences between operations, discussing and sharing experiences with the comparison partner company. Benchmarking was chosen as a suitable method because of its familiarity among the decision-makers in the focal company as well as its apparent simplicity. Thus, Jarzabkowski and Kaplan's (2015) statement of "selection of tools being influenced by the degree to which they are simple and easy to remember and use" is reinforced. The two companies are not direct competitors, but there is some level of comparability as they both operate as networked manufacturing companies.

As Jarzabkowski and Kaplan (2015) state, tools are used as essential devices enabling actors to focus attention on and make sense of focal issues for themselves and for others. Also in this case, the themes for benchmarking helped to map on the existing essential interests of the actors in the focal company. Here, the themes to be benchmarked were design, congruence of design criteria and documentation, product development project, make or buy, supply chain, manufacturing, life cycle and training. The list of themes was quite broad, but it was decided to start with this extensive view to be further focused later.

The 3P BM was used as a tool to find solutions for company-specific development needs, for example, recognized poor process operability. Using benchmarking, new ways of acting as well as successful practices were sought over the organizational boundaries. Benchmarking was found to be a useful tool to support collaborative culture among the participating companies and for its part enabling knowledge sharing and creation between different organizations. Thus, benchmarking tool can be seen as a boundary object "opening eyes" and providing a common language for conversation between actors across different boundaries, as Jarzabkowski and Kaplan (2015) also state.

Benchmarking Theory

According to Reider (2000), benchmarking is a method to learn success; that is, it is a learning method which is accomplished by transferring knowledge from one company to another. Inter-organizational benchmarking requires common knowledge and understanding (Grant 1986), therefore also overcoming the possible knowledge boundaries between organizations (Carlile 2004). Boundary objects are concrete or abstract "bridges" that allow contributing to a more comprehensive objective between groups with different perspectives and aims (Star and Griesemer 1989; Star 2010); thus, they should be taken into account while designing, for example, methods for knowledge sharing. A philosophical definition of benchmarking is that "it is the practice of being humble enough to admit that someone else is better at something, and being wise enough to learn how to match them and even surpass them at it" (APQC 1993).

The justification of benchmarking lies in the question "why re-invent the wheel?" (Kleemola 2005). In principle, benchmarking is setting goals and learning from others. Bhutta and Huq (1999) and Andersen et al. (1999) have used the phrase "benchmarking wheel" (see Fig. 10.1), adopting Deming's plan-do-change-act (PDCA) approach, to describe the process of benchmarking. The steps of the wheel are (1) plan the study, (2) search for benchmarking partners, (3) observe the partners' process, (4) analyze the gaps in performance and the causes of them, and (5) adopt the best practice.

There are different benchmarking types, for example, internal, external, competitor, functional and industry benchmarking (Bendell et al. 1993). Cooperative and collaborative benchmarking are the most talked about (Boxwell and Boxwell 1994). In cooperative benchmarking, an

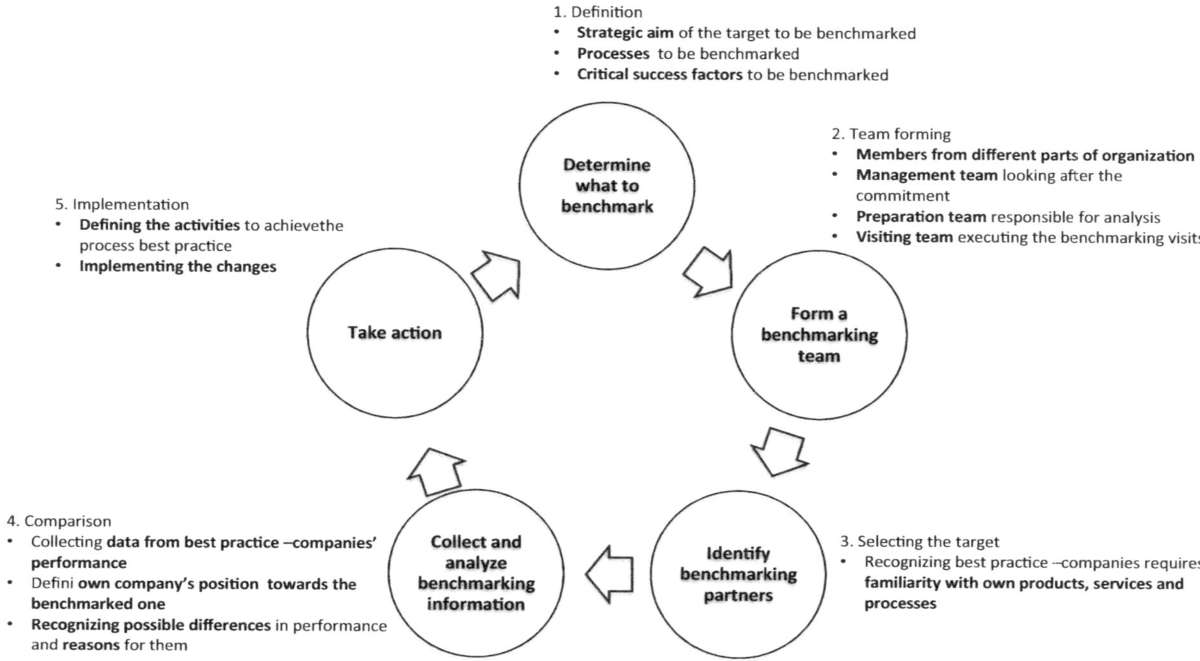

Fig. 10.1 The benchmarking wheel (adapted from Camp 1989 and Bhutta and Huq 1999)

organization that wants to improve a particular activity through benchmarking contacts the target firms and asks them if they are willing to share knowledge with the benchmarking team. Usually, the target companies are not direct competitors of the benchmarking company which secures better cooperation. However, some level of comparability should be found between the companies. The benefits and learning success are often unidirectional—from the target company to the benchmarking company—in cooperative benchmarking. Thus, the targets typically give more than they receive. In practice, the benchmarking process is often a mixture of several benchmarking types.

As Kleemola (2005) has stated, the whole benchmarking process might feel quite difficult from the benchmarking organization's viewpoint. The organization has to learn the process of benchmarking and train the whole team to do it. It also has to know the possible tools and techniques to handle the gathered information. It must have sufficient understanding to pick up the appropriate method for the information it has and for the analyzing to be done. As the benchmarking process interacts with and involves the different entities of the organization(s), a systematic approach is needed when full benefits of the benchmarking process are aimed for.

In a benchmarking process, there are usually two or more different organizations sharing knowledge and learning from one another. However, when the worlds of these organizations intersect, a difficulty may appear. Thus, boundary-spanning actors and activities are needed to overcome organizational or other boundaries to enable reciprocal knowledge sharing and learning. Boundary objects are artifacts, documents and vocabularies that can help people from different organizations to build a shared knowledge. In the context of benchmarking, the most appropriate boundary object would be a standardized form (Star and Griesemer 1989).

The theory of knowledge creation and the model of knowledge spiral, from socialization to externalization to combination and finally to internalization (SECI), by Nonaka and Takeuchi (1995) can be applied to benchmarking. Socialization is the process of sharing tacit knowledge of individuals. Before the participants of benchmarking process gather together to answer the focal questions (to fill the form), they have shared their knowledge with other people in their organization. Externalization is a process articulating tacit knowledge into explicit knowledge. It is often triggered by dialogue using metaphors, analogies, concepts and different models, that is, boundary objects, helping in their articulation. Combination takes place through editing and systemizing or combining different pieces of explicit knowledge. During a benchmarking visit, one company gives pieces of information to another company which edits and combines it to its existing knowledge. In internalization, the newly created explicit knowledge is converted into the tacit knowledge of individuals. After learning the better ways of doing activities, the company applies the new knowledge into its own processes, products and organization. The explicit knowledge converts to tacit knowledge of individuals through learning by doing, training and simulation (Kleemola 2005).

There are several enabling factors essential for benchmarking processes and also affecting the success of knowledge creation and learning. Simatupang and Sridharan (2005) propose three collaborative enablers, namely information sharing, decision synchronization and incentive alignment. Kleemola (2005) also suggests three enabling factors as prerequisites for benchmarking process. First, motive is a natural factor in benchmarking process as in all development programs. Second, openness is a key factor when the exchange of information is dependent on communication and willingness to share knowledge. Third, past experience is a basis in benchmarking process because the only way to learn is to produce new knowledge by using existing knowledge. Also, knowledge creation is dependent on the cultural factors such as organization's cooperative and collaborative abilities, and it requires the willingness of participants to collaborate and share knowledge to mutual benefits.

Third-Party-Supported Benchmarking

A benchmarking process traditionally follows a five-step procedure (definition, team forming, selecting the target, comparison and implementation, cf. Matters and Evans 1996). The developed 3P BM process complements the traditional procedure in three central ways: first, the focus in this procedure is on knowledge sharing and learning both on intra- and inter-organizational level. Second, the focal role of process coordination and support implemented by an outside professional third party (i.e. research organization) deserves attention. Third, the boundary objects are central as the systematic benchmarking process itself forms a boundary-spanning object, and also, the used questions, blueprints, pictures and diagrams act as boundary objects helping people from different organizations to learn and build a shared knowledge. Furthermore, this procedure is systematic; that is, the five main steps of benchmarking are included (Fig. 10.2).

Case: Finding Solutions for Company-Specific Development Needs

Purpose

The proposed 3P BM process is based on a pilot that aimed at developing novel methods and solutions to support innovation management in local and global R&D networks of an industrial manufacturing company. The main objective was to find solutions for quite a broad set of company-specific development needs in R&D.

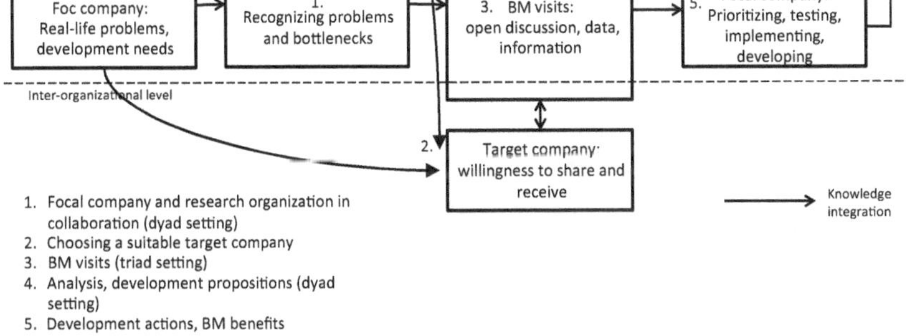

Fig. 10.2 Process of third-party-supported benchmarking

Benchmarking was chosen as a development tool because new ways of acting as well as successful practices were sought over the organizational boundaries. The aim was to detect and utilize good, existing practices instead of developing everything from scratch. Benchmarking was also found a useful tool to support collaborative culture among the participating companies.

Starting Point and Objectives

The preparation team in the focal company made self-assessment and formed a list of bottlenecks and problems to be resolved. The list of activities to be benchmarked was quite broad (see Fig. 10.3), but it was decided to go on with this extensive view to get a big picture and to be further focused later.

Based on the identified bottlenecks and problems, the following list (see Table 10.1) of more detailed questions was delivered to the target company before the actual benchmarking visit. The list was developed based on the focal company's internal, tacit knowledge and information needs. Articulating these needs in an explicit manner ensured that the most important, "right", questions were asked.

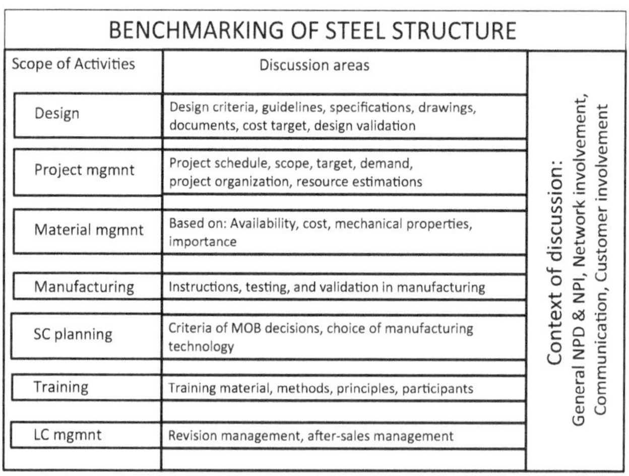

Fig. 10.3 Activities to be benchmarked

Table 10.1 Themes and questions to be discussed

Problem	What is needed? Information request for the benchmarking partner
Design	
The strengths and weaknesses of different organization models of design and product development	How are R&D, product development and supply planning organized?
Where to get information about global requirements and opportunities?	Where to get information about requirements and opportunities in different continents, and tolerances and country-specific materials?
Possibilities to utilize prototypes and product testing	Producing prototypes? How else to ensure validation?
Managing customer changes in supply project	How to manage changes in delivery specifications?
Congruence of design criteria	
There are no common design criteria	Example of documented design criteria
No sufficient feedback between parties	Network's internal feedback system
Lack of common design criteria is not seen as a problem or a necessity	Good justification for common design criteria
Congruence of documentation	
Documentation is cultural	Example of operating between different cultures
Tacit knowledge does not transfer along the documents	Way of listening to the partner, model of transferring both know-how and tacit knowledge
Changes do not transfer between parties	Network's internal knowledge sharing, example of managing changes
Product development project	
	How and who starts a new product development project?
	What kind of project team formulated?
	Who owns/funds the project? Who has the biggest decision-making power?
	How is the need for resources evaluated?
	How are R&D, research and product development projects interconnected?
	Official regulations and qualification approvals?

(*continued*)

Table 10.1 (continued)

Problem	What is needed? Information request for the benchmarking partner
	How to consider possible special applications in product development phase?
Make or buy	
Criteria for decision-making. How does the chosen technology affect?	What are the focal criteria for selection?
	How does the manufacturing technology affect selection?
Supply chain	
Supply chain management and communication in project development phase	How do subcontractors bring their own know-how into product development project?
	Supplier ramp-up and organizing support
	Inspections and approvals
	How to manage the direct deliveries from supplier to customer?
	How to manage subcontractor's subcontractors?
Manufacturing	
How can production best support product development project?	How much resources from production are involved in production development phase?
	How and where are manufacturing instructions made?
	Tools and device investments? Are they part of product development project?
	How is testing in production phase defined and validated?
	Are incoming goods also inspected?
	How long does the product development process last? Up to first ones are completed, delivered, …?
Life cycle and training	
Preconditions and resources for preparing training material	In what phase is training material prepared?
Change management during the life cycle	How to cope with version management?
Different functions (service, production, procurement, technical descriptions) may have different needs	What kind of documentation is there? Separate for service, production, procurement, …?

The immediate objective for benchmarking was to compare differences between the operations, to discuss and to share experiences. Also, the aim was to get acquainted with working practices to help in solving the bottlenecks and problems of the focal company. The long-term target was to develop the quality and profitability of the participants as well as to support the formation of a collaborative culture and ongoing development in the network.

Comparison Partner

The target company was selected as a comparison partner on the following grounds:

1. Global company should be known for its good and working practices.
2. Information sharing was supposed to be easier than with straight competitors.
3. Both companies were participating in the same research program and project.
4. Both companies shared an interest toward R&D collaboration.
5. Both companies were interested in managing supplier networks and supplier partners.

Schedule and Activities in BM Process

The steps and schedule for 3P BM process were as follows:

1. Self-evaluation in focal company, 4–8 weeks
2. Analysis and further actions planned (choosing the themes to benchmark, questions to be asked), 4–6 weeks
3. The first comparison visit was organized three months after self-evaluation
4. The second visit was organized four months after the first visit

5. Aftermaths (analysis, choosing the solutions to be piloted, preparing an action plan for improving the focal company's practices, reporting), 10–12 months after starting the BM process

The roles and activities for the third-party professional actor (research unit) and participating companies are shown in Fig. 10.4.

Benchmarking Partners, Comparison Visit and Development Plans

The focal company requested the opportunity to benchmark with the target company which is known for its good practices. Furthermore, both companies saw benchmarking as a beneficial development tool. Planning, congruence of design criteria and documentation, R&D project, make or buy, supply chain, production, life cycle and training were chosen as the topics for the first benchmarking visit. The members of the preparation team and the experts of each benchmarking topic attended the benchmarking visit. The collected information was processed in workshops and

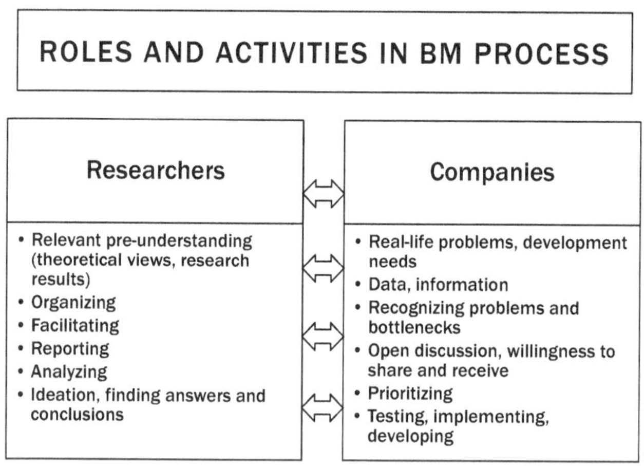

Fig. 10.4 Roles and activities in 3P BM process

used as a benchmark when evaluating the workability of current operations as well as in planning improvements for current procedures. Based on analysis the solutions to be piloted were chosen and an action plan for improving the focal company's practices was made.

Conclusions

As stated by Jarzabkowski and Kaplan (2015), social processes, such as 3P BM, produce multiple potential outcomes. Often the outcomes are known only in the long run, but in the short term, use of tool may, for example, help the organization to move forward, increase internal discussion, help to gain support for particular views as well as help moving from suboptimization toward a more holistic view as was the case here. Along the pilot, the similarities and differences were detected during the course of process (BM visits 1 and 2), and as a result, development propositions related to the focal company's product processes, R&D management, supplier collaboration, as well as modeling, testing and training were named. Immediately after the benchmarking process, three out of five development propositions were launched.

At the end of this process, the third-party actor (research unit) discussed with the focal company's key actors to summarize the reasons for the company to choose benchmarking at the first place, to find out what was expected from the process and what will follow from it. All in all, the focal company representatives found the piloted process quite successful along with benefits identified from the process. This kind of client satisfaction is one relevant outcome of the use of the tool (cf. Jarzabkowski and Kaplan 2015). In relation to the identified benefits, people from the focal benchmarking participant commented that 3P BM process

increased internal discussion
made to look into the mirror
helped to identify the stimulants
reinforced the assumptions
increased the development of operations on the whole instead of sub-optimizing.

The piloted 3P BM tool connects a systematic approach of benchmarking, third-party attendance as well as a suitable set of both boundary objects and participants to collaborate in a network for reciprocal learning and to find solutions for specific practical problems. In the 3P BM tool, a systematic approach and the third-party attendance are emphasized as the organizations often lack the capabilities and resources to learn the process of benchmarking, use possible tools and techniques to handle the gathered information and train the whole team to do it. The experience of the use of 3P BM tool encourages applying it to other improvement and development projects too.

References

American Productivity and Quality Center. (1993). *The benchmarking management guide*. Portland, OR: Productivity Press.

Andersen, B., Fagerhaug, T., Randmæl, S., Schuldmaier, J., & Prenninger, J. (1999). Benchmarking supply chain management: Finding best practices. *Journal of Business & Industrial Marketing, 14*(5/6), 378–389. doi:10.1108/08858629910290139.

Bendell, T., Boulter, L., & Kelly, J. (1993). *Benchmarking for competitive advantage*. London: Financial Times/Pitman Publishing.

Bhutta, K. S., & Huq, F. (1999). Benchmarking-best practices: An integrated approach. *Benchmarking: An International Journal, 6*(3), 254–268. doi:10.1108/14635779910289261.

Boxwell, R. J., & Boxwell, R. J. (1994). *Benchmarking for competitive advantage* (p. 30). New York: McGraw-Hill.

Camp, R. C. (1989). *Benchmarking: The search for industry best practices that lead to superior performance*. White Plains, NY: Quality Resources.

Carlile, P. R. (2004). Transferring, translating, and transforming: An integrative framework for managing knowledge across boundaries. *Organization Science, 15*(5), 555–568. doi:10.1287/orsc.1040.0094.

Elmuti, D., & Kathawala, Y. (1997). An overview of benchmarking process: A tool for continuous improvement and competitive advantage. *Benchmarking for Quality Management & Technology, 4*(4), 229–243. doi:10.1108/14635779710195087.

Grant, R. M. (1986). Toward a knowledge-based theory of the firm. *Strategic Management Journal Winter, 17*(109), 109–122. doi:10.1002/smj.4250171110.

Hong, P., Hong, S. W., Jungbae Roh, J., & Park, K. (2012). Evolving benchmarking practices: A review for research perspectives. *Benchmarking: An International Journal, 19*(4/5), 444–462. doi:10.1108/14635771211257945.

Jarzabkowski, P., & Kaplan, S. (2015). Strategy tools-in-use: A framework for understanding "technologies of rationality" in practice. *Strategic Management Journal, 36*, 537–558. doi:10.1002/smj.2270.

Kleemola, A. (2005). Group benchmarking as a model for knowledge creation in supply management context. Doctoral thesis. Tampere University of Technology. Publication 555.

Matters, M., & Evans, A. (1996). *The nuts and bolts of benchmarking*. Benchmarking Link-Up Australia. available at: www.ozemail.com.au/~benchmark/nuts.bolts.html

Nonaka, I., & Takeuchi, H. (1995). *The knowledge-creating company: How Japanese companies create the dynamics of innovation*. New York: Oxford University Press.

Reider, R. (2000). *Benchmarking strategies: A tool for profit improvement*. New York: John Wiley.

Simatupang, T. M., Sridharan, R. (2005). Supply chain discontent: *Business Process Management Journal, 11*(4), 349–369.

Star, S. L. (2010). This is not a boundary object: Reflections on the origin of a concept. *Science, Technology & Human Values, 35*(5), 601–617. doi:10.1177/0162243910377624.

Star, S. L., & Griesemer, J. R. (1989). Institutional ecology, translations' and boundary objects: Amateurs and professionals in Berkeley's Museum of Vertebrate Zoology, 1907–39. *Social Studies of Science, 19*(3), 387–420. doi:10.1177/030631289019003001.

11

Value Proposition Co-development

Juho Ylimäki and Jukka Vesalainen

Introduction

As companies increasingly focus on their core business, they often develop a need to outsource service functions that were once carried out in-house. When outsourcing needs go further and edge closer to critical services, outsourcing companies face important questions around which service functions are safe and efficient to outsource, and whether there are some functions that would be risky to outsource. The value potential of an outsourcing project is often unclear because it is difficult to establish in advance how well a potential services partner could meet the project requirements. These issues are more critical when the services in question involve high levels of collaboration and when they are strongly tied with customer processes. Some services such as basic cleaning or real estate maintenance have only a weak connection to a purchasing company's

J. Ylimäki (✉) • J. Vesalainen
University of Vaasa, Vaasa, Finland

J. Vesalainen et al. (eds.), *Practices for Network Management*,
DOI 10.1007/978-3-319-49649-8_11

core processes and are easy to manage, whereas other service functions such as machinery repairs or scheduled maintenance closely affect core processes and, thus, have the potential to cause major problems when unexpected issues arise.

It is typical for a firm aiming to outsource aspects of its business to evaluate the value potential in service outsourcing itself. The problem with that one-sided practice is that the outsourcing company is not aware of the most suitable service available, which means it is not necessarily making very reliable decisions on service outsourcing. Furthermore, when a firm invites tenders based on a one-sided evaluation of value potential, the tendering service providers' knowledge of the customer's specific needs is limited and those service providers cannot offer the optimal service solution owing to the information asymmetry.

We suggest that a relational business approach applied to evaluating outsourcing value potential would help to unify the outsourcing customer's need information (information about market need) and the service provider's how information (information about how to serve that need) in an objective analysis. It follows that to achieve relationality in outsourcing projects, firms need new boundary objects designed for collaboration.

To provide a solution to the challenging question of *how service providers and customer companies could collaborate to systematically evaluate potential outsourcing value, and to find the best mix of outsourced services*, we take a practical view and describe a tool for the joint evaluation of the outsourcing value of service functions with the potential to be outsourced. The tool has been developed by us, university researchers, in collaboration with two companies, factory maintenance service provider (acronym Serv used further on) and manufacturing company (acronym Manu used further on), and aims to ensure that outsourcing decisions are based on objective evaluation, sufficient knowledge sharing, and joint sense making. The used methodology represents a design science approach as the research led to the construction of a scientifically grounded tool that was then used to solve a practical business problem, meaning it was validated by members of the project from the company side. The tool developed is an effective boundary object that facilitates knowledge sharing, knowledge integration, and joint sense making.

Following this introduction, the second section explains the need for relationality and co-creation in outsourcing projects. The third section then presents the tool for collaborative evaluation of outsourcing potential and it explains its use. The fourth section presents the case that prompted the development of the tool. The chapter then concludes with a discussion of the developed tool and its potential in the area of collaborative outsourcing projects, and of some further potential applications.

Theoretical Basis for Joint Evaluation of Outsourcing Value Potential—The Relational View of Strategy and Value Co-creation

The theoretical basis for the tool and its application in general lies in the relational view of strategy. According to that relational view (Dyer and Singh 1998; Lavie 2006), companies can achieve benefits that in turn create collaborative advantage through joint actions and functional, long-term relationships. These benefits can only be achieved when companies collaborate. Such benefits are based on relation-specific assets and capabilities, knowledge-sharing routines, complementary resources, and relational governance. These elements are interconnected and can create a self-strengthening cycle as the collaboration progresses. To achieve the benefits of collaboration, companies should avoid arm's-length, market-type relationships, and move toward relationships that include attributes that boost commitment and long-term relationships.

In the setting of a decision whether to outsource services, the potential benefits of collaboration derive from factors such as the service provider having a highly developed knowledge of the other party's needs and capabilities, efficient communication flowing from a developed joint language, and from the usage of resources applied in the relationship being optimized. Knowledge of the other party's needs and capabilities develops over time as companies collaborate and resolve everyday issues related to the services produced. Daily communication helps companies to adapt to each other's language and terminology, which in turn enhances the efficiency of the communication. In addition, the optimal resource combination allocated to collaboration is typically finalized only after the parties have learned about each other's capabilities in practice, which usually involves a trial-and-error learning process. Furthermore, sometimes inflexible contracts, which are typical of arm's-length relationships, can hinder such learning and development.

Although the mechanisms behind the collaborative benefits are path dependent and require time to evolve, this tool takes a view that the development of sources of joint benefits can be facilitated to a remarkable degree by using systematic tools to enhance collaboration. The tool described in this chapter could assist companies to create collaborative advantage by facilitating knowledge sharing and enhancing the search for complementary resources. As a prerequisite, companies need to have evolving relational governance, which means that they need to trust each other and share similar targets for the collaboration (Ylimäki and Vesalainen 2015). If, as a result of the analysis, firms implement an outsourcing project, they are committing themselves to developing relationship-specific assets and capabilities. As an example of the interconnection of collaborative elements that create benefits, these relationship-specific assets and capabilities further enhance knowledge sharing (Shou et al. 2013) and mitigate the risks posed by opportunism (Williamson 1985).

Another basis for the tool presented in this chapter is derived from the value co-creation literature (Prahalad and Ramaswamy 2000; Grönroos 2011). As companies collaborate in the realm of services, they co-create value when both parties contribute in the area of service production. Depending on the viewpoint, either the customer (Heinonen et al. 2010) or the service provider (Prahalad and Ramaswamy 2000) can leverage service production by using the other party's competences. It should be noted that value co-creation is not about consuming the other party's competences to take advantage of a reduced workload in an organization. In contrast, involving a partner in value creation should improve the service experience while requiring less overall effort in the relationship owing to the optimization of capabilities.

In outsourcing projects, seamless collaboration in terms of value creation is essential, and both parties to the collaboration have essential roles in its success. Service providers seeking new customers aiming to outsource services formerly produced in-house need to find out how to efficiently manage the co-creation of solutions with their customers.

Similarly, from the customer's perspective, the buyer (the outsourcing company) should have a clear understanding of how to engage the service provider efficiently in the co-creation of an optimal package of outsourced service functions. Although co-creation leans on a sound logic, its application can in practice be challenging. Scholars have, for example, questioned whether customer companies can actually communicate their needs in a fully understandable way (Nordin and Kowalkowski 2010), and thus, it is not clear if service providers can really understand the challenges faced by their customers. The tool for the co-evaluation of outsourcing value potential assists companies intending to co-create value as it helps to define which service functions to keep in-house and which should be carried out externally.

Evaluating Service Outsourcing Value Potential

The tool presented in this chapter balances two essential dimensions in the analysis of outsourcing possibilities: risk level and outsourcing value. The former is further divided into elements of criticality and probability and the latter into elements of cost efficiency and utility value. These elements, in turn, consist of eight factors that are evaluated in relation to the current way of organizing services. All service modules being considered for outsourcing are analyzed individually and the outcome is a chart presenting the relative positions of these modules in terms of achievable outsourcing value and risk level.

Utilizing the tool involves four stages. First, the entities to be evaluated are selected. These should be service functions that could either be outsourced or produced in-house. The current way of organizing these entities does not matter as the analysis does not preclude functions that are currently organized via external service providers.

Second, the analysis must identify the most important factors affecting outsourcing decisions. Following discussions with the case companies involved, two main dimensions were identified: outsourcing value and risk. Including risk dimension to the tool was particularly in the interest of Manu. To balance these dimensions and to ensure sufficiently broad analysis, the first half of the evaluated factors should consider outsourcing value from four different viewpoints and the second half should incorporate four risk measures. Combining these two aspects makes it possible to build a two-dimensional analysis to support the selection of the service functions best suited to outsourcing. We found evaluating eight factors made assessing the different service functions both simple and efficient. Outsourcing value was broken down into cost efficiency and utility value sub-dimensions. These, in turn, were divided into cost, efficiency, special expertise, and lead time. On the risk side, two sub-dimensions were identified, namely, probability and criticality. Then, these were further divided into quantity of objects, malfunction probability, tied capital, and degree of criticality of the process. Figure 11.1 presents the structure of these eight factors used in our Manu—Serv case. When utilizing the tool, the above eight factors should be modified to fit the case-specific environment.

Third, the service provider and customer firms jointly rate the selected eight factors in the evaluation process for each service function that might be outsourced. All ratings are agreed in collaboration and should represent a joint opinion on the effects of outsourcing each service function compared to organizing it internally. In our case study, agreeing the rating for some service functions was simple, whereas evaluating others

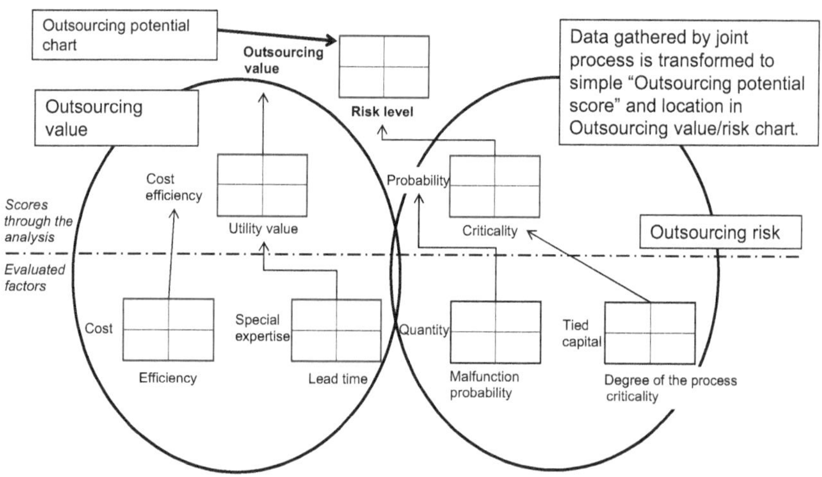

Fig. 11.1 Structure of the systematic evaluation of outsourcing potential

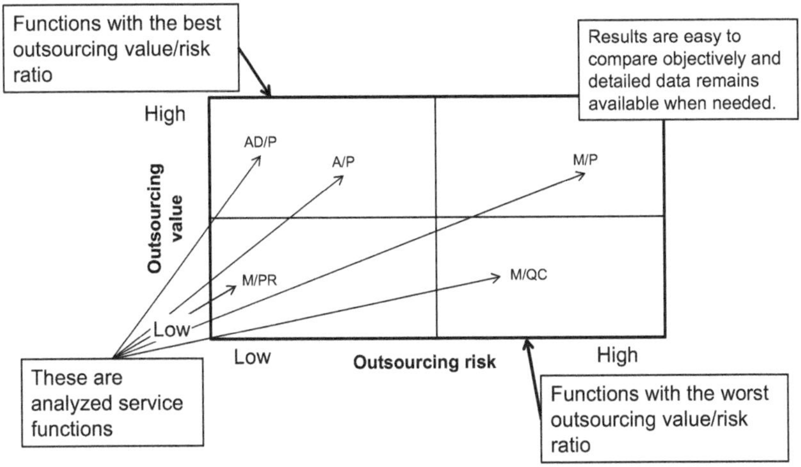

Fig. 11.2 Outsourcing potential chart

required considerable discussion before agreement was reached. In the Manu—Serv case, the rating exercise was conducted at a joint meeting using a web-based tool to ease the data handling and gathering process, and that method enabled all participants to concentrate on the evaluation discussion.

Fourth, the data are analyzed and an outsourcing potential chart (Fig. 11.2) created. In this fourth stage, the outsourcing potential chart acts as a boundary object that facilitates joint sense making in terms of the optimal organization of a broad service solution. Comparison of the outsourcing potential of different service functions is simple because their position on the outsourcing potential chart is based on reliable and well-grounded information that is jointly agreed upon.

Following a joint discussion, systematic outsourcing decisions can be made by the buyer company and possible implementation can then be discussed with the service provider. In the Manu—Serv case, systematic analysis led to adjustments in the organization of factory maintenance. However, it did not support the initial idea of broadly outsourcing factory maintenance to Serv.

Finding an Optimal Mix of Factory Maintenance Functions for Outsourcing

The tool is connected to a case in which two industrial companies and a team of university researchers developed a broad collaborative process for service development. This process included five stages. First, companies jointly checked each other's orientations in the relationship. Second, they analyzed the present state of the collaboration. At the third stage, companies evaluated outsourcing value potential. At the fourth stage, companies designed service process, and at the final stage, they planned the relational governance to support continuous development in relationship.

This chapter focuses on the third stage and especially on the outsourcing evaluation tool developed in collaboration with the university researchers. At that stage of the overall process, the three-party collaboration resulted first in the development of the evaluation tool and then in its implementation into an actual evaluation of outsourcing value potential.

The development work involved an industrial company Manu that needed to evaluate the potential to outsource its factory maintenance and a service solution provider Serv that was willing to assist in the evaluation process and to co-develop a tool for the joint evaluation of potential outsourcing value. The companies agreed that deep and open collaboration would serve as a good basis for the development.

It is noteworthy that, in this case, the time invested in developing the new tool was justified by reasons that went beyond the evolving collaboration: the service provider wanted to find new ways that it could incorporate into its marketing to other customers and the industrial company was interested in possible approaches to systemizing outsourcing evaluation in a broad sense.

The two firms had dealt with each other before entering the evaluation process. Serv had delivered ad-hoc services and some small service components for Manu. The relationship was relatively long but was underdeveloped as Manu had unfilled needs in areas where Serv operated. The situation was well set for collaboration on the development and application of the outsourcing evaluation tool.

Factory maintenance was originally organized by an internal maintenance department and services purchased in a transactional manner from up to 40 service providers including Serv. This way of purchasing services from a relatively broad group of suppliers led to high transaction costs for Manu. Serv's business is concentrated on factory automation and providing maintenance services for machinery and tools. In this case, Serv was willing to broaden its business focus to include full-service solutions for factory maintenance, and thus, was interested in finding ways to establish the partnership with Manu.

The development of the tool required two joint development meetings in which representatives of both companies and university researchers were present, three interviews of company decision-makers, and feedback via email on the initial versions. The tool was also refined during piloting, which involved reducing the original 16 factors to eight factors and evaluating all the factors by comparing the current way of organizing to an outsourced option instead of evaluating both separately. The initial aim was to evaluate each factor independently at both companies, but co-evaluation seemed to be beneficial because it facilitated discussion and the companies sharing understanding.

The discussions guided by the evaluations and the analyzed data led to the following main findings: (1) the direct cost of the workforce was the same under the evaluations of Manu and Serv; (2) in the case of some service functions previously bought on a transactional basis, direct costs could increase because of repeated profit margins; (3) the increased flexibility in the outsourcing model could improve efficiency in the use of the workforce; (4) more expert knowledge would be available under the new model; (5) the new model might enhance efficiency of the supervision and coordination of the maintenance workforce (including external personnel); (6) the total maintenance cost would be more accurately accountable; and (7) Serv would have to increase the service level by making investments that would be beneficial only in the relationship in question, which would reduce its flexibility on costs.

The usage of the outsourcing potential evaluation tool enhanced joint problem solving and knowledge sharing as it allowed the parties to avoid rigid buyer and seller roles. In light of these findings and of the accompanying discussions, it became clear that the service provider was only able to offer limited improvements in the context of outsourcing the whole factory maintenance department. However, in the case of some service functions, outsourcing looked to be beneficial. At the beginning of the collaboration, Manu's representative had explicit and tacit knowledge of the plant's maintenance requirements and of existing practices, and Serv's representatives possessed explicit and tacit knowledge of various types of maintenance services and the applicability of various specialized manufacturing and maintenance technologies. During the evaluation process, these different accumulations of knowledge were shared and the parties were able to form a mutually held view of the optimal combination of outsourced service functions. Overall, joint analysis led to a shared understanding of value creation in factory maintenance, and of the most critical maintenance functions.

Conclusions

The analysis tool developed offered a beneficial platform for discussion. It systematically supported decision making in terms of which service functions it would be beneficial to outsource. The tool also revealed the critical characteristics of different service functions in terms of a value/risk score. The analysis guided Manu to make the right outsourcing decisions and Serv learned valuable information about the areas it would have to work on to attract Manu and other similar industrial companies.

Applying the tool developed served as a relational practice that facilitated joint learning (Huikkola et al. 2013). The tool supports all three elements of joint learning: joint sense making, knowledge sharing, and knowledge integration (Selnes and Sallis 2003). The structure of the evaluation process enhances the commitment to the results as each rating is jointly discussed and agreed upon after both parties presented their arguments at each step, which enhanced joint sense making. Furthermore, joint evaluations increased the knowledge sharing between the companies as both parties explained their assumptions and the known facts underpinning them. Analysis of the ratings and the documented outsourcing potential chart assisted the companies to integrate created knowledge into the relationship. This information helped the companies not only to make the outsourcing decisions but also to shed light on the enhancements of the most suitable service functions and their elements. These dimensions of joint learning are elements that strengthen the relationship themselves and are essential factors in the creation of collaborative advantage.

The tool was developed to address a scenario where firms were aiming to optimize service outsourcing of factory maintenance. However, the same tool could easily be used in outsourcing decisions related to other services that involve high levels of uncertainty or when it is difficult to formulate an optimal service solution. The essential phase then is to carefully select the outsourcing value and risk factors to be evaluated. The tool and its basic idea could be further modified to assist in any service purchase. In that case, companies might also want to adjust the main dimensions (value and risk) to meet their specific needs. These modification options enable the broad usage of the core of the developed tool and the accompanying evaluation process.

References

Dyer, J., & Singh, H. (1998). The relational view: Csooperative strategy and sources of interorganizational competitive advantage. *Academy of Management Review, 23*(4), 660–679.

Grönroos, C. (2011). Value co-creation in service logic: A critical analysis. *Marketing Theory, 11*(3), 279–301.

Heinonen, K., Strandvik, T., Mickelsson, K.-J., Edvardsson, B., Sundström, E., & Andersson, P. (2010). A customer-dominant logic of service. *Journal of Service Management, 21*(4), 531–548.

Huikkola, T., Ylimäki, J., & Kohtamäki, M. (2013). Joint learning in R&D collaborations and the facilitating relational practices. *Industrial Marketing Management, 42*(7), 1167–1180.

Lavie, D. (2006). The competitive advantage of interconnected firms: An extension of the resource-based view. *Academy of Management Review, 31*(3), 638–658.

Nordin, F., & Kowalkowski, C. (2010). Solutions offerings: A critical review and reconceptualisation. *Journal of Service Management, 21*(4), 441–459.

Selnes, F., & Sallis, J. (2003). Promoting relationship learning. *Journal of Marketing, 67*(3), 80–95.

Shou, Z., Yang, L., Zhang, Q., & Su, C. (2013). Market munificence and inter-firm information sharing: The moderating effect of specific assets. *Journal of Business Research, 66*(10), 2130–2138.
Williamson, O. E. (1985). *The economic institutions of capitalism*. New York: The Free Press.
Ylimäki, J., & Vesalainen, J. (2015). Relational development of a service concept: Dialogue meets efficiency. *Journal of Business & Industrial Marketing, 30*(8), 939–950.

12

Relational Factors as Part of Network Relationship Evaluation

Rainer Breite, Sari Mäenpää, Anu Suominen, and Mika Perho

Introduction of the Problem

Nowadays, network management is becoming more and more delicate. However, the demands for network management are still increasing. The demands for different networks vary, but in general, networks should be more flexible, efficient, effective, and easily managed. In this context, the Supplier Evaluation System tool is presented. The overall purpose of the tool is to map the level of relational factors in order to evaluate the potentiality for increasing self-direction between network parties and decrease the need for the focal company's control. That is, the higher the level of the relational factors is, the more capable the network parties are to share the focal company's control tasks. After the mapping, the improvement measures of flexibility factors of the network can be considered and the potentiality to reduce the need for control contemplated. This tool

R. Breite (✉) • S. Mäenpää • A. Suominen • M. Perho
Tampere University of Technology, Tampere, Finland

J. Vesalainen et al. (eds.), *Practices for Network Management*,
DOI 10.1007/978-3-319-49649-8_12

utilizes the theoretical framework that includes the examination aspect of social capital. In this tool, together the relational factors, including both relational properties and relational behavior aspects, form a platform that enables or restricts self-direction. Relational properties are trust, commitment, collaboration, and power. Relational behavior includes six various aspects: initiating behavior, signaling behavior, disclosing behavior, interaction frequency, richness, lateral involvement, and vertical involvement. The development process of the tool includes the features of design science (Simon 1996). That is, it has been developed with the help of practitioners for specific practical network relationship problems (Holmström et al. 2009). For this purpose, the theoretical framework has been created by the researchers. Correspondingly, the relevance of its functionality has been tested in the case company's supply network.

The practical and managerial purpose of the tool is to evaluate and give an overall view on whether there is potential to decrease the need for the control in a network, especially in cases with multiple smaller and larger suppliers. Due to the complex business environment and largish supply network, the network management can be demanding, requiring resources and time. Therefore, the long-term purpose of the focal company could be to decrease the need for network control. That is, the overall objective is diminishing the control of the focal company by transferring control to its suppliers. Then, with the help of the tool, the focal companies can estimate the circumstances and possibilities to reduce their own network control. However, due to the result of the company's external and internal contingency factors, the usage and applications of the tool vary. As Jarzabkowski and Kaplan (2015) have mentioned, the affordance of the tool varies among organizations, and its usage and applications depend upon the agency of actors.

In the piloted case, the overall objective was to evaluate the levels of the relational factors in a pursuit to transfer the focal company's project control to suppliers in the future. Here, this tool was found to be useful to evaluate the relational factors, and based on the evaluations, project control and management tasks transferred to the suppliers. That is, with the help of the tool, the relational properties between the network parties can be estimated in the systematic way.

Theoretical Background of the Tool

Social capital comprises both the network and the assets that may be mobilized through the network (cf. Burt 1992). Social capital is owned jointly by the parties in a relationship, and although it has value in use, it cannot be traded easily (Nahapiet and Ghoshal 1998). Social capital can be seen as the "relational glue" in inter-organizational relationships and a focal antecedent for collaboration. Burt (1992) and Loury (1977) have conceptualized social capital as a set of social resources embedded in relationships. A broader definition includes not only social relationships but also the norms and values associated with them (Coleman 1988; Putnam 1995).

According to Krause et al. (2007) and Lawson et al. (2008), building social capital is important for achieving benefits in an inter-organizational relationship. Social capital resides in relationships, and relationships are created through exchange (Bourdieu 1986). Frequent inter-organizational interactions between parties on different hierarchical levels promote the sharing of information, leading to faster problem resolution and synchronized inter-firm processes. Several scholars have studied how building social capital creates value for companies participating in collaborative relationships (Villena et al. 2011; Krause et al. 2007; Cousins et al. 2006; Cousins and Menguc 2006). Among others, these scholars suggest that building social capital between buyers and suppliers allows them to gain access and leverage the resources embedded in their relationships. They also highlight the fact that social capital reduces the likelihood of conflicts and promotes collaboration because of its association with shared objectives, trusting relations, and social ties.

Partnership-type relationships require antecedents, that is, "soft" factors, that current practices do not consider sufficiently (Agostini and Nosella 2015). Relational properties are embedded in social capital, which makes it possible to achieve something that cannot be achieved without it in social exchange process in business context as well. Relational properties concern matters that are reflecting and affecting to relationship(s) between two or more interrelated actors. A relationship can be characterized in part by relational properties. Relational properties like trust, commitment, collaboration, and power differ from each other by the nature and scale (see Ivens 2006; Gummesson 2008; Leuthesser 1997; Leuthesser and Kohli 1995). Therefore, relational properties of a relationship must be on a good enough level to form and develop a well-functioning network relationship in the purpose of becoming the integrated part of the key partner supply network. In network context, control and governance are easier to implement and manage when relational properties are in a good state. This, in turn, allows reducing the amount of effort and resources in the controlling and monitoring tasks and activities within a network.

Leuthesser and Kohli (1995) found at least three important aspects of relational behavior from literature review of group theory, marketing, and organization behavior. The first aspect relates to the type of information a supplier obtains from and provides to a buyer. Behaviors that appear to be central in this respect are *initiating*, *signaling*, and *disclosing behaviors*. The second aspect of relational behavior relates to the *frequency of interaction* and the *richness* of the medium of that interaction. The third aspect of relational behavior indicates the extent of *lateral* and *vertical involvement* in interactions between organizations' functions and hierarchical levels. (Leuthesser and Kohli 1995, 221–222) Relational properties can be seen as a foundation for a business relationship and relational behavior part as an apparatus to uphold customer's satisfaction in continuous relationship. In relational skills, both relational behavior and properties are taken into account. The better the relational skills an actor has the better the aspects of relationship are taken into account with continuous desire to improve the relationships.

Supplier Evaluation System with Relational Factors

In order for the focal company to reach the ultimate goal of reducing some or all control to its supplier, there are many phases. The process consists at least of four steps, but the supplier evaluation system with relational factors regards the first three of these steps (see Fig. 12.1):

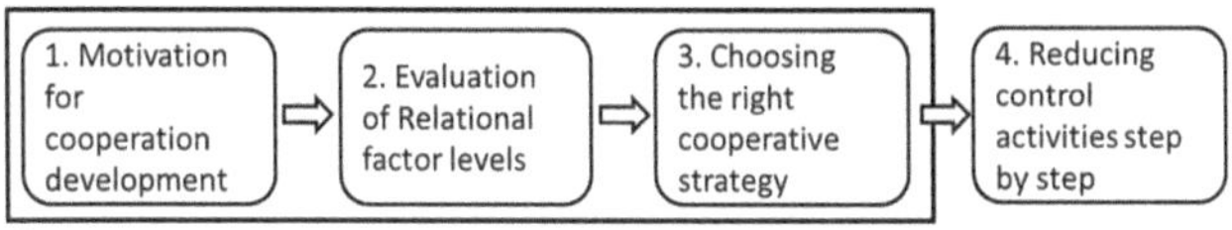

Fig. 12.1 Steps for the estimation of the potential control reduction by the focal company

1. *Motivation for cooperation development*: key suppliers' motivation for long-term cooperation is preliminary estimated, together with the network constellations, that is, which company controls certain activities within the network, also the participants for the evaluation are chosen.
2. *Evaluation of Relational factor levels*: the levels of relational factors are evaluated. During this step, suppliers' potential of the cooperation and readiness to take responsibility are defined. This definition is made by using the chosen relational factors.
3. *Choosing the right cooperation strategy*: the cooperation strategy between the company and suppliers is defined. The chosen strategy is based on the idea that the level of relational factors is identified and suppliers have potential to cooperate together and they are ready to take more responsibility.
4. *Reducing control activities step by step*: the company and its supplier make a plan on how some or all of the control of activities is transferred from the focal company to its suppliers.

This tool operates in the area of social capital and its purpose is to define the level of the relational factors in a focal company led supply network. With the tool, the level of relational factors, including relational properties of trust, commitment, collaboration, and power, together with relational behavior aspects of initiating, signaling, and disclosing behaviors, frequency of interaction and richness of the medium of that interaction, and lateral and vertical involvement are evaluated. Thus, with the results of the tool the network's suppliers' readiness for more self-directness, and in turn, the focal company's possibility to decrease the need for control can be determined. The theoretical and empirical background of the tool lies in Leuthesser's and Kohli's (1995) and Perho's (2015) model of relational behaviors and properties (see Fig. 12.2).

The tool consist of phasis:

Phase 1. *"Motivation for cooperation development"*:

The estimation and improvement measures are carried out according to three steps:

(a) *"Defining the partners/actions"*: the actions that have partners are identified.
(b) *"The Defining the Network Constellations"*: the network constellations, that is, which company controls certain activities within the network (see Fig. 12.2) are defined. The ways company's suppliers cooperate together and position themselves in the network, strongly affect the company's network management. For this purpose, this is an important part of the tool. At this stage, the mutual relations of the network partners are examined. Figure 12.2 is an example of the mutual relations. It illustrates a relationship constellation between three participants. The main point of this phase is illustrating participants' relative position and affection with respect to each other (cf. Johnston et al. 2004).
(c) "Selecting participants": the participants that should be a part of the relational factor evaluation are selected. *"Which are the right or best suppliers for the company?"*, is the fundamental question for the successful network companies. This question makes room for "*Selecting*

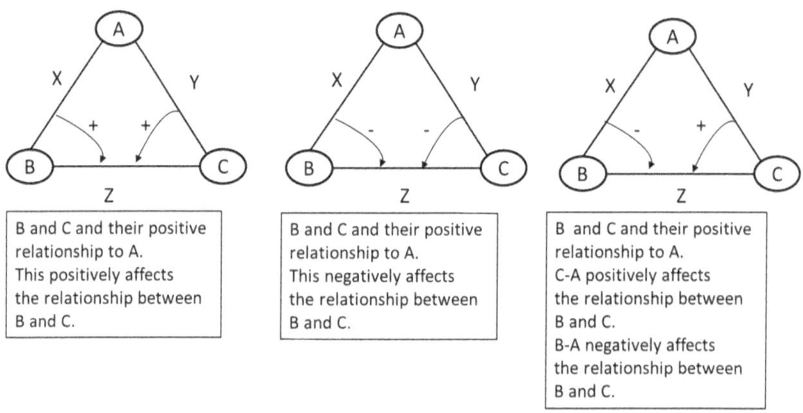

Fig. 12.2 An example of relationship constellations

participants" that forms one of the main elements of the tool. The basic idea is to scan the company's potential suppliers. For this purpose, suppliers' importance for the company's business and their willingness for long-term cooperation are preliminary estimated.

Phase 2. *"Evaluation of Relational factor levels" (Fig. 12.3)*:

(a) The relational factors, that is, relational properties (C) of trust, commitment, collaboration, and power, together with relational behavior (A) of initiating, signaling, and disclosing, frequency of interaction and richness of the medium of that interaction, and lateral and vertical involvement are evaluated on a scale of 1–5 or with verbal evaluation. The evaluation questions are presented below (evaluation questions).
(b) The level of the relational factors is presented to a focal company.

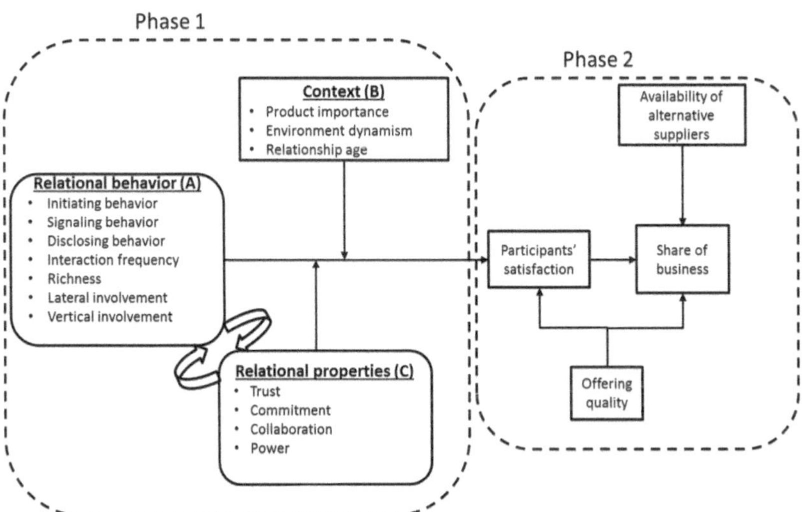

Fig. 12.3 Relational factors and their consequences (modified from Leuthesser and Kohli 1995; Perho 2015)

Evaluation questions:

Triad objectives (O) flexibility, good cooperation, technology and economic benefits.

Function of the focal company + supplier SS + [supplier S1, S2, S3, S4, S5]

Backgrounds (B)

1. size of company, domain, turnover, and profitability
2. interviewee's role/position/task
3. cooperation organizations: primary customer/supplier/subcontractor, others
4. collaboration form
   a. how did collaboration start?
   b. duration (years, months)
   c. based on project, annual or partnership contract?
   d. how many projects

Relational factors for evaluating possibilities to cooperate in triad

Relational properties in survey: trust, commitment, collaboration, and power

Trust (T)

1. Do suppliers trust each other and how does it appear?
2. Do suppliers trust the buyer and how does it appear?
3. Has there been any reliability problems with the organization or personnel, what?
4. Describe reputation of the cooperation organization?
5. Describe reputation of the counterparty person in the other organization?
6. What kinds of experiences and impressions have been got from the cooperation so far?
7. What is the basis of trust?
   A. affective
   B. cognitive

   1. prediction of behavior (calculated),
   2. perceive consistent behavior (knowledge), or
   3. mutual understanding and common values (similarity).
8. Level of trust (1–5): poor(1), adequate(2), good(3), very good(4), excellent(5)
   (a) F - S
   (b) S - F
   (c) S - SS
   (d) SS - S
9. Is there reciprocity in the relationship, what kind?
10. Is there solidarity in the relationship; how does it occur?
11. How do the organizational culture and norms differ in organizations?
12. Does principal control work too little, enough, or too much?

Commitment (Com)

1. Is the supplier committed to the cooperation and common target of another supplier; how does it occur?
2. Are both parties aiming for a long-term collaborative relationship?
3. Are suppliers committed to work together to achieve common objectives?
4. Have objectives been accepted together?
5. Have relation-specific investments been made? (e.g., equipment, training, certificates)
6. Level of commitment (1–5): poor - excellent.
   (a) F - S
   (b) S - F
   (c) S - SS
   (d) SS - S
7. Does the supplier keep agreed schedules?
8. Estimate the supplier's attitude (1–5) in task execution?
9. Estimate the supplier's motivation (1–5) in task execution?
10. How has cooperation affected desire to cooperate in future (increased—decreased)?

Collaboration (Col)

1. Describe communication with counterparty:
   (a) open?
   (b) confidential?
   (c) informal or formal?
   (d) frequency, regularity?
2. Describe communication between suppliers.
3. Is there enough information exchange?
4. Have the objectives set together?
5. Which of the following describe the relationship best: new, expanding, troublesome, static, or lifeless?
6. How has collaborative relationship evolved over time?
7. How frequent are conflict situations (0–5) and how are they resolved?
8. Is there opportunism in relationships?
9. Does the supplier have the will and capability to more autonomous and self-directedness way of doing business?
10. How would you describe the short- and long-term flexibility of resources for changes in requirements and demand?
11. Do the counterparties have common social relations outside of business; for example, what kind of hobbies?
12. How well is the collaboration going? Estimate between 1 (poorly) and 5 (excellently)
13. How important is the collaboration in future? Estimate between 1 (it is not important) and 5 (it is very important)

Power and responsibility (P)

1. Does the supplier take responsibility of its own and co-partner's work and how does it occur?
2. Does the supplier have competence and will to take care of increasing project management responsibility?
3. Are the tasks assignment, order, and responsibility clear to all actors?
4. Who coordinates the whole and how?
5. Has there been abuse of power?
6. How much has the actor had to adapt in cooperation (0–5)?
7. Has the actor been forced to submit to demands (0–5)?

8. Can the supplier be empowered to do work self-directly? How does it happen?
9. How is the suppliers' cooperation achieved?
10. What changes triad business model causes in the current tasks and job descriptions (in the focal company) compared to the current dyadic business model?

Relational behavior (R)

1. Do personal and social characteristics have conducive, none, or restrictive impact on doing business?
2. Is building and maintaining of personal relationships important (0(not at all)–5(very important))?
3. Does the supplier act proactively in finding needs and requirements of the customer and contribute to the competitiveness of the customer; how does it occur?
4. Do suppliers communicate horizontally with each other (0(not at all)–5(very much))?
5. Do suppliers communicate vertically with each other (0(not at all)–5(very much))?
6. To what extent does the actor provide sensitive/confidential information about itself and is the information withheld from others?
7. Quality of relational behavior
    (a) initiative
    (b) advance notice of intended and impending changes
    (c) disclosure of sensitive information
    (d) attraction
        (economic benefits, access to important resources, and social compatibility)
    (e) personal chemistry match
    (f) total satisfaction
    (g) interaction frequency (times/week), and
    (h) richness (face-to-face, others)
8. How does another (what?) actor-actor relationship effect on cooperation in own dyadic relationship?

The ways in which the network companies can really achieve partnership and estimate the possibilities for the relationship developments are the basic aspects of the competitive advantage. For this reason, Supplier Evaluation System with Relational Factors focuses on describing the evaluation process for the successful partnership.

Case: From Functional Project Management to Visualized Network Management

The empirical material is a case study of one supply network of maritime organizations in project-based industry, producing massive constructions with extreme quality requirements. This case has been documented in more detail in Mika Perho's master thesis (Perho 2015). The focal company's supply networks consist of around twenty key suppliers and plenty of minor suppliers. The focal company of this network operates in project business. Typical for project business is that the contracts are principally bid and (re)negotiated for each project. However, the length of the relationships with the focal company and subcontractors has been even up to 20 years. The organizations have a long-term view on collaboration and the effects of relational factors on cooperation. The case company operates in a complex of oil and gas business. With high-risk level and varying capacity requirements, the project control is a major issue for both focal company and its suppliers. Thus, the number of potential suppliers is limited.

Motivation for cooperation development:

a. *Defining activities and purposes*. In this phase, the case company defined the common activities and purposes with its suppliers. After that, the context was decided. In this case, the context was formed according to five key activities and one support activity that are strongly related to the chosen key activities. Furthermore, subcontractors who have been in the long-term relationship with the case were chosen. The suitable relational factors, both relational properties of trust, collaboration, commitment, and power and relational behavior of initiating, signaling, and disclosing behaviors, frequency of interaction and richness of the medium of that interaction, and lateral and vertical involvement were chosen according to social capital literature.

b. *Defining the Network Constellation.* The relationship constellation was carried out the following way: first the case company's network was roughly described and the key suppliers and their relative positions and affection with respect to each other were defined and the common service supplier (SS) was discovered (see Fig. 12.4a). Next, the triad constellation was described for the relationships between the case company (F), key supplier (S1, S2, S3, S4, S5), and key supplier of support activities (SS) (see Fig. 12.4b). The aim of this step is to define the context or framework where the possibilities of the control shift and further collaboration with the suppliers will be examined.
c. *Selecting participants.* In this phase, six key subcontractors were selected. One subcontractor represented support activity and five other subcontractors represented the key chosen activities. Every subcontractor has a long-term relationship with the case company and they were estimated to have potential for a long-term strategic partnership with the case company in the future.

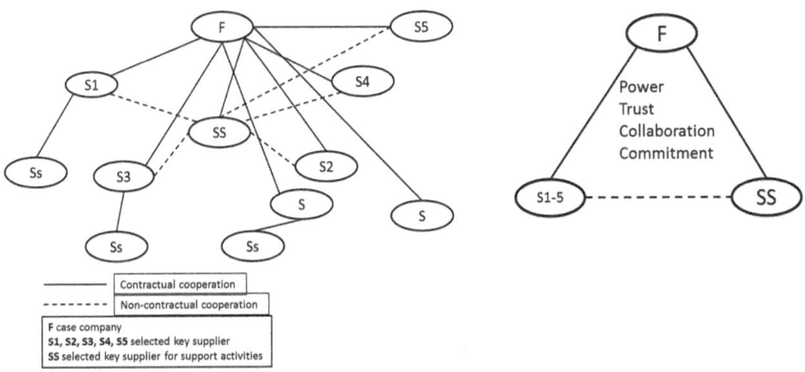

Fig. 12.4 **(a)** A part of the case company's supply network (on the left-hand side). **(b)** The context of the relationship definitions (on the right-hand side).

Evaluation of Relational factor levels. The relational factors were decided to evaluate and map in the context of the triad framework. According to this context, the query with questions and discussion themes was carried out above (*Evaluation questions*). At this phase, the suppliers' potential for cooperation and readiness to take responsibility were evaluated according to the results.

Choosing the right cooperation strategy. The company's purpose, according to the results from phase 2, was to figure out the subcontractors' readiness to cooperate together, whether the suppliers are at a level where they can be allowed to take more responsibility of project control.

Reduce control activities step by step. This has not been done yet. In the future, the focal company and its supplier will plan how a part of control activities can be transferred from the focal company to the suppliers. Furthermore, in project management, it will be taken into account that the need for the network-based control activities will decrease.

Benefits for the Case Company

Although the use of the tool brings new needs for the company's network and project management, several benefits can clearly be indicated. (1) Its network management is more visual that, in turn, is simplifying network management itself. (2) The need for the control of project activities may be decreased in the future that, in turn, is simplifying project management. (3) Cost saving is expected. The expectations are based on the conception that project management is more efficient, improved cooperation between subcontractors, and the area of subcontractors' responsibility is more explicit.

Conclusions

Companies' competitive advantage is based more and more on their network management. Therefore, demand, and also utilizing the possibilities of the network, is increasing all the time. For this reason, the tool has been developed. It brings the new systematic way to utilize relational factors when the project is developed for transferring project control within the network. The theoretical background of the tool is based on social capital and its role in relational factors. Although the tool has been applied to only one company, the results of its usage are reassuring. It has helped case company to see network and network management from the different point of view, it has brought the systematic way to improve and utilize company's relationship management.

The experiences of the use of the tool encourage us to apply it to other network development projects. We suggest that this tool can be applied to the cases where the focal company would benefit from insight to the level of the supplier relationships, or is in process to transfer more project control to its suppliers. As Jarzabkowski and Kaplan (2015) have brought forward, tools provide space for collecting data for decision making and different solutions. But they have also emphasized the dynamics of tools in use, and therefore, the affordance of the tool varies and the agency of actors affects the use and application of the tool and final outcomes. For example, some of the statements and questions have to be tailored case by case, but most of them are generally quite easy to use and apply for other cases. These cases can be both at network levels (i.e., multilateral relationships) and in pure dyadic relationships.

References

Agostini, L., & Nosella, A. (2015). Interorganizational relationships in marketing: A critical review and research agenda. *International Journal of Management Reviews*, 1–20.

Bourdieu, P. (1986). The forms of capital. In J. G. Richardson (Ed.), *Handbook of theory and research for the sociology of education* (pp. 241–258). New York: Greenwood Press.

Burt, R. S. (1992). *Structural holes: The social structure of competition* (313 p). Cambridge: Harvard University Press.

Coleman, J. S. (1988). Social capital in the creation of human capital. *American Journal of Sociology, 94*, 95–120.

Cousins, P. D., Handfield, R. B., Lawson, B., & Petersen, K. J. (2006). Creating supply chain relational capital: The impact of formal and informal socialization processes. *Journal of Operations Management, 26*(6), 851–863.
Cousins, P. E., & Menguc, B. (2006). The implications of socialization and integration in supply chain management. *Journal of Operations Management, 24*, 604–620.
Gummesson, E. (2008). *Total relationship marketing* (3rd ed.). Amsterdam: Elsevier.
Holmström, J., Ketokivi, M., & Hameri, A.-P. (2009). Bridging practice and theory: A design science approach. *Decision Sciences, 40*(1), 65–87. doi:10.1111/j.1540-5915.2008.00221.x.
Ivens, B. S. (2006). Norm-based relational behaviours: Is there an underlying dimensional structure? *Journal of Business & Industrial Marketing, 21*(2), 94–105.
Jarzabkowski, P., & Kaplan, S. (2015). Strategy tools-in-use: A framework for understanding 'technologies of rationality' in practice. *Strategic Management Journal, 36*, 537–558.
Johnston, D. A., McCutcheon, D. M., Stuart, F. I., & Kerwood, H. (2004). Effects of supplier trust on performance of cooperative supplier relationship. *Journal of Operations Management, 22*, 23–38.
Krause, D. R., Handfield, R. B., & Tyler, B. B. (2007). The relationships between supplier development, commitment, social capital accumulation and performance improvement. *Journal of Operations Management, 25*, 528–545.
Lawson, B., Tyler, B. B., & Cousins, P. D. (2008). Antecedents and consequences of social capital on buyer performance improvement. *Journal of Operations Management, 26*(3), 446–460.
Leuthesser, L. (1997). Supplier relational behavior: An empirical assessment. *Industrial Marketing Management, 26*(3), 245–254.
Leuthesser, L., & Kohli, A. (1995). Relational behavior in business markets: Implications for relationship management. *Journal of Business Research, 34*, 221–233.
Loury, G. C. (1977). A dynamic theory of racial income differences. In P. Wallace & A. LaMont (Eds.), *Women, minorities and employment discrimination* (pp. 153–186). Lexington, MA: Lexington Books.
Nahapiet, J., & Ghoshal, S. (1998). Social capital, intellectual capital and the organizational advantage. *The Academy of Management Review, 23*(2), 242–266.

Perho, M. (2015). Forming and developing triads in supply network. Master of Science thesis, Tampere University of Technology.

Putnam, R. (1995). Bowling alone: America's declining social capital. *Journal of Democracy, 6*(1), 65–78.

Simon, H. (1996). *The sciences of the artificial* (3rd ed.). Cambridge, MA: MIT Press.

Villena, V. H., Revilla, E., & Choi, T. Y. (2011). The dark side of buyer-supplier relationships: A social capital perspective. *Journal of Operations Management, 29*, 561–576.

13

A Tool for Increased Cognitive Ergonomics in Operative Supplier Selection in a Global Context

Tomi Nokelainen, Magnus Hellström, and Robin Wikström

Introduction

It is common for buying organizations, especially those with a global reach, to have multiple suppliers for the products, components, or subassemblies (henceforth called *components* for simplicity) they procure. Reasons for doing so may include, for example, a desire to limit the volume of purchases from any given supplier, maintaining bargaining power toward suppliers with multiple available suppliers, or using different suppliers for different customer projects because of their different locations, and therefore, their geographical proximities to a given project (e.g., Berger et al. 2004).

While such an approach undoubtedly comes with a number of benefits, especially in complex products and engineer-to-order supply chains, or more commonly project business, it also creates certain challenges. In

T. Nokelainen (✉) • M. Hellström • R. Wikström
Åbo Akademi University, Turku, Finland

J. Vesalainen et al. (eds.), *Practices for Network Management*,
DOI 10.1007/978-3-319-49649-8_13

a multi-supplier context, it is important to be able to determine which of the available suppliers best fit a given *particular* supply need—in contrast to generally, on average, or in a typical case—such as a new customer project (c.f. Kauffman and Leszczyc 2005). That is, some suppliers may be outright unsuitable due to a lack of tangible capabilities (such as required production facilities, equipment, or specific production technology), or may be economically sub-optimal for a specific sourcing need despite being highly viable suppliers with an excellent strategic fit to the buyer organization in general.

Thus, when making the procurement decision, in a buying organization, there must be an established practice for ascertaining need-supplier fit in concrete specific cases. Such a practice must enable buyer's procurement personnel to access all necessary information available, both about the requirements of the procured components and the available suppliers' corresponding relevant capabilities and other pertinent properties. Naturally, this issue is accentuated in a global and globally dispersed (sourcing) context.

Large corporations strive to cope with this issue by introducing formal supplier evaluation practices with explicit evaluation criteria, as well as centralized purchasing schemes in an attempt to leverage synergies such as bargaining power through increased purchasing volumes (Rozemeijr 2000). Such formal practices, however, often focus on relatively higher-level supplier characteristics, such as financial health and product and process certifications. Moreover, such practices often are engaged only in the very beginning of a buyer-supplier relationship (evaluating supplier fit), or periodically (e.g., once a year, to reassess supplier fit). Such practices, quite evidently, are neither appropriate nor designed for the needs of *specific* procurement decisions such as those typical in complex and customized products', or projects' supply chain.

Furthermore, according to a rather recent study, the most common supplier evaluation criteria proposed by academic research include high-level constructs like quality, delivery accuracy, price/cost, general manufacturing capability, service, management, R&D, finance, flexibility, and reputation (Ho et al. 2010). While such characteristics certainly are important and serve as good proxies for general-level capabilities, they may tell very little about the tangible, actual "low-level" capabilities, such as production equipment maximum capacities for pieces of certain geometry or achievable tolerances in a specific application, which are required to produce specific sourced components in specific quantities with sufficient efficiency, or even at all. Such low-level capabilities are especially relevant in manufacturing and assembling complex products with bespoke designs (Stinchcombe and Heimer 1985; Hobday 1998).

Academic research, in turn, has tended to focus on formal decision-making models of a mathematical nature, often criticized for being incompatible with the highly emotion- and intuition-driven practice of actual purchasing work (de Boer et al. 2001). It is argued, however, that the increased complexity and strategic importance of the purchasing function requires a systematic approach (rather than pure judgment), the incorporation of qualitative (as opposed to only quantitative) and configurable (as opposed to static and pre-determined) criteria (Huang and Keskar 2007), more flexible models encompassing the entire purchasing process rather than only the selection itself (de Boer and van der Wegen 2003).

In other words, there seems to be a need for a systematized methodology that supports actual sourcing practice by providing an appropriate mixture of formal and informal approaches (i.e., bringing structured criteria-based procedures to supplier selection while allowing for human judgment). Such methodology would, at the same time, complement human judgment by applying pre-determined criteria for "easy" or more mechanistic aspects of the decision at hand, and leverage the human ability to manage vast amounts of "fuzzy" information, which is difficult if not impossible to codify in any criteria-based system.

Furthermore, putting more emphasis on such low-level capabilities and informal criteria are likely to promote relational (rather than arm's length or transactional) business practices. Nevertheless, to constitute a fully-blown inter-organizational or (organizational) boundary-spanning practice, such appropriate buyer need-supplier capability fit requires mutual adjustment and selection practices. For example, suppliers can proactively increase their fitness if they can exercise foresight in terms of buyer's needs (both quantitatively and qualitatively) in the future. Correspondingly, buyer's fitness judgment is enhanced by visibility to supplier's capacity utilization in the relevant period into the future. (Tuomikangas and Kaipia 2014) Such capabilities require inter-organizational practices built on inter-organizational information access and exchange which, in turn, requires significant trust and mutualistic commitment to the relationship (c.f. Butler 1999).

We, however, maintain that it is essential to develop such practical systematic procurement practices first internally within an organization before making an attempt to extend such practices to inter-organizational or (organizational) boundary-spanning settings. This is because required sense making is more challenging and complex in multi-organizational settings (c.f. Lundgren-Henriksson and Kock 2016) with representatives from different (organizational) discourses (Mantere 2013), procedures for decision-making (Jarzabkowski and Seidl 2008), and governance structures and organizational cultures (Jarzabkowski and Wilson 2002). For this reason, as Tsvetkova, Nokelainen, Gustafsson, and Eriksson in their respective chapter in this volume also suggest, inter-organizational practices, and especially changes in those, are markedly different from organizational ones (e.g., Lounsbury and Crumley 2007). In effect, following Gomez and Bouty (2011), we maintain that through mindful and demonstrably performance-appropriate practice development within an organization, an organization is in a significantly better (influential) position to subsequently affect inter-organizational practices.

In other words, we posit that the practices and especially the supplier selection tool put forth in this chapter constitute a necessary platform upon which inter-organizational practices and accompanying tools or systems may be built. Correspondingly, we refer to this intra-organizational practice development as "Stage 1," and the inter-organizational or boundary-spanning setting as "Stage 2." The majority of this chapter is concerned, consistent with our empirical case, with Stage 1 development, with extensions into Stage 2 discussed toward the end of the chapter.

The Stage 1 decision support system we put forth outlines a supplier selection system which aims at complementing human judgment in specific supplier selection cases by weeding out inappropriate suppliers for the purposes of a customer project while letting the user exercise full judgment over the remaining ones. This approach is also motivated by our observation of supplier selection in project-based business, often as much a question about "avoiding the worst" as about "selecting the best."

That is, performance-wise, supplier relationship management is often as much about avoiding wrong choices as about distinguishing between the best and the second-best choices.

Regarding the informational side of the proposed system, while supplier-related documentation is often stored in corporate intranets and made accessible to purchasing personnel, especially in large corporations, it often predominantly includes high-level information such as supply and pricing agreements and process certification documents. In other words, such documentation may not provide relevant tangible information about suppliers' actual low-level capabilities to support operative-specific procurement decisions. Needless to say, in project business, a misinformed purchase decision which fails to identify necessary low-level capabilities may ruin the project time schedule and undermine the supplier's and/or buyer's profitability and customer satisfaction. This, in turn, may damage the relationship between the supplier(s) involved, and once damaged, the focal organization may be exceedingly difficult and/or time-consuming to restore (c.f. Bell et al. 2002).

Experienced purchasers, however, typically do possess large amounts of relevant low-level information required in making informed supplier selection decisions. This information is accumulated over time through repeated interactions with suppliers and by visiting them, and most likely as a result of learning from some misinformed erroneous decisions as well.

While such experience-based information undoubtedly is a great asset for the buying organization, it is not readily accessible for other employees because it is tacit (i.e., not codified) (Haldin-Herrgard 2000). Thus, new purchasing personnel must accumulate this store of information themselves through interaction with the experienced individuals and the supplier base over a prolonged period of time, and most likely through making some misinformed decisions themselves. Moreover, if an experienced purchasing employee leaves the organization, his or her non-codified decision-relevant information is no longer available in the organization in any form (Droege and Hoobler 2003).

Taking the preceding discussion together, there is often a need for a decision support system which codifies and makes the following readily accessible:

1. Suppliers' relevant capabilities—notably including the low-level ones—and other characteristics needed to assess suppliers' suitability for any given specific purchasing need, such as a customer project.
2. Components' requirements which are consequential with regard to selecting the most suitable supplier in any given specific purchasing need.
3. The relevant linkages between the above (i.e., their meaning).

In short, the aims of the system described here are to provide purchasing employees with all relevant information so that they can relatively effortlessly match available suppliers with procurement needs for the best overall results. Consequently, one of the particular aims of the system is to eliminate erroneous or otherwise inappropriate supplier selection decisions in specific cases due to lack of decision-relevant information. A simple example of such an inappropriate decision would be to order large components from a supplier, which, in principle, is capable of producing those, but whose automated production machines can only manufacture smaller components, which then leads to long lead time and variable quality due to the high amount of manual labor required. In this case then, on a high level, the supplier is an appropriate selection for the assignment, but if one takes the low-level capabilities into account, appropriateness is not at all evident.

Therefore, we maintain that there is a practice-motivated need for a tool providing cognitive ergonomics in operative supplier selection, which to our best knowledge is a novel way of approaching supplier selection problematics. The tool aims at an appropriate balance between criteria-based ranking and filtering ("avoiding the worst"), and leveraging purchasing professionals' expertise and human judgment ("selecting the best").

In terms of organizational practices (Simpson 2009), the tool can be understood just as such: a tool to organize daily (or frequently occurring) routine praxis (c.f. Kaplan 2011). Or, if one emphasizes the software manifestation of the tool (e.g., user interface, tight coupling with computer equipment in actual use), the tool can be fruitfully perceived even as an artefact which shapes practitioners' perceptions of the organizational and inter-organizational reality (Jarzabkowski et al. 2013). In such capabilities, the tool serves also as a platform for Stage 2 extensions into inter-organizational praxis, as noted above.

The tool has been developed at a case company, a marine product manufacturer with global operations and a globally dispersed supplier network. From the very beginning of its development, the intention at the case company has been consistent with what has been said above—to increase cognitive ergonomics in procurement by 'automatically' filtering out clearly inappropriate supplier selection choices while allowing the corporate procurement professionals to exercise full judgment concerning the ultimate selection, with subsequent Stage 2 extensions following successful Stage 1 adoption and refinement in the case organization itself. At the time of writing, the tool is being transitioned into Stage 1 implementation.

Supplier Selection Tool as Increased Cognitive Ergonomics

Cognitive ergonomics refers to ergonomics in general, or the study of how to design products and systems so that they are suitable to be used by humans, given the distinctly human qualities (Dui et al. 2012). While ergonomics is more commonly known in terms of physiological suitability, cognitive ergonomics is about the very same phenomenon, but in terms of psychological suitability.

The need and rationale for cognitive ergonomics emerges from fundamental human psychological qualities, and in one way or another, these qualities essentially have to do with departures from perfect rationality and infinite computing power. Examples of such departures include, for example, bounded rationality (Simon 1991) and various cognitive heuristics and biases (Kahneman et al. 1982). Put differently, the aim of cognitive ergonomics is to design systems which take into account and complement the inherently human cognitive "limitations." A very simple example of such a cognitive ergonomics aid is a checklist, which is in widespread use in situations such as surgery (Urbach et al. 2014), nuclear plant operation (Roth 1997), and aviation (Degani and Wiener 1993).

Hence, cognitive ergonomics in this case means incorporating the use of the checklist in workflow, thereby outsourcing some of the required memory and recall to the "system" (Ely et al. 2011).

Thus, attempts at increasing cognitive ergonomics typically take the form, or otherwise involve, a tool or an artefact through which the focal practice (i.e. the actual behavior of the practitioners involved) is shaped (c.f. Kaplan 2011). Or more generally, cognitive ergonomics can be seen as being about changing the perceptions of the practitioners "about the world" in ways deemed appropriate (c.f. Jarzabkowski et al. 2013).

To date, studies specifically related to cognitive ergonomics are rather sparse. However, with the increasing collaboration between machines and humans in both business and consumer domains, there will undoubtedly be a surge in this line of inquiry. The increasing importance of cognitive ergonomics is also motivated by the transfer of *systemic outsourcing* from physical tasks (e.g., physical tools, automation, and robotization) where the development is quite mature already, to mental or cognitive tasks, where it is significantly less mature. Indeed, while there were some notable fears decades ago over automatization- and robotization-induced blue collar unemployment (e.g., Kinoshita and Yamada 1989), the discussion has more recently shifted to software-induced white collar unemployment (e.g., Brynjolfsson and McAfee 2011) (i.e., systemic outsourcing of cognitive tasks). As cognitive tasks are, no doubt, more complex and less readily codified and automated, at least fully, cognitive ergonomics will be needed as a mediator between the domain of the software and that of the human (Brinkman and Neerincx 2011).

The cognitive ergonomics perspective of the supplier selection tool we put forward also includes outsourcing the most readily codifiable elements of the decision-making process to the system and supplying the user with sufficient decision-relevant information to exercise his or her judgment concerning the rest of the process. To give a very simple example, supplying a cast part that is seven meters in diameter is simply impossible for a furnace with a diameter of five meters, no matter how good a strategic fit a supplier has with the buyer. This aspect of the decision process can be outsourced to the system with no ambiguities whatsoever, and all associated errors due to a factor like inattentiveness, for example, can be removed. However, at the other end of the continuum, all social considerations such as not allocating an order to an appropriate and capable supplier in order to "make a point" because of a recent inappropriate behavior may be outright impossible to capture formally, and thereby, best left for human judgment.

This noted, we will turn next to outlining the system (the Stage 1 supplier selection tool) in more detail.

The Stage 1 Supplier Selection Tool Described

As suggested, the supplier selection tool put forward and described in this section is basically a decision support system which aims at increasing cognitive ergonomics in operative, specific supplier selection decisions. More tangibly, it is a repository of decision-relevant information with an appropriate user interface for convenient access. Thus, the tool constitutes an "electronic artefact" (Jarzabkowski et al. 2013) which is intended to shape the operational organizational procurement practice in desired ways.

In the focal case organization, the manifestation of the system is a functional module in the web-based corporate supplier portal to which purchasing personnel have access. Consistent with the view that detailed or micro-level aspects are highly relevant in organizational practices and their outcomes (Rouleau 2005), the tool described in some detail (though not by any means exhaustively because of space limitations).

The system consists of four basic elements:

1. Supplier capability database
2. Component database
3. Database of manufacturing (i.e., suppliers') process descriptions
4. User interface

Figure 13.1 illustrates the mutual relationships between these elements.

Of the four basic elements, for each purchased component, the supplier capability database includes all the suppliers with which the organization has an established relationship as well as categorically arranged information about their relevant capabilities, essentially including their

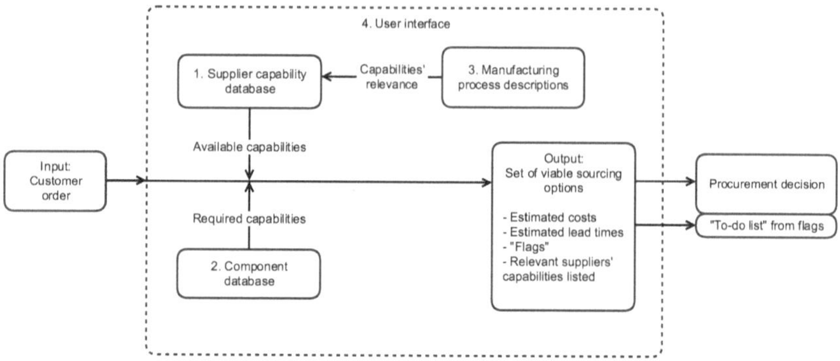

Fig. 13.1 The basic elements (1…4) of the Stage 1 supplier selection tool

Table 13.1 An exemplary subset of supplier capabilities for a bronze cast component

Capability	Measure
Primary furnaces	Count
Primary furnace capacity	Tons
Secondary furnaces	Count
Secondary furnace capacity	Tons
Available cooling floor area	Square meters
Breadth of moulding box	Meters
Length of moulding box	Meters
Pattern technology	One or several: (1) wooden (2) polystyrene (3) patternless
Valid certifications	One or several: Certification body A + valid through date Certification body B + valid through date Certification body C + valid through date ....

relevant low-level capabilities. At the case organization, this is not to serve as a "master database" of suppliers (because such a database already exists there, which is likely to be the case in large organizations in general), but instead to focus on tangible supply-related low-level capabilities which are the most consequential in operative purchasing decisions.

Table 13.2 An exemplary subset of properties of a bronze cast component

Property	Measure
Finished weight	Tons
Cast weight	Tons
Cast unit cross-section	Square meters
Assembly type	One of the following: (1) single piece (2) modular
Components in end product	Number

For example, in the context of the case organization, Table 13.1 presents an exemplary subset of supplier capabilities recorded for suppliers of a bronze cast component.

Next, the component database lists, again for each purchased component, all the purchasing-relevant properties. This information may already be codified and readily available in a buying organization if, for example, relevant component properties can be easily inferred from selling-related product databases. In such a case, the system must link to such databases. Otherwise, a component property database must be constructed so that each component property has a relevant purchasing decision-related linkage.

For example, in the context of the case organization, an exemplary subset of properties for a bronze cast component is listed in Table 13.2.

The purpose of manufacturing (i.e., suppliers') process descriptions is to facilitate assigning meaning to supplier capabilities. This is needed because the relevance of some such capabilities may not be immediately obvious, especially for inexperienced purchasing personnel. Figure 13.2 illustrates the basic manufacturing process for a bronze cast part.

In addition to a basic process diagram, Fig. 13.2 importantly depicts the process descriptions, including those of all the process phases, along with illustrative photographs, typical phase durations and their main determinants, typical quality risks, and associations to other phases in the process. In sum, the process descriptions are intended to help the sourcing professional *understand* how suppliers' tangible capabilities are related to and may affect the sourcing choice at hand.

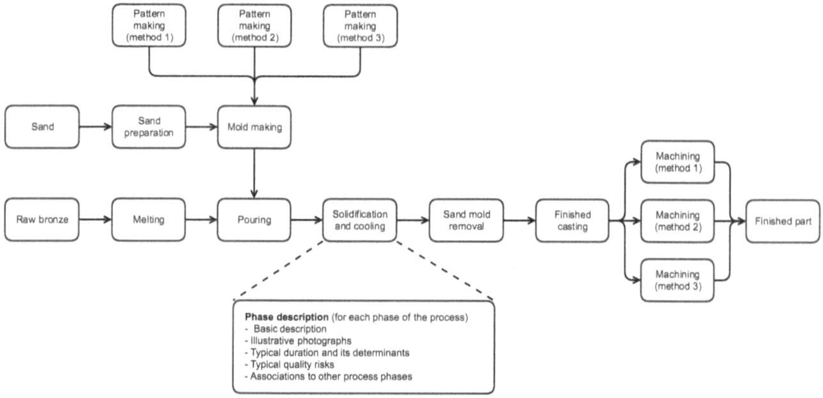

Fig. 13.2 The basic manufacturing process for a bronze case part

Referring to the Fig. 13.2, it is straightforward to ascertain that a supplier with one 10-ton primary furnace and one 5-ton secondary furnace is unable to supply a component with a casting weight of 20 tons because there is not enough furnace capacity to melt the metal for the cast required. However, the real meaningfulness of the process descriptions becomes evident in more complex considerations. To give a relatively simple example, a customer's order of six products of a certain type may imply a need for 24 cast components of a certain size to be procured (component database). Given a set of 24 components, it turns out (process descriptions) that the most cost-efficient way of manufacturing these is typically with a combination of pattern-making method 2 *combined with* machining method 3, though the combination of pattern-making method 1 combined with machining method 2 will save a certain amount of time. In both cases, the throughput time is dependent on how much floor area a supplier has for solidification and cooling (supplier capability database), because this determines how many casts can be done in a batch. Furthermore, once assembled, the procured component has such properties that road transportation requires a special truck delivery necessitating permits from road traffic authorities, whereas sea transportation requires an open top container which, in turn, necessitates a specially arranged placement on a containership which must be reserved several weeks before the shipment ("flags").

Hence, certain suppliers can be automatically filtered out of a consideration set based on their unambiguous capability mismatch with the requirements of the order at hand (supplier capability database, component database), thereby "avoiding the worst" being outsourced to the system. However, the mutual degree of appropriateness between the suppliers within the remaining consideration set may be a very complex question not amenable to algorithmic ranking. It is here where the proposed supplier selection tool complements (as opposed to replaces) human judgment by supplying the user with ample information to support his or her human judgment.

As noted above, very experienced buyers are likely to possess most of this information already, as it accumulates over time in such decision-making processes, though most likely through erroneous decisions, a powerful yet potentially costly "tool" for learning (Sitkin 1992). Yet, not all organizational buyers are very experienced—at least in the long term—and even the most experienced ones are subject to fundamental human cognitive limitations (c.f. Simon 1991; Kahneman et al. 1982). Furthermore, from the knowledge management perspective, the supplier selection tool can serve as a means of codifying this tacit experiential knowledge for wider organizational access and retention.

Current Status and Envisioned Stage 2 Extensions

As noted, at the time of writing, the Stage 1 tool has been jointly specified with the research team and the case company, and is in the process of being transitioned into implementation.

Like in any information system development and adoption project, it must not be assumed that a preconceived system with seemingly apparent benefits will ultimately succeed in being embraced by the users (or practitioners) as a part of their daily workflow (or praxis). User resistance can result from things like difficulty of use, little or no perceived benefits in comparison to current practices, perceived loss of status (e.g., if current practice is seen as a form of "craft" or "art"), or gradual obsolescence of available information if not appropriately updated (c.f. Legris et al. 2003).

Moreover, in practice-based research, it has been noted that it is fairly common that the developers of tools aimed at changing organizational practices are disconnected from actual praxis, and therefore, tend to develop tools which are not entirely relevant for the target practitioners (Moisander and Stenfors 2009).

For this reason, both development and implementation must be seen as a non-trivial organizational and social psychological process, visibly embraced and tangibly supported by the organization, especially the (top) management (Nah et al. 2001). Especially consequential individuals are the most experienced intended users because (1) their expertise to a large degree constitutes the content to be codified in the system, and therefore, (2) they are likely to feel the most threatened by it. In addition, (3) such individuals often are looked up to by their peers, and hence, may serve as opinion leaders in their department or other such organizational unit.

As noted earlier, at Stage 2, the system should be taken in a significantly more relational direction by opening up some relevant aspects of it to the suppliers. In other words, at Stage 2, the aim is to develop the tool to facilitate inter-organizational practice for the benefit of both the focal buyer and its (selected) suppliers. The basic rationale for doing so is to achieve better and more transparent access to and flow of information between the focal buying organization and the suppliers, so that all the involved organizations can make better-informed decisions because of more and better available information. In the case of the suppliers in particular, this essentially enables planning with foresight and proactive improvement of fit.

Doing so-that is, extending the tool to incorporate inter-organizational information sharing and interaction—requires trust in, and strategic commitment to, the relationship from both the buyer and the supplier(s), because increased informational exposure quite automatically implies increased exposure to abuse as well (Butler 1999).

The first envisioned step toward this direction is to open the order books of the respective organizations—the focal buyer and the selected strategic suppliers—so that they can prepare their operations with knowledge of each other's order books. Figure 13.3 illustrates such Stage 2 extensions (denoted with inverse colors).

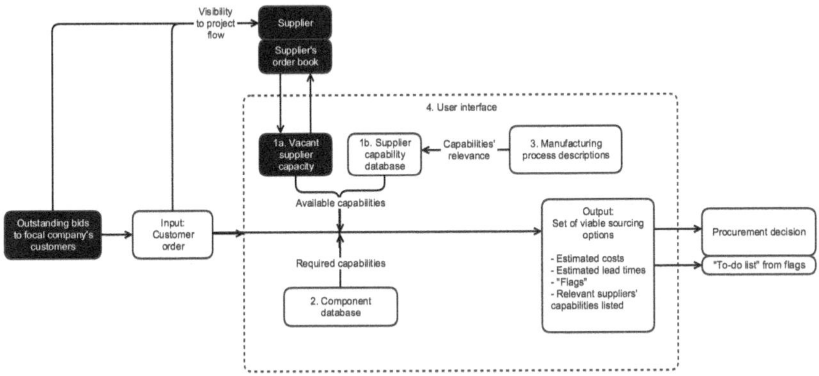

Fig. 13.3 Selected relational Stage 2 extensions to the selection tool

For the focal organization, this allows for a more mindful allocation of orders because it is possible to estimate how a given order would fit a given supplier's foreseeable production schedule. For a supplier, in turn, this allows for a more mindful bidding and accepting of orders because of an improved visibility to the expected flow of orders from the buying organization. But, as said above, this requires mutual long-term commitment to the relationship and mutual trust because of the increased informational exposure. Moreover, such openness must be supported by inter-organizational communication and other trust-inducing practices (see e.g., Panteli and Sockalingam 2005) on top of mere order book access. For example, communication may include a mutual discussion about what a given buyer's order book situation likely means (e.g., what the buyer's intentions are, given the situation) for a given supplier, and a good-faith discussion if a given intention does not materialize in concrete order as expected.

In any event, in this manner, the supplier selection tool can and is intended to serve, at Stage 2, as a platform for better relational business by enabling tangibly meaningful informational transparency and communications between a focal buyer and its (strategic) suppliers. However, we underscore that it does not constitute a sufficient practice enabling this in and of itself. Rather, it must be seen as a means—or a mediating artefact (Jarzabkowski et al. 2013; Kaplan 2011) in a web of related practices—toward this end.

Discussion and Conclusions

In the contemporary global purchasing context, and especially in project business with non-recurring deliveries, selecting the most appropriate suppliers is arguably more crucial, and at the same time, harder than it was previously. Often, established corporate sourcing practices focus predominantly on suppliers' high-level capabilities and other characteristics that are not very useful in ascertaining suppliers' actual, tangible appropriateness for the idiosyncratic needs of a particular customer project. In other words, existing sourcing practices are not entirely appropriate to the routine praxis—a typical situation with respect to practices instituted by organizational members other than the focal practitioners (c.f. Moisander and Stenfors 2009).

To bridge this practice-praxis gap, we have put forth and outlined a tool, a mediating artifact, for supplier selection in *specific* procurement decisions (as opposed to supplier "fit" in general, or on average), with a particular focus on suppliers' tangible capabilities. The overarching general aim of the tool is to structure routine sourcing praxis by increasing cognitive ergonomics of this work by automatically filtering out unambiguously inappropriate suppliers for a given specific procurement need. In addition, the tool aims to provide the procurement professional with ample information to support his or her expert human judgment concerning the relative goodness of different options within the remaining consideration set. Consistent with established practice-based research underscoring the consequentiality of the very micro-level or organizational practices (Rouleau 2005), the tool is premised on an assumption that the devil is in the details regarding success or failure in a given *specific* procurement decision, and consequently, procurement professionals, especially less experienced ones, should have ample informational assistance at their disposal when making these decisions.

In this manner, the tool goes a long way toward codifying the decision-making logic of the experienced purchasing professionals of an organization, as both the information to be included in the system and their interconnections are to a large degree based on what the experienced individuals have found useful over time. Thus, the buy-in of such individuals is crucial for the success of the project because their reluctance can thwart the project at any stage of its life cycle (design, construction, adoption, and use). For this reason, they must be seen as the primary stakeholders of the project from the very beginning. In this manner, it is also possible to avoid the typical practice-praxis disconnect (c.f. Moisander and Stenfors 2009), whereby developed tools are not entirely appropriate for actual daily work.

The tool, as stated, must not be perceived only as a Stage 1 tool for the focal organization to conduct its business more economically on a transactional basis but also—importantly—as a platform which can enable, at Stage 2, a deeper and more mutualistic relationship between a focal buying organization and its suppliers. This entails opening up the informational contents of the tool *in both directions* between the suppliers and the focal organization for increased transparency and more meaningful inter-organizational practices. This, however, requires (but also supports) a high level of trust and long-term commitment between the organizations, and can by no means be accomplished with a tool alone. Thus, we remind again that the tool, by no means, constitutes a sufficient practice enabling inter-organizational practices with beneficial outcomes in and of itself. Rather, it must be seen as a one piece in a web of related practices toward this end.

References

Alavi, M., & Leinder, D. E. (2001). Review: Knowledge management and knowledge management systems: Conceptual foundations and research issues. *MIS Quarterly, 25*(1), 107–136.

Bell, G. G., Oppenheimer, R. J., & Bastien, A. (2002). Trust deterioration in an international buyer-supplier relationship. *Journal of Business Ethics, 36*(1), 65–78.

Berger, P. D., Gerstenfeld, A., & Zengh, A. Z. (2004). How many suppliers are best? A decision-analysis approach. *Omega, 32*(1), 9–15.

Brinkman, W. P., & Neerincx, M. (2011). Cognitive ergonomics for situated human-automation collaboration. *Interacting with Computers, 23*(4), iii–iiv.

Brynjolfsson, E., & McAfee, A. (2011). *Race against the machine: How the digital revolution is accelerating innovation, driving productivity, and irreversibly transforming employment and the economy.* Lexington, MA: Digital Frontier Press.

Butler Jr., J. K. (1999). Trust expectations, information sharing, climate of trust, and negotiation effectiveness and efficiency. *Group & Organization Management, 24*(2), 217–238.

Demirkan, H., & Delen, D. (2013). Leveraging the capabilities of service-oriented decision support systems: Putting analytics and big data in cloud. *Decision Support Systems, 55*(1), 412–421.

de Boer, L., Labro, E., & Morlacchi, P. (2001). A review of methods supporting supplier selection. *European Journal of Purchasing and Supply Management, 7*(2), 75–89.

de Boer, L., & van der Wegen, L. (2003). Practice and promise of formal supplier selection: A study of four empirical cases. *Journal of Purchasing and Supply Management, 9*(3), 109–118.

Degani, A., & Wiener, E. L. (1993). Cockpit checklists: Concepts, design, and use. *Human Factors, 35*(2), 345–359.

Droege, S. B., & Hoobler, J. M. (2003). Employee turnover and tacit knowledge diffusion: A network perspective. *Journal of Managerial Issues, 15*(1), 50–64.

Dui, J., Bruder, R., Buckle, P., Carayon, P., Faizon, P., Marras, W. S., et al. (2012). A strategy for human factors/ergonomics: Developing the discipline and profession. *Ergonomics, 55*(4), 377–395.

Ely, J. W., Graber, M. L., & Croskerry, P. (2011). Checklists to reduce diagnostic errors. *Academic Medicine, 86*(3), 307–313.

Engelbrecht, A. P. (2007). *Computational intelligence: An introduction.* Chichester: John Wiley & Sons.

Gomez, M., & Bouty, I. (2011). The emergence of an influential practice: Food for thought. *Organization Studies, 32*(7), 921–940.

Haldin-Herrgard, T. (2000). Difficulties in diffusion of tacit knowledge in organizations. *Journal of Intellectual Capital, 1*(4), 357–365.

Hassal, M., Xiao, T., Sanderson, P., & Neal, A. (2015). Human factors and ergonomics. In J. D. Wright (Ed.), *International encyclopedia of the social & behavioral sciences* (pp. 297–305). Oxford: Elsevier.

Ho, W., Xu, X., & Dey, P. (2010). Multi-criteria decision making approaches for supplier evaluation and selection: A literature review. *European Journal of Operational Research, 202*(1), 16–24.

Hobday, M. (1998). Product complexity, innovation and industrial organization. *Research Policy, 26*(6), 689–710.

Huang, S. H., & Kerskar, H. (2007). Comprehensive and configurable metrics for supplier selection. *International Journal of Production Economics, 105*(2), 510–523.

Jarzabkowski, P., & Seidl, D. (2008). The role of meetings in the social practice of strategy. *Organization Studies, 29*(11), 1391–1426.

Jarzabkowski, P., Spee, A. P., & Smets, M. (2013). Material artifacts: Practices for doing strategy with 'stuff'. *European Management Journal, 31*(1), 41–54.

Jarzabkowski, P., & Wilson, D. C. (2002). Top teams and strategy in a UK university. *Journal of Management Studies, 39*(3), 355–381.

Kahneman, D., Slovic, P., & Tversky, A. (1982). *Judgment under uncertainty: Heuristics and biases*. Cambridge: Cambridge University Press.

Kaplan, S. (2011). Strategy and PowerPoint: An inquiry into the epistemic culture and machinery of strategy making. *Organization Science, 22*(2), 320–346.

Kauffman, R. G., & Leszczyc, P. T. L. P. (2005). An optimization approach to business buyer choice sets: How many suppliers should be included? *Industrial Marketing Management, 34*(1), 3–12.

Kinoshita, S., & Yamada, M. (1989). The impacts of robotization on macro and sectoral economies with a world econometric model. *Technological Forecasting and Social Change, 35*(2–3), 211–230.

Ko, M., Tiwari, A., & Mehnen, J. (2010). A review of soft computing applications in supply chain management. *Applied Soft Computing, 10*(3), 661–674.

Legris, P., Ingham, J., & Collerette, P. (2003). Why do people use information technology? A critical review of the technology acceptance model. *Information & Management, 40*(3), 191–204.

Lounsbury, M., & Crumley, E. T. (2007). New practice creation: An institutional perspective on innovation. *Organization Studies, 28*(7), 993–1012.

Lundgren, E. L., & Kock, S. (2016). A sensemaking perspective on coopetition. *Industrial Marketing Management, 57*, 97–108.

Mantere, S. (2013). What is organizational strategy? A language-based view. *Journal of Management Studies, 50*(8), 1408–1426.

Marra, M., Ho, W., & Edwards, J. S. (2012). Supply chain knowledge management: A literature review. *Expert Systems with Applications, 39*(5), 6103–6110.

Moisander, J., & Stenfors, S. (2009). Exploring the edges of theory-practice gap: Epistemic cultures in strategy-tool development and use. *Organization, 16*(2), 227–247.

Nah, F. F. H., Lau, J. L. S., & Kuang, J. (2001). Critical factors for successful implementation of enterprise systems. *Business Management Journal, 7*(3), 285–296.

Panteli, N., & Sockalingam, S. (2005). Trust and conflict within virtual interorganizational alliances: A framework for facilitating knowledge sharing. *Decision Support Systems, 39*(4), 599–617.

Roth, E. M. (1997). Analysis of decision making in nuclear power plant emergencies: An investigation of aided decision making. In C. E. Zsambok & G. Klein (Eds.), *Naturalistic decision making* (pp. 175–182). New York: Routledge.

Rouleau, L. (2005). Micro-practices of strategic sensemaking and sensegiving: How middle managers interpret and sell change every day. *Journal of Management Studies, 42*(7), 1413–1441.

Rozemeijr, F. (2000). How to manage corporate purchasing synergy in a decentralized company? Towards design rules for managing and organising purchasing synergy in decentralised companies. *European Journal of Purchasing & Supply Management, 6*(1), 5–12.

Shim, J. P., Warkentin, M., Courtney, J. F., Power, D. J., Shadra, R., & Carlsson, C. (2002). Past, present, and future of decision support technology. *Decision Support Systems, 33*(2), 111–126.

Simon, H. A. (1991). Bounded rationality and organizational learning. *Organization Science, 2*(1), 125–134.

Simpson, B. (2009). Pragmatism, Mead and the practice turn. *Organization Studies, 30*(12), 1329–1347.

Sitkin, S. B. (1992). Learning through failure: The strategy of small losses. *Research in Organizational Behavior, 14*, 231–266.

Stinchcombe, A., & Heimer, C. (1985). *Organization theory and project management: Administering uncertainty in Norwegian offshore oil.* Oslo: Norwegian University Press.

Trent, R. J., & Monzcka, R. M. (2003a). International purchasing and global sourcing—What are the differences? *Journal of Supply Chain Management, 39*(3), 26–36.

Trent, R. J., & Monzcka, R. M. (2003b). Understanding integrated global sourcing. *International Journal of Physical Distribution & Logistics Management, 33*(7), 607–629.

Tuomikangas, N., & Kaipia, R. (2014). A coordination framework for sales and operations planning (S&OP): Synthesis from the literature. *International Journal of Production Economics, 154*(4), 243–262.

Urbach, D. R., Govindarajan, A., Saskin, R., Wilton, A. S., & Baxter, N. N. (2014). Introducing surgical safety checklists in Ontario, Canada. *New England Journal of Medicine, 370*, 1029–1038.

Wagner, W. P., Otto, J., & Chung, Q. B. (2002). Knowledge acquisition for expert systems in accounting and financial problem domains. *Knowledge-Based Systems, 15*(8), 439–447.

Part III

Networks-as-Value-Generating Entities

14

Introduction to Part III—Moving Toward Mutual Benefits and Increased Total Value

Magnus Hellström

In order to achieve business goals, companies are more and more seeking help from their external relationships. In some cases, these relationships form a system of their own with a common goal (i.e., a meta-goal). Such system-level goals, on the one hand, require input from more than one company and, on the other hand, they come with an expectation of higher total value (cf. Zott et al. 2011). By definition, organizing networks of companies for meta-goals and higher total value means avoiding sub-optimization and focusing on synergies rather than only on pure self-benefits, a viewpoint that often entails developing a long-term perspective. The essence of this part of the book is managing networks as value-generating entities (the right side of the main triangle in Fig. 14.1) and aiming at enhanced value co-creation and maximum value capture by the network actors.

M. Hellström (✉)
Åbo Akademi University, Turku, Finland

J. Vesalainen et al. (eds.), *Practices for Network Management*,
DOI 10.1007/978-3-319-49649-8_14

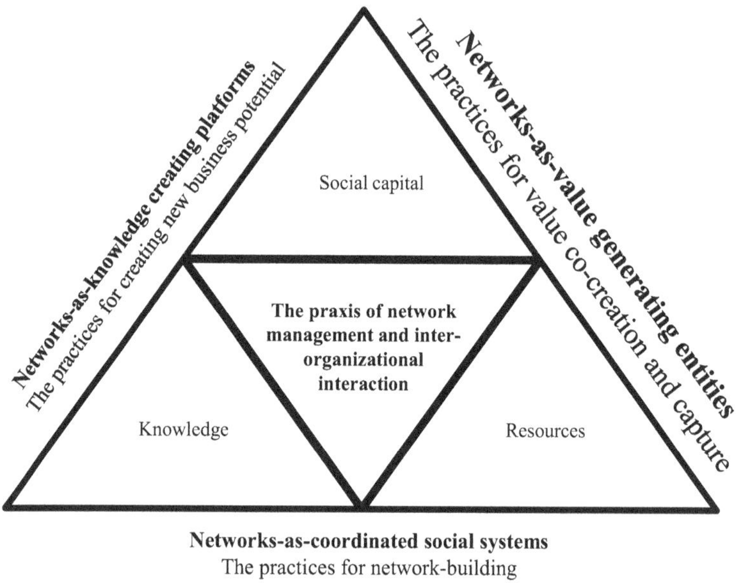

Fig. 14.1 The networking system (adapted from Fig. 1.2)

Managing networks as value-generating entities borders on and combines the knowledge and capability aspects of networking and the social system point of view. Hence, the tools presented in this section focus on the capabilities for enhanced system-level value creation and the structures and mechanisms that lead networks toward common goals. In other words, they present network management practices that turn their networks' tangible resources and knowledge into customer value (with the help of social capital or other similar intangible resources). To act intentionally, networks need a common understanding of the strategic and operative goals to be achieved and the means to implement the objectives that are set. It is our belief that such understanding can be enhanced through various managerial activities through which networks find their goal-oriented and intentional character.

Network management, however, differs from the management of organizations in that it does not possess the ownership- and authority-based power that organizations do (Gulati et al. 2012). Acknowledging this fact as a starting point, we distinguish among three types of network management: (1) network or relationship-level strategic and operative management; (2) network leadership and relationship management; and (3) network governance. This section offers tools for the first type of network management, which consists of "hard" managerial issues like relationship-specific investments, integration of information systems, developing joint service offerings, strategic analysis, or building network-level operations systems. Network leadership, on its part, refers to the "soft" side of relational issues, like the development of trust, unity, and commitment of and between partners (considered in Part I of this book). By network governance, we mean legal or other formal agreements having a special character known as *relational contracting* (touched upon in Chap. 6). As there are no positions called *network managers*, network management occurs through the activities of boundary-spanning actors.

The system level of networks, nevertheless, comprises a bundle of single dyadic relationships. For this reason, the idea underlying the tools presented in this part of the book is to provide the means to measure, manage, and communicate value co-creation, first at the level of single relationships and then at a consolidated network or system level. When analyzing value creation in networks, we can differentiate the communication of the proposed and potential value, on the one hand, and the measurement of the created value, on the other hand. In network relationships, the communication of the added value of certain products and services is challenging, as their features often are (a) seemingly intangible, (b) long-term and relational, and (c) complex and may concern several parties beyond the immediate buyer and seller.

It is also challenging to master the sales of such products and services, as doing so requires careful direction and follow-up within the supply organizations. For this reason, in the DIMECC REBUS program, we have developed tools for both planning and communicating as well as measuring and monitoring the added value. This discussion presents seven such tools, all of which can be positioned along a continuum where the one end centers on the more operative development and communication of value and the other end focuses on strategic analysis and follow-up so that the devised relational investment creates value for both (or all) involved parties. Figure 14.2 summarizes and positions the chapter along this same continuum.

Communication

Tool	Description
Chp. 15. Life cycle cost calculation	P: How to change thinking and the sourcing criteria of customers towards life-cycle costs S: LCC tool configured and tested with customers
Chp 16. The service configurator	P: How to identify the optimal service scope and communicate its value? S: Configurator as a tool for value-driven selling utilized at two interfaces i) internally between delivery and sales, and ii) externally between a salesman and a customer
Chp. 17. The value-based sales approach	P: A new kind of logic needed in solutions sales S: A solution design process with three distinct stages
Chp. 18. Value co-creation analysis	P: How to analyze the most valuable customers, on which the relational practices should be focused? What kind of value we should create to our customers. S: Value functions and value creation process based measurement
Chp. 19. Value curve as a multipurpose tool	P: Evaluation of business performance, customer satisfaction, differentiation, value proposition redesign, and business strategy S: Value curve tool using two dimensions: Horizontal dimension for the individual value elements and vertical for the rating of each individual dimension
Chp. 20. A framework for ecosystemic strategizing and change	P: How to change and overcome the inertia of established but sub-optimal business ecosystems? S: A three-stage framework that ranges from current state analysis to performance metrics for new ecosystems coming into being.
Chp. 21. Network performance management	P: How to overcome barriers related to asymmetric information in value potential evaluation of service outsourcing projects? S: Evaluating services against the criteria for risk and performance.

Follow-up

Fig. 14.2 The tools positioned along the communication—follow-up continuum

The chapters also feature a number of other issues and phenomena present during system- or network-level value creation. The first three chapters are what could be classified as sales tools.

- The first one, "Life Cycle Cost Calculations as the Means for Value Communication in Networks" (Chap. 15), adopts a life cycle perspective on the evaluation of product benefits and provides the seller (and buyer) with a quantified value proposition.
- The application area of the tool in the next chapter, "The Service Configurator—How to Optimally Split Project Scopes" (Chap. 16), is similar in that it strives to see benefits an (service) offering from a broader angle. It adopts a "best-for-the-project" mentality and elucidates qualitative value propositions.
- The service configurator is developed to go along with the solution design process presented in the third chapter, "The Value-Based Sales

Approach—Design Process, Tools, and Needed Capabilities to Create a Solution" (Chap. 17). This process enables the co-creation of innovative and problem-based solutions with customers.

The next three chapters, in turn, provide tools for market and industrial analyses.

- The fourth chapter, "Value Co-creation Analysis in Customer-Supplier Network Relationships" (Chap. 18), offers insights into how co-creation can be facilitated through better understanding of the customer's value creation logic.
- In the fifth chapter, "Value Curve as a Multipurpose Tool—From Self-Assessment to Forming Collaborative Networks" (Chap. 19), the authors have adopted a well-known strategy tool (the value curve) for analytic use in a network context.
- The sixth chapter, "A Framework for Ecosystemic Strategizing and Change" (Chap. 20), is also analytical by nature, but rather than considering customers or competitors as in the previous chapter, it adopts a business ecosystem perspective and asks how the functionality of an entire industry (or sector) can be improved.

Finally, we take a look at network performance as a whole.

- The last chapter, "Network Performance Management: Measurement, Scorecard, and Boundary Processes" (Chap. 21), shows academic ambition by addressing the network performance measurement issue.

References

Gulati, R., Puranam, P., & Tushman, M. (2012). Meta-organization design: Rethinking design in interorganizational and community contexts. *Strategic Management Journal, 33*(6), 571–586. doi:10.1002/smj.1975.

Zott, C., Amit, R., & Massa, L. (2011). The business model: Recent developments and future research. *Journal of Management, 37*(4), 1019–1042. doi:10.1177/0149206311406265.

15

Life Cycle Cost Calculations as the Means for Value Communication in Networks

Susanna Kunttu, Outi Kettunen, and Tero Välisalo

Introduction

Today industrial production systems, buildings, working machines, and so on are created by a network that contains several companies that provide the different components of the end product. Thus, the value of an end product is the result of the combined work of all these companies, and the value created by one partner in the network is not necessarily transparent to other participants. In such a network-based environment, there is a need for methods and tools to enhance understanding of the value created by the different actors.

Roughly speaking, the role of companies in networks can be categorized into three main types, namely, equipment manufacturers, subsystem assemblers, and end users (see Fig. 15.1). All companies have the objective of a profitable business, but because of their different positions

S. Kunttu (✉) • O. Kettunen • T. Välisalo
VTT Technical Research Center of Finland, Tampere, Finland

J. Vesalainen et al. (eds.), *Practices for Network Management*,
DOI 10.1007/978-3-319-49649-8_15

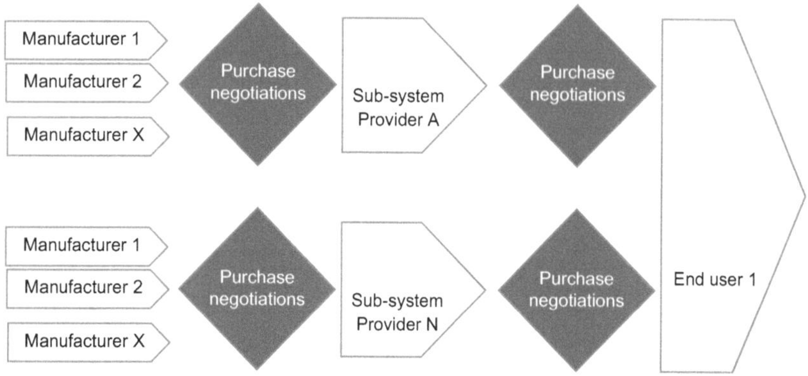

Fig. 15.1 Structure of the industrial network(s)

in the network, they do not necessarily have a common goal, such as minimizing the cost of ownership, the goal of end user. This aspect makes it challenging for a single company, especially if it is a small- and medium-sized enterprise (SME), to manage or influence its network (Valkokari et al. 2013). Different managerial tools, such as a life cycle cost (LCC) tool, can be utilized as a boundary-spanning objective (i.e., a means of communication by SME companies) (Valkokari and Valkokari 2014).

A demonstration of the value that one company can provide to the end user is typically required in purchase negotiations, where a sub-system provider is selecting equipment and components for its offering, or the end user is selecting solutions. Business-to-business negotiations are typically dominated by the purchase price, especially in cases where the other negotiation partners are not responsible for operation and LCCs. The situation can be challenging for a manufacturer who is producing high-quality products with relatively high purchase prices, as well as for an end user whose interest is to get the best solution from the cost- of -ownership perspective. One reason for focusing on purchase price has been the lack of LCC information, which we are now trying to eliminate by presenting the approach of using a LCC applied to industrial networks.

The LCC calculation is one possible tool to use for presenting the value of a solution in monetary terms, which is widely used as decision criteria. Purchase prices are basically always available in any decision-making situation, but other benefits that can be achieved by different solutions are typically communicated by more abstract value propositions, such as less downtime, longer life, and short reaction time for failures. Obviously those kinds of promises are desirable and easily seen and accepted as important objectives. On the other hand, these value propositions are often presented only on a general level without any clear or precise indication of their effects on end user business. Thus, the information is not particularly useful where the goal is to compare alternatives or decide whether to buy or not. To make such benefits more concrete and provide explicit indicators, all companies in the network should be able to transform at least part of these effects to actual monetary values, which then can clearly indicate whether the provided solution is worth the cost in money.

The LCC Calculation

The goal of LCC is to recognize and estimate all lifetime costs rather than only investment or purchase costs (Woodward 1997). As the lifetime of a system could be upward of several decades, usage/operating costs (such as the cost of energy and maintenance) can end up being several times higher than the original acquisition price. A typical case for LCC calculation is a decision-making situation where the aim is to select an optimal alternative among different options. By taking into account LCCs instead of pure purchase price, decision makers have a better opportunity of optimizing the total cost of ownership and achieving better profitability in the long term.

Economic values of alternatives can be compared by using LCC or life cycle profit (LCP) calculations. The focus of LCC calculations is on costs and can be used in those cases where the aim is to minimize costs. In cases where the objective is to select an option that gives the best profit, for example, investments to increase capacity, LCP calculations provide the required information needed to select the best option (e.g., Götze et al. 2008). For example, an air-conditioning system, that is described later in more detail in the case section, does not increase the capacity of a production system (e.g., in a food factory), and thus, the appropriate question is which solution will minimize the total cost of air conditioning. For this kind of case, the proper method is LCC estimation. LCCs emphasize the objective of minimizing total costs instead of individual cost items. For example, a product with a higher purchase price may need less maintenance when lower LCCs can be achieved.

Phases That Calculate LCC

LCC calculation sounds like a simple task—just sum up all costs related to the product and/or service in question. Especially in industrial networks, the challenge may be how to consider all relevant cost factors and how to create reliable estimates for different factors. The IEC standard (IEC 60300-3-3 2004) presents the general process, using five main steps to establish LCC calculation. This systematic process is also applicable for establishing LCC calculations in a networked environment to ensure both quality and usefulness of results.

Definition of a Calculation Case

A clear definition of the calculation case will help one focus on essential costs and avoid extra complexity in other calculation phases. Definition needs to be done for the utilization of results to ensure the usefulness of the full LCC estimations. There are questions to be answered before calculations: Who will utilize the results, and what kind of information is useful for the various companies? Is the calculation case unique, and does it aim to support one decision situation or is the case more general and one that can be repeated in different situations by changing relevant parameters according to each case? Which product of a product family do the calculations cover? Is the calculation case a product of one company or a larger entity created by several companies?

LCC calculations are typically done purely for a physical product by taking into account basic operation and maintenance costs. However, it should be noticed that in addition to better physical features, LCCs can also be reduced by relevant services. Thus, where applicable, available services provided by the manufacturer or another company in the network be included in the calculation.

Product-service systems (PSS) can be distinguished as three main types: (a) product-oriented services, which are centered on product sales, including additional services like maintenance and take-back agreements; (b) user-oriented services, which are based on product leases, rentals, sharing, and pooling; and (c) result-oriented services, which provide specific outcomes, such as the creation of a pleasant climate in offices (Tukker and Tischner 2006).

The Cost Breakdown Structure

The second step is to create a cost breakdown structure as a hierarchical representation of costs related to the case in question. It divides a rather abstract LCC value into more concrete and thus more easily estimated cost elements. Level of structure details are kept practical (e.g., in purchase negotiations), the purchase price is available as such, and there is no point in dividing it into detailed cost factors like design and manufacturing, although those elements do belong to the LCC.

To ensure comprehensive consideration of all relevant aspects related to cost factors, a cost breakdown structure should be created by a group of experts from different areas of expertise. Depending on the case, needed expertise can be found inside one company or inside the industrial network. A company having the role of manufacturer as described in the Fig. 15.1 might have the required information on cost factors inside the company. A sub-system provider typically needs more communication with other stakeholders though they necessarily do not have all the required competencies for the products of other partners.

Estimation of the Calculation Parameters

The third step includes the definition of reliable data sources and the collection of numerical values for elements of the cost breakdown structure. Numerical values for calculation parameters can be estimated by either qualitative or quantitative methods (e.g., as presented by Niazi et al.

2006). Depending on the case, statistical data can be available for estimation or numerical values need to be produced by expert judgments. The quality of results is entirely dependent on the quality of cost estimates, so sufficient effort for data collection is required. On the other hand, the typical aim in practice is a comparison of alternatives when the correct magnitude is more important than precise values. The estimation of values is balancing the quality of estimates and the practical limitations of the actual available data.

As the definition of a cost breakdown structure requires cooperation between the companies in the industrial network, the same holds for the estimation of calculation parameters. Companies in the network have different knowledge and data. For example, end users can provide the best estimates for unavailability costs, and manufacturers will have a better ability to estimate maintenance costs.

Sensitivity Analysis

LCC calculations are typically used to support decision-making, which means that these calculations are performed before the costs are realized, and the calculations are based on estimates of future values, which are inherently uncertain. The robustness of the LCC calculation results for the change in cost parameters can be evaluated, however, by a sensitivity analysis (e.g., Saltelli et al. 2008). The simplest way to conduct a sensitivity analysis is to change the variable values to demonstrate the best or worst case and then re-calculate the results (i.e., a what-if analysis).

Presentation of Results

The last phase defines which result indicators are presented and how they are presented. The main indicator is obviously the estimate of the LCC, but estimates of the main cost categories and the accumulation of costs are also relevant information for decision-making. Utilization and the users of results need to be considered when designing a presentation of results. Do the different network actors need different information, and how can all the various information needs be best fulfilled? Visualization of results provides a quick way to adopt the main information. When designing this visualization, it is essential to consider the usefulness of graphs and focus on relevant information while avoiding unnecessary decorations that might hinder the best interpretation of the results (e.g., Cleveland 1985).

Barriers to LCC Calculations

LCC calculation methods have been developing for decades and are quite well established. Despite that history, however, many companies still do not widely and systematically utilize LCC calculations in their decision-making processes (Korpi and Ala-Risku 2008). Different companies have various reasons why they do not utilize LCC calculations. Some of the common reasons are a lack of reliable data, uncertainty related to predictions, and limited resources to establish the calculations.

All these barriers are relevant for a single company case as for a network of companies. In a networked environment, the challenge is to collect reliable data. In networks, the required data and expertise is spread to several companies, so the collection of good quality data can be a laborious task, further hampered if companies are strictly protecting their data. Thus, all participating companies should be willing to provide the relevant data they have to ensure the reliability of data used in calculations. Reliability of data is crucial in any analysis; bad data do not lead to good or accurate results.

LCC calculations are usually done during a decision phase before costs are realized when it is obvious that even at best, LCC values are only predictions and inherently uncertain. Sensitivity analysis is a tool to use to assess how much the results will change if the values of calculation parameters are not realized as estimated. Sensitivity analysis can produce a range of values for the most profitable acquisitions. One of the challenges with LCC calculations is its uniqueness because detailed cost structures and calculation values will vary case by case, and laborious calculations need to be established from the beginning every time. Thus, it is important to consider those cases where the value of the calculation results is worth the used resources. In a networked environment, one way to overcome this particular barrier is to consider which company has the best possibilities to establish its calculations and collect data and also utilize its ready calculations on more than one case. For example, a manufacturer can utilize well-structured calculations for several cases by changing certain customer-specific parameter values.

A Practical Case for LCC Implementation

We conducted a case-specific implementation of the LCC tool with a manufacturer of air-conditioning equipment. The company is the largest in Finland and operates internationally. It produces cold water stations that can be delivered with remote access service that makes it possible to remotely monitor and access the cold water station control system. By using this remote access, company experts can ascertain the status and history of the cold water station, change parameters, resolve failure situations quickly, and react rapidly to certain abnormalities in the performance of a cold water station. The case is described in more detail by Kunttu et al. (2015).

The case company's challenge was how to communicate to its customers and/or end users the benefits of its high-quality products that are more expensive to purchase originally compared to competitors, as well as how to communicate the benefits of their unique remote access service. That challenge is even more demanding due to the complexity of the network. (see Fig. 15.1). In the construction business, the network of actors is often quite extensive. In addition to a supplier, there are architects and engineering designers that become involved in the sales process. They can influence the customer's final decisions by making designs with certain types of equipment. This choice means that the supplier often needs to convince the designers first. There are also various kinds of customers. The buyer might be a construction company or one of its subcontractors. It can also be a real estate investor or another kind of building owner, and especially with the service being offered, the customer can even be a property maintenance company. Sometimes the customer of the product and the service supplier are the direct users of the building (e.g., a hospital, hotel, or industrial company). Thus, the network involved in using a LCC tool can be extensive with the actor having its own views on the solution's pros and cons. In order to optimize value creation and capture it at the network level successfully, this kind of tool enabling communication over varying organizational boundaries is required (see Introduction, Fig. 15.1).

To fully support the ability of the case company to communicate the value of its products to other companies in its industrial network, it was decided to establish LCC calculations for the premium product. The LCC method was selected since purchase decisions are typically based on monetary values. This first calculation case was limited to the premium product, however, since it was considered to benefit this kind of communication approach the most.

The goal of the case can thus be divided into two main objectives. The first aim was to establish a LCC calculation for the product service system containing the cold water station and the remote access service. Detailed LCC calculations for this case were conducted by following the previously noted steps. The main working method chosen was workshops between experts who were familiar with the air-conditioning systems and researchers who were familiar with the structured development of LCC.

The second aim was to develop specifications and a prototype for a tool that supported fluent progress of meetings with customers. This tool includes a cost breakdown structure, all cost parameters with default values, and formulas to calculate the required results. Some of the calculation parameters were customer-specific and needed to be defined for each individual customer case, and some of the cases needed adjustment of the default values. The tool also includes an interface for data input, which provides an easy way to change the parameter values and also create a natural situation for discussing the factors that affect LCCs. In the top of its form, the second interface created in the tool contains a determination of the product service systems to be compared, and at the bottom of the form, a presentation of results (see Fig. 15.2). Results are updated instantly if any options are changed by hitting buttons at the top of the form; thus, it is very simple to compare different options instantaneously when meeting with a customer.

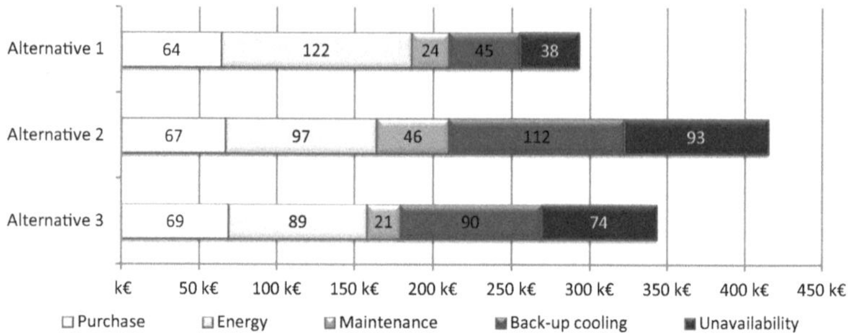

Fig. 15.2 Interface for the selection of alternatives and the presentation of results for customers

Summary of User Feedback

Toward the end of the development process, the tool was tested with key actors in the manufacturer's network. These included architects, engineering designers, constructors, and final users. The purpose was to ensure that the tool would be easy to use for all necessary actors in the network and thus facilitate their cooperation. The tests were conducted at actual sales events where the main goal was to promote the manufacturer's equipment to the customer; however, these customers were informed before the meeting that the main aim was to test the tool.

The general feedback from the network companies was very positive. The LCC topic presented in this way was considered to be novel and very useful. It opened the eyes of the participants to be better able to think about the whole life cycle of the product. The tool was seen as providing information that was clearly visualized and thus supported decision-making. Customers also pointed out that this kind of information increased the understanding of proper usage and the available benefits for professional adjustments and service of the physical product. Customers' trust in the results, however, might still be an issue for this kind of calculation when not all calculation parameters are presented and not all stakeholders have the necessary deep competence to assess the reliability of all the parameters.

It was also seen that in this industrial branch, it is very rare to have this kind of precise tool. However, it is an emerging issue, and interest is growing strongly. For some customers, the LCC information already has had an effect on their decision-making.

Conclusions

In this chapter, we presented the basics of the LCC calculation, its role in an industrial network, and an example of a tool that supports positive discussion in a construction sector network consisting of a service provider, an architect, an engineering designer, and various types of potential end customers. The main aim of the LCC calculation and the tool in this context is to improve the ability of the network actors to communicate the key factors affecting operating costs and the value of different solutions in terms of LCCs. Therefore, the tool can support a network's operation as a "value-generating entity" with shared understanding about any solutions' pros and cons and the viewpoints of all the network actors.

Calculation of LCCs is basically simple mathematics; the real challenge is how to reliably estimate costs that will actually be realized over a long period following the investment decision. Sometimes this uncertainty is even used as an excuse to omit life cycle calculations. Despite this inherent uncertainty, estimates of LCCs do provide relevant information on the magnitude of costs and the differences between alternative solutions. By collecting this relevant data, more accurate estimates can be produced and offered. Thus, the design of data collection over organizational boundaries is part of the LCC calculation in this kind of case when the calculations are intended to be repeated over a long period.

Another challenge is the uniqueness of the cases. Cost structures and cost values need to be created or at least tailored to every case. In networks, LCC calculations should be established by those companies who have the best possibilities of gathering the required data and who are able to re-utilize the established calculations in other cases with the smallest modifications. For example, in the case study presented in this chapter, the case company can use the calculations several times by just adjusting the value of a few case-specific parameters or/and selecting different components and services.

According to the feedback given in the use case, product service providers, together with other network partners, can support their customers' decision-making and increase their knowledge about the factors affecting operating costs, by using LCC estimates for different solutions. The tool facilitates the discussion between different actors in the complex network of the construction business. The partners considered information produced by the tool as trustworthy even though all calculation parameters are not visible to customers. Currently, similar approaches to communicate LCCs at a network level are sparse. It is expected that customers will become more and more interested in utilizing LCC information for their purchase decisions. Thus, providing this kind of information as a network can give a company a competitive edge.

In addition to the above-mentioned benefits achieved through communication with customers and other network actors provided by this kind of LCC information, the development process itself can be a valuable opportunity for networked companies to develop the calculations to improve their understanding of cost composition. The development process stimulates discussion and the exchange of information between companies, different departments, and organizational levels, as the tool building process requires the participation of other key actors in the network during the testing phase.

LCC calculations offer an industrial network the means to discuss cost structure and demonstrate both positive and negative financial effects of different solutions. It also helps to communicate the LCC viewpoint (i.e., the pros and cons of a solution over its life cycle) for decision makers at different companies in the network. Thus, it can be a valuable tool to use for supporting customers and helping them make their most appropriate purchase decisions.

References

Cleveland, W. S. (1985). *The elements of graphing data*. Belmont, CA: Wadsworth Publishing Co Inc.

Götze, U., Northcott, D., & Schuster, P. (2008). *Investment appraisals methods and models*. Berlin Heidelberg: Springer-Verlag.

IEC 60300-3-3. (2004). *Dependability management—Part 3-3: Application guide—Life cycle costing* (2nd ed.). Geneva.

Korpi, E., & Ala-Risku, T. (2008). Life cycle costing: A review of published case studies. *Managerial Auditing Journal, 23*(3), 240–261.

Kunttu, S., Reunanen, M., Raukola, J., Frankenhaeuser, K., & Frankenhaeuser, J. (2013). Executing sustainable business in practice—A case study on how to support sustainable investment decisions. In P. W. Tse (Ed.), *Engineering asset management—Systems, professional practices and certification. Proceedings of the 8th World Congress on Engineering Asset Management (WCEAM, 2013) & the 3rd International Conference on Utility Management & Safety (ICUMAS)* (pp. 1095–1107). Switzerland: Springer International Publishing.

Kunttu, S., Välisalo, T., Kettunen, O., & Aulanko, S. (2015). Life cycle cost calculations supporting service offering; A case study of air conditioning systems. In K. T. Koskinen, H. Kortelainen, J. Aaltonen, T. Uusitalo, K. Komonen, J. Mathew, & J. Laitinen (Eds.), *Proceedings of the 10th World Congress on Engineering Asset Management (WCEAM, 2015)* (pp. 381–388). Verlag: Springer International Publishing.

Niazi, A., Dai, J. S., Balabani, S., & Seneviratne, L. (2006). Product cost estimation: Technique classification and methodology review. *Journal of Manufacturing Science and Engineering, Transactions of the ASME, 128*(2), 563–575.

Saltelli, A., Ratto, M., Andres, T., Campolongo, F., Cariboni, J., Gatelli, D., et al. (2008). *Global sensitivity analysis: The primer.* Chichester, UK: John Wiley & Sons Ltd.

Tukker, A., & Tischner, U. (2006). Product-services as a research field: Past, present, and future. Reflections from a decade of research. *Journal of Cleaner Production, 14*(17), 1552–1556.

Valkokari, K., & Valkokari, P. (2014). How SMEs can manage their networks—Lessons learnt from communication in animal swarm. *Journal of Inspiration Economy, 1*(1), 111–128.

Valkokari, K., Valkokari, P., Rantala, T., Palomäki, K., Kunttu, S., & Reunanen, M. (2013). How to co-create sustainable solutions within manufacturing networks. In *Proceedings of the XXIV ISPIM Conference—Innovating in Global Markets: Challenges for Sustainable Growth* (pp. 1–14). Helsinki: Lappeenranta University of Technology Press.

Woodward, D. G. (1997). Life cycle costing—Theory, information acquisition, and application. *International Journal of Project Management, 15*(6), 335–344.

16

The Service Configurator—How to Optimally Split Project Scopes

Magnus Hellström, Víctor A. Sifontes Herrera, Robin Wikström, and Johnny Långstedt

Introduction of the Problem

The transition from products to services continues to be a challenge for manufacturing companies (Kowalkowski et al. 2015). Many project companies have widened the scope of their offerings from mere equipment to full-fledged turnkey or engineering, procurement, and construction (EPC) solutions, and a wide variety of hybrids in between. However, one size does not fit all; customers require individual solutions, starting from the *scope of supply*, which not only includes hardware but also project-related services (such as procurement management, safety management, and quality management) with varying degrees of *intensity* (the extent to which the supplier will assume responsibility for a given aspect of the project). At the same time, too much customization leads to a situation

M. Hellström (✉) • V.A. Sifontes Herrera • R. Wikström • J. Långstedt
Åbo Akademi University, Turku, Finland

J. Vesalainen et al. (eds.), *Practices for Network Management*,
DOI 10.1007/978-3-319-49649-8_16

in which the supplier may not be able to establish a common way of delivering different services and therefore may not be able to reap the benefits of scale economies. How, then, should one choose an appropriate scope of supply that both satisfies the customer need and leans on an established, high-quality way of working? Ideally, the scope formation would depart from (1) the needs of the project (i.e., a best for the project mentality) and (2) shared responsibility in the way that tasks (risks) are handled by the stakeholder most capable of dealing with the respective risk.

The problem often is that the determination of the scope of project-related services takes place at an early stage, when there is not enough information about the needs and competencies required by the project and the customer. It is often the case that some services impact the project more deeply than others, and so a precipitate service offering during sales may have negative consequences on overall performance: for example, a technically simple project running on a very tight schedule might depend more on time management than on engineering-related services. However, a contractor rarely possesses enough knowledge in the early sales phases of the project, and the pursuit of *just the adequate offering* is thwarted by

- lack of information flow between sales and delivery divisions (Savolainen and Ahonen 2014);
- different incentive strategies for sales and delivery; while the former is typically awarded for margins sold, the latter is for the project's final margins;
- inability of the sales team to translate the contextual factors into appropriate sales arguments; that is, the contextual factors should be utilized in the mapping of customer needs rather than merely relying on the output/promise of the given product;
- overemphasis on cost-related selection criteria by the purchaser;
- lack of knowledge of the value and purpose of the services among the sales personnel; and
- inability of the delivery team to communicate the value of the services it provides.

Theoretical Background

As such, the lack of information flow between sales and delivery is a classical case in cross-functional integration (Galbraith 1973). In the specific context of delivery projects and project business, studies of the sales-operations (projects) interface has been approached as a resource (i.e., capacity) problem, which can be solved using common operations scheduling tools (Cooper and Budd 2007). Turkulainen et al. (2013), in turn, adopt an information processing perspective to develop a contingency framework for choosing among different integration mechanisms. They developed propositions for the use of a specific integration mechanism in the sales phase along all four contingency dimensions: (1) uniqueness is associated with the use of liaison persons, (2) ambiguity and (3) complexity with managerial-level cross-functional teams and meetings, and (4) dispersion with co-location. These recommendations are undoubtedly ideal and analytically powerful. However, and according to our experience, sales seldom lets itself be restricted by either the shortage of resources or the lack of a suitable integration mechanism. Hence, we would like to introduce another, perhaps more practical, tool to bridge the sales-delivery gap, and more generally, to provide an approach to solve all the above-mentioned problems.

Decision-Making

Essentially, the tool aims at supporting decision-making during the sales phase of projects. Given that construction projects are often one-off endeavors that are executed in various contexts, the project team cannot exclusively rely on automatic responses or assumptions. However, research shows that people's reflective capabilities are considerably restricted in even slightly stressful situations (Greene 2013). Therefore, sales and project teams need support in sorting out the elements that affect the project: *Is the project knowledge-intensive? What kind of customer are they facing? What competencies can be found locally?* The stressful and sometimes confusing first contacts with the project increase the sales team's cognitive burden and render them more prone to react to situations rather than to reflect on them. In order to cope with the stressful environment, sales teams need a clear framework that alleviates the burden they bear in order to reflect on their responses. Unfortunately, such a clear framework rarely exists because the continuous shifts scope of supply that occur in projects requires that newcomers become acquainted with the context, and the scope is therefore constructed in parallel with the project.

To address this, and building on the notion of cues derived from sense-making (Weick 1995), our tool provides the sales team with an initial understanding of the context in which it operates. Because project managers are not usually involved from the beginning of the sales of the project, it becomes the salesman's task to chart the critical factors in the project. In order to provide focus on critical factors and to improve the information exchange between sales and delivery departments, the knowledge of both divisions should be properly collected and made subsequently available throughout the execution phase; that is, a knowledge transfer layer should be incorporated in addition to decision-making support.

The Need to Support and Facilitate Decision-Making

Developing solutions and tools that support and aid decision-making processes has emerged as a vital activity, not only in research but among practitioners as well. As explained before, it is often the salesperson's task to chart the critical factors of a potential project. Thus, our aim was to produce a tool that could aid salespersons and project managers in charting the service requirements of a project by providing a framework on which to focus their knowledge and insights, while simultaneously decreasing stress and confusion and increasing efficiency. In other words, we are striving toward making people think and encouraging them to actually take time to reflect upon the situation at hand: a successful decision support tool would facilitate the information assimilation and improve the information flow between sales and delivery (Aharoni et al. 2011).

The need for different decision support tools is further supported by the fact that human brains are not suitable for handling uncertainty and are even worse when making big and well calculated decisions

(Gray 1999). Providing the user with a tool based on historic project information can make the whole process more efficient in time and quality by (1) decreasing the amount of uncertainty and (2) aiding in characterizing the project. With the configurator, we are assisting the user in finding the *perfect bundle* for the customer—a rather complex task, where most of the information and clues are provided in batches (face-to-face meetings, e-mails, etc.). Therefore, a tool that can aid the user to concentrate their thoughts and pick up the relevant cues after receiving a batch of information is essential. With this, the goal is to diminish the overlooked critical factors by drafting a profile of the project.

Configurators

Configurators are one specific type of decision support systems, initially developed to enhance product development decisions and to enforce the use of standard parts and modules in an assembly; that is, to manage the variety in the order acquisition and fulfillment process (Forza and Salvador 2002; Riitahuhta and Pulkkinen 2001). Configuration as such can be seen as an engineering activity where certain configurations (constellations) of a product or system are developed by choosing from a platform of more or less standard modules or building blocks (Riitahuhta and Pulkkinen 2001). Rogoll and Piller (2003) describe a configurator as a tool by which a product/service is modeled to correspond to a specific customer's needs, or in other words, a tool used for customizing product/service configurations. Configurators can belong to a larger group of computer-aided selling (CAS) tools aimed at achieving customer integration (i.e., the idea of utilizing the customer as a co-designer), as they enable fast visualization and simulation of different product configurations.

A prerequisite of configurators is a modular product architecture (Riitahuhta and Pulkkinen 2001), which allows one to configure customized solutions from a set of *standard modules* that can be combined in various ways. Earlier studies found that modularity is a suitable approach for typical construction project services such as logistics (Bask et al.

2011), engineering services (Rahikka et al. 2011) and delivery management (Hellström 2014).

In a recent study by Hellström et al. (2016), the following general design rules for configurators for knowledge-intensive and complex services were outlined:

1. Must address problems that the project or customer deem valuable (Brady et al. 2005), for example, project risks (Edkins et al. 2013);
2. Must take into account uncertainty (Edkins et al. 2013; Winch 2015) and the co-creative nature (Ramirez 1999; Vargo and Lusch 2004) of the project front-end; and
3. Must be based on a modular service architecture (Riitahuhta and Pulkkinen 2001; Salvador 2007).

Method

The idea of developing the service configurator came about when the case company, engaged in the delivery of large engineering projects, had expressed an interest in capitalizing on information from previous projects to improve its service-offering strategies. Viewed from the angle of the *tools-in-use* framework for examining *existing* strategy tools (Jarzabkowski and Kaplan 2015), our approach responds to a different implementation of the framework; we do not focus on long-established strategy tools, but instead on directing the results of our observations to the actual development of the configurator (i.e., our stance is more akin to that of *tools-in-development*). In other words, we collect insights along the three stages mentioned in the framework (selection, application, and outcomes of tools) for directly influencing the affordances of our tool. This connection will become clearer in the following sections, where we illustrate how the tool is tested in an ongoing project (application), the extent to which its output resembles the project's current service offering (outcomes), and how the tool could find a niche within the processes of the case company (selection). Our research strategy is problem-centric rather than product-centric: we identify common, real-life challenges that projects face and link them to the case company's current service offering, which includes services such as project management, engineering, logistics, and installation supervision. This means that customized services are a response to customer and project needs, rather than standard product (or service) features.

We analyzed data from 203 projects with 619 reported challenges collected during a three-year period from the case company. The data were analyzed, and 143 questionnaire items were constructed according to the process visualized in Fig. 16.1. In order to avoid biases, the challenges were analyzed individually by three researchers. The researchers attributed each challenge to a service that would respond to its requirements (e.g., some delays could be attributed to logistics or engineering or both, depending on the causes of the delays and what service would prevent such delays). Next, the researchers discussed diverging attributions and merged similar challenges. The challenges within the services were thematically and hierarchically ordered when they were attributed and merged. The interdependent nature of services required us to ensure that changes in one service impact the scope of other services, too. For example, the extent of engineering impacts construction services, as non-standard design implies that standard ways of working may not be applicable, which, in turn, tends to increase resource requirements. The end result of the research process is a dynamic and structured interactive questionnaire that is embedded into a predefined logic for selecting the most relevant services based on the user's answers.

Finally, a logic and process was developed around the tool, as explained in the next section. This logic was further refined during the practical implementation of the tool (see further below).

Description of the Configurator

The tool we developed is aimed at proposing an optimal (i.e., best for the project) scope of project-related services by charting customer needs in terms of project requirements, aiding in the subsequent identification of the required services and extent of requirement. This logically demands a precise definition of the supplier's service portfolio (corresponding to the *standard modules* mentioned above) so that connections between requirements and services can be properly established. A number of factors

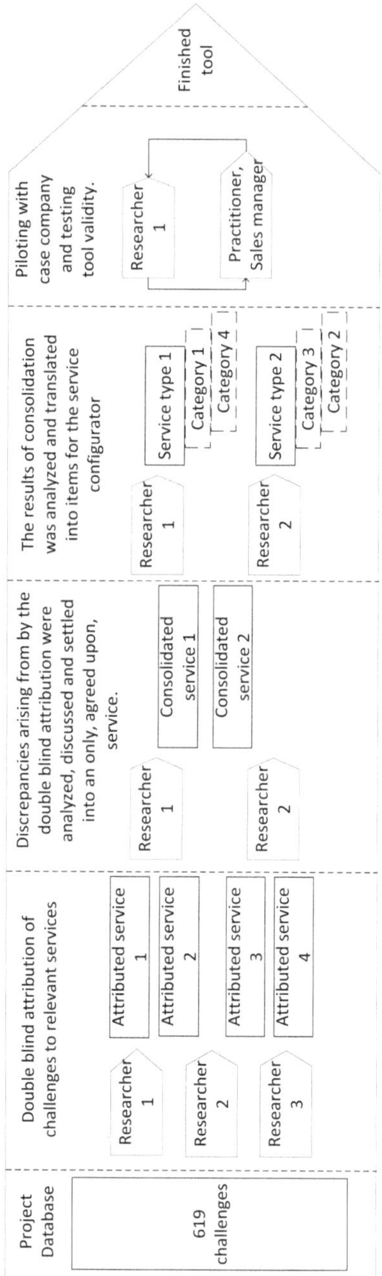

Fig. 16.1 The research process

impact customer needs and the optimal scope, such as institutional factors, customer capabilities, project needs, and supplier capabilities.

The charting of customer needs and project requirements is achieved by presenting parameters to assess and efficiently manage the requirements of the customer and the project context at large; these parameters take the form of questions such as "Is the customer contract-oriented?", implying a focus on transactional arrangements rather than relational ones (Müller and Turner 2007). The tool then processes this assessment and suggests a breakdown of services related to the project and the critical tasks that should be in the supplier's scope in order to guarantee the overall performance of the project.

In more detail, this tool, referred to as the configurator, is an interactive questionnaire that aims at (1) collecting relevant information available at the initial stages of the project while simultaneously (2) prompting the user (sales representative, project manager, etc.) to reflect upon the requirements of the customer and the project itself. The output of this initial phase is a tentative bundle of services (hereafter referred to as the "basic bundle"). In the following phase, the basic bundle is fine-tuned with a second round of more specific questions that are answered as more information becomes available. This second phase has an iterative character, and the user can re-evaluate the questions as many times as needed. That is, as more knowledge is acquired regarding the project, the configurator can be utilized over and over again. The final result is a service offering that closely matches the requirements of the project and that the sales team can use as the foundation for the final offering (i.e. the "customized bundle"). Figure 16.2 shows an overview of the configuration process with the configurator tool acting as a facilitator of sales–customer interaction and a hub for collecting and processing information; as information becomes available (through meetings, conversations, e-mails, etc.), it is fed into the configurator tool and tentative service bundles are proposed—these tentative bundles constitute the basis of further negotiations that enable a deeper understanding of the needs of the project. In fact, the process shown in Fig. 16.2 is adapted from the corresponding process of value-based selling presented by Luotola et al. in Chap. 17 of this book (see also Liinamaa et al. 2016).

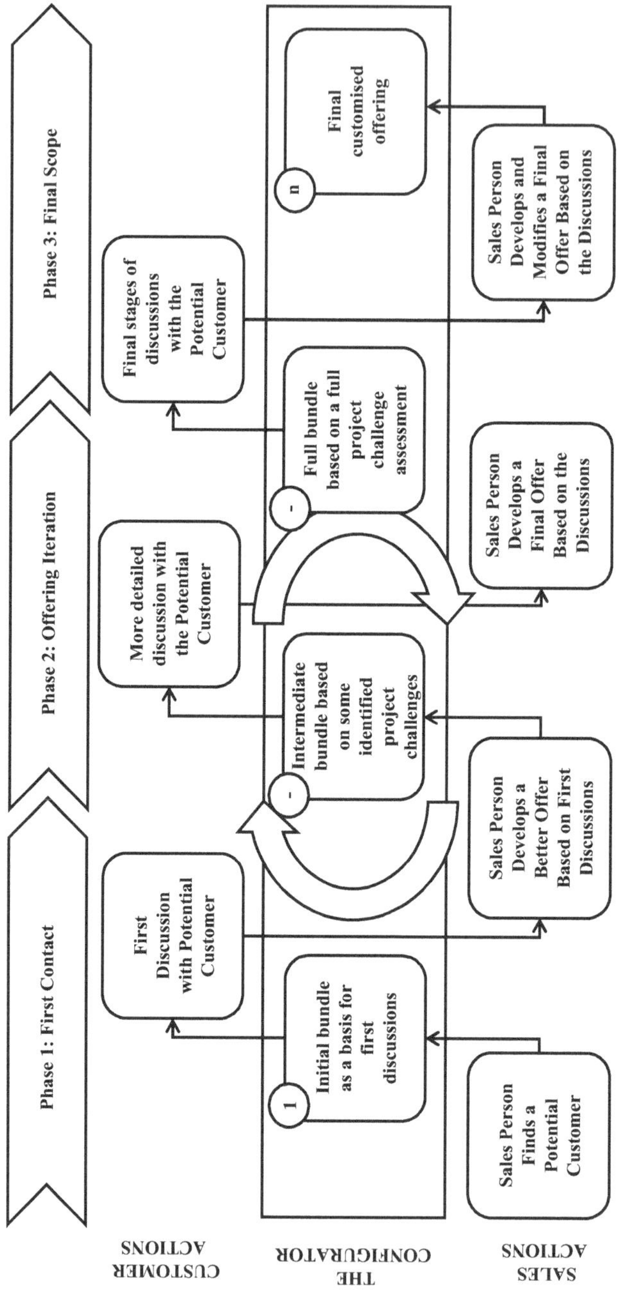

Fig. 16.2 The configuration process

Practical Implementation of the Web-based Application

The tool was created so that the project participants would have a functioning demo to test and discuss. The tool is web-based and works together with all major web browsers, meaning that all project participants with the login details can access the tool from anywhere in the world and test the newest version.

On the start screen of the configurator, the user is able to freely navigate through the different stages of the questionnaire, from basic questions to detailed ones, with continuous adjustment of preliminary and final outputs. The tool has an input phase, consisting of three main steps: map (as certain countries have specific requirements and thus trigger specific questions); meta-questions (basic-level questions that trigger other questions and result in the *basic bundle*); and sharpening questions (more detailed questions meant for fine-tuning the output, resulting in the *customized bundle*). An internal risk check can also be included in the third step to ensure that the output does not contain any major risks for the supplier itself. The output consists of a graphical illustration showing the service need of the project and a qualitative description of the project at hand. The outputs change as the user modifies the inputs; this is iterative and can be done and redone as much as the user wants (see Fig. 16.2).

The goal of the meta-questions is to create an as-good-as-possible output with as few questions as possible. Furthermore, the questions should be of such a character that the user could also fill in the answer using qualified guesses. Mostly, we employed yes/no alternatives, scales, and predefined choices. After the initial input data (geographical location and meta-questions) have been collected, the model will already produce an output (the *basic bundle*). Naturally, as the input from the user at this stage has been rather limited, the output will also be rather rough and so should be considered to point in the right direction. The tool provides two kinds of output: a scope of supply for the service part and an accompanying value proposition; the value proposition reads along the following lines (a hypothetical example):

In this project…

- *Especially the construction appears to be challenging.*

For the purpose…

- *Construction management service provides an effective means for selecting the best subcontractors, controlling their progress and supervising their work so as to complete the project on time, within budget, and according to customer requirements.*

In general, …

- *The package offers a proven, bankable solution with effective transfer of both performance and completion risks with a single point of contact and responsibility.*
- *It provides an efficient means for a customer who wishes to concentrate on business and leave the rest to an experienced team.*

If the outputs do not please the salesperson or if more information becomes available, he/she can move on to the sharpening stage, where the user can open up the different services and answer further questions related to that service (one question can trigger more than one service, thus creating links between services). A set of service-specific (i.e., regarding the project management service) questions are listed in Table 16.1. The basic bundle, produced with the input from the map and meta-questions, can therefore be further refined and become more realistic.

The model behind the outputs is rather straightforward: each question is connected to one or more services and carries a certain weight depending on its impact on the service. We then implemented a scoring system, in which answering a certain question in a certain way increased or decreased the different service levels proportionally by weight. Naturally, one needs to answer a certain amount of questions connected to a service to activate that service; that is, if the user did not answer any question regarding a specific service, it will not be triggered.

As points are accumulated, different service levels are activated: higher-demand levels are suggested as more points are assigned to a given service.

Table 16.1 Sharpening questions for the project management service

Project management sharpening questions	
There are many influential stakeholders in the project	Yes/No
The customer or financier insists that the project be executed in a consortium	
The project scope-split or set-up will be unclear or complex	
The customer has implied needs or hidden expectations	
There will likely be issues with the customer's organization	
The customer has a very tight schedule or expects a fast-track delivery	
The client makes reference to a certain scheduling technique (e.g., client's own scheduling system)	
A party in the project requires daily or weekly planning and reporting routines on site	
The client emphasizes the role of quality in the project (e.g., already has a preferred quality system)	

The final output of the tool is the scope of supply for project services and their demand and risk levels: what services are needed and to what extent they are needed in order to avoid or tackle challenges?

The Case of an Evolving Scope of Supply

During the later phases of tool development, we conducted a workshop with a senior salesperson from the case company. The goal was to test the developed tool and method on a real case.

The chosen test case was an ongoing sales lead in Mexico. Together with the salesperson, we went through the configuration process two times. The first time, we went with the mindset and knowledge they had at the early stages of the negotiations; the second time, we used the knowledge they had at the moment of performing this test.

This exercise found that in the beginning of the negotiations, the customer was planning (hoping) to conduct the project using the minimum amount of services. Yet the project context appeared challenging, for example, in terms of meeting local design standards, which normally would be a task of the supplier: that is, demanding the corresponding service prompted by positive ("Yes") responses to statements in the configurator, such as "demanding local standards or special industrial requirements apply" and "the customer has demanding standards and procedures." Hence, the first iteration resulted in a bundle containing a number of services with high levels of engagement (in particular, in the engineering part of the project, which deals with standards). However, during a year of negotiations and further investigations that followed the initial discussions, it turned out that neither the customer nor the local authorities required specific design standards. Hence, the positive responses were changed to negative ones (i.e., "No"; see Table 16.1), and consequently, the case company was able to offer its ordinary engineering module at a competitive price. To successfully finalize the project based on the *initial* negotiations would have required many more services, and if the case company would have rushed into the deal at an early stage, it is likely that the project would have resulted in red bookkeeping numbers. The salesperson that performed this exercise was impressed by the fact that the configurator managed to point out the issues they had overlooked in the beginning. As soon as the case company discovered the actual scope of the project, they approached the customer differently and were able to negotiate a deal that was better for both parties.

Based on the experience gained from the test, the salesperson noted that the configurator would be especially beneficial in situations where an inexperienced person is participating in a potential project negotiation, such as those intended for projects in new and unfamiliar sectors or countries. This makes the configurator a suitable tool for identifying general issues despite the difficulties that it might have in pinpointing very unique cases or problems.

Conclusions

We believe that the mechanisms underlying the use of decision-making support tools have not been studied sufficiently. There seems to be considerable literature on decision-making support in IT-related fields, yet the effects that these tools have on a sense-making level have been studied to a much lesser degree. We are of the opinion, therefore, that there is an obvious need, from practical and academic points of view, to develop more tools like the one presented in this chapter. Moreover, in order to give continuity to this work, the *tools-in-development* stance taken in this article of course gives rise to the scientifically interesting situation in which a follow-up of the final tool would take the form of the tools-in-use framework advocated in the introduction of this book, thus providing a contrast on how strategy tools are developed and how they are actually used.

Our objective was not only to advance a tool meant for assisting salespersons and project managers but also to bring forth a field of interest within management that addresses the question, "How do the tools actually work and why?" Here, the focus is not on different techniques but rather on the mental results (stress alleviation, faster integration, knowledge diffusion, etc.) that could originate from implementing a certain tool (cf. tools-in-use), especially those that would enable both the sales and the project teams to share the cues that they are required to understand in order to sell and execute projects successfully. It seems that theory would support the notion of such tools as stress alleviators, and, by transitivity, as reflection enablers, through the notion of having an elementary understanding of the project from the get-go, regardless of changes in the teams' structure or the project team's absence in the sales process. Such tools can even function as initial socialization frameworks where project teams are introduced to the project setting through a shared set of initial cues (i.e., the knowledge the sales teams have acquired is available to the project team in a structured and shared framework).

By first mapping the reoccurring problems in project-based settings and then modularizing/generalizing them, we created the foundations of the tool. With the foundations in place, our decision support tool is able to create a setting in which both sales and delivery could (with little effort) get a good overview of the project at hand. Furthermore, the tool would aid in creating the optimal project scope, which in turn would provide the customer with maximum value. To properly address the mutual benefit aspects of network tools (advocated in the introduction of this book), would certainly be an area that requires further action-oriented research.

Acknowledgments We are very grateful for the collaborative disposition of our case company and for the cooperation with members of their staff: this constituted the core of our research. Furthermore, we would like to acknowledge Dr. Magnus Gustafsson for providing relevant and important insights. Finally, the collaboration of our programmers, Mr. Mikael Sand and Mr. Robert Syring, is gratefully acknowledged.

References

Aharoni, Y., Tihanyi, L., & Connelly, B. L. (2011). Managerial decision-making in international business: A forty-five-year retrospective. *Journal of World Business, 46*(2), 135–142. doi:10.1016/j.jwb.2010.05.001.

Bask, A. H., Lipponen, M., Rajahonka, M., & Tinnilä, M. (2011). Modularity in logistics services: A business model and process view. *International Journal of Services and Operations Management, 10*(4), 379–399. doi:10.1504/IJSOM.2011.043463.

Brady, T., Davies, A., & Gann, D. M. (2005). Creating value by delivering integrated solutions. *International Journal of Project Management, 23*(5), 360–365. doi:10.1016/j.ijproman.2005.01.001.

Cooper, M. J., & Budd, C. S. (2007). Tying the pieces together: A normative framework for integrating sales and project operations. *Industrial Marketing Management, 36*(2), 173–182. doi:10.1016/j.indmarman.2006.03.005.

Edkins, A., Geraldi, J., Morris, P., & Smith, A. (2013). Exploring the front-end of project management. *Engineering Project Organization Journal, 3*(2), 71–85. doi:10.1080/21573727.2013.775942.

Forza, C., & Salvador, F. (2002). Managing for variety in the order acquisition and fulfilment process: The contribution of product configuration systems. *International Journal of Production Economics, 76*(1), 87–98. doi:10.1016/S0925-5273(01)00157-8.

Galbraith, J. R. (1973). *Designing complex organization.* Reading, MA: Addison-Wesley.

Gray, J. R. (1999). A bias toward short-term thinking in threat-related negative emotional states. *PSPB, 25*(1), 65–75. doi:10.1007/BF02985213.

Greene, J. (2013). *Moral tribes: Emotion, reason, and the gap between us and them.* New York: Penguin Books.

Hellström, M. (2014). Solution business models based on functional modularity—The case of complex capital goods. *Journal of Service Management, 25*(5), 654–676. doi:10.1108/JOSM-07-2013-0198.

Hellström, M., Wikström, R., Gustafsson, M., & Luotola, H. (2016). The value of project execution services: A problem and uncertainty perspective. *Construction Management and Economics*. Retrieved April 28, 2016, from http://www.tandfonline.com/eprint/GWdGQnfAXCmhGMsHruB2/full#.VyJ3KsA3Ju4.mendeley

Jarzabkowski, P., & Kaplan, S. (2015). Strategy tools-in-use: A framework for understanding "technologies of rationality" in practice. *Strategic Management Journal, 36*(4), 537–558. doi:10.1002/smj.2270.

Kowalkowski, C., Windahl, C., Kindström, D., & Gebauer, H. (2015). What service transition? Rethinking established assumptions about manufacturers' service-led growth strategies. *Industrial Marketing Management, 45*, 59–69. doi:10.1016/j.indmarman.2015.02.016.

Liinamaa, J., Viljanen, M., Hurmerinta, A., Ivanova-Gongne, M., Luotola, H., & Gustafsson, M. (2016). Performance-based and functional contracting in value-based solution selling. *Industrial Marketing Management, 59*, 37–49. doi:10.1016/j.indmarman.2016.05.032.

Müller, R., & Turner, J. R. (2007). Matching the project manager's leadership style to project type. *International Journal of Project Management, 25*(1), 21–32. doi:10.1016/j.ijproman.2006.04.003.

Rahikka, E., Ulkuniemi, P., & Pekkarinen, S. (2011). Developing the value perception of the business customer through service modularity. *Journal of Business & Industrial Marketing, 26*(5), 357–367. doi:10.1108/08858621111144415.

Ramirez, R. (1999). Value co-production: Intellectual origins and implications for practice and research. *Strategic Management Journal, 20*(1), 49–65.

Riitahuhta, A., & Pulkkinen, A. (2001). *Design for configuration a debate based on the 5th workshop on product structuring*. Berlin: Springer.

Rogoll, T., & Piller, F. (2003). *Konfigurationssysteme für Mass Customization und Variantenproduktion: Strategie, Erfolgsfaktoren und Technologie von Systemen zur Kundenintegration*. Munich, Germany: Think Consult.

Salvador, F. (2007). Toward a product system modularity construct: Literature review and reconceptualization. *IEEE Transactions on Engineering Management, 54*(2), 219–240.

Savolainen, P., & Ahonen, J. J. (2014). Knowledge lost: Challenges in changing project manager between sales and implementation in software projects. *International Journal of Project Management, 33*(1), 92–102. doi:10.1016/j.ijproman.2014.04.003.

Turkulainen, V., Kujala, J., Artto, K., & Levitt, R. E. (2013). Organizing in the context of global project-based firm: The case of sales-operations interface. *Industrial Marketing Management, 42*(2), 223–233. doi:10.1016/j.indmarman.2012.08.004.

Vargo, S. L., & Lusch, R. F. (2004). Evolving to a new dominant logic for marketing. *Journal of Marketing, 68*(1), 1–17.

Weick, K. E. (1995). *Sensemaking in organizations*. London: Sage.

Winch, G. M. (2015). Project organizing as a problem in information. *Construction Management and Economics, 33*(2), 106–116. doi:10.1080/01446193.2015.1021703.

17

The Value-based Sales Approach—Design Process, Tools and Needed Capabilities to Create a Solution

Hanna Luotola, Maria Ivanova-Gongne, and Johanna Liinamaa

Introduction

Today a majority of industrial manufacturing companies claim to provide solutions with their products and services. This means that solution providers sell offerings that consist of technology components, maintenance, training, business consultancy and financial services aiming to produce customer value surpassing prior product-based technology offerings (Storbacka 2011). Such complex structure of a solution has led to increased attention to value-based selling techniques among business practitioners. In value-based selling, sellers seek to understand customer problems and communicate how their solution generates higher profits for the customer. Still, the novel character of solution business and the solution concept often leads the customer unclear on how the claimed solution actually solves any business problem per

H. Luotola (✉) • M. Ivanova-Gongne • J. Liinamaa
Åbo Akademi University, Turku, Finland

J. Vesalainen et al. (eds.), *Practices for Network Management*,
DOI 10.1007/978-3-319-49649-8_17

se, or how the supplier solution generates higher profits for the customer. This inadequacy was driving us to investigate how solution sellers should first identify the value potential of the customer's business and second, to demonstrate and create value during the sales process. However, we have noted that the solution to a problem does not always arise from the plethora of a supplier offering, nor from the existing needs of the customer firm. Instead, the economic functionality of a customer solution begins by understanding market insights and business environments, which may generate value to a customer (Hellström et al. 2016). This means that solution sales call for the managerial capability to change the underlying business logic, including pricing, revenue sharing mechanisms and a functional contracting mechanism (see Chap. 6. for further details on functional contracting) for settling the solution.

We believe that being able to impact on the value creation requires a structured sales process, which would enable reaching the desired aims in a straightforward and comprehensive manner. For meeting the abovementioned demands, design thinking was adopted in order to solve industry problems, including creative methods and tools that enable developing a functional solution for the customer. Design thinking enabled a solution-focused way of working meaning that the rules and mechanisms for ensuring system value were created. Design thinking gave us tools and perspectives to support our Rebus clients when they were struggling to define pathways to succeed as solution providers. In addition, design thinking helped us refining new strategic guidelines as we changed the solution business environment toward the optimal one. Our way of working with the companies is a good example of a design process: we found and were given a set of problems in order to seek what is the solution that would best make sense in economic terms and enable productivity for its business ecosystem actors. We regard business ecosystems as value-creating and value-capturing systems (Dalziel 2007), where various actors serve a certain role for solution development. As an example, when the supplier promised to increase the investment net cash flow, the customer was forced to consider whether they believed the supplier explanation and facts to cover all the points of uncertainty regarding the value of the solution. At first, there was no definite certainty about the value, as unforeseen situations and new problems occurred. In addition, the customer had doubts regarding the functionality and benefit of the service, that was one element of the solution. For solving the doubts, the sales team and researchers were forced to develop proven fact-based sales arguments demonstrating the added value to a customer. In other words, the team guaranteed that the contractually agreed earnings will increase through the supplier's solution. Without the revenue guarantee, the scope of supply to the customer would in practice equal the scope of a traditional product supplier's offering, which only guarantees the technical functionality of the product. Offering the above-mentioned service guarantees included both downside and upside risks. If the supplier was not able to succeed in the solution delivery, the incomes for neither itself nor the customer were not achieved. However, in the case of success the potential for extra earnings was significant for both parties. Therefore, the lack of customer certainty was one of the main barriers in the sales situation unless the supplier company was able to communicate the fact-based measures of the added value.

Our investigation at various companies suggests that firms that are successful in selling solutions are the ones that can first of all identify customer's business problems and barriers. We believe that a solution cannot only consist of a supplier's offering, as the current offerings do not address customer problems nor impact on the revenue side. Instead, the solution should evolve from the customer's business case as the supplier and customer seek together the match between the customer's business problems and the supplier's solution components and capabilities. The customer and supplier then together integrate the components into a value-creating solution. This means that successful solution providers understand that the key capability here is being able to handle complexity and uncertainty on business ecosystem level, and to understand customer revenue sharing mechanisms. In addition, leading solution sellers are driven by value, meaning that they are able to orchestrate the business in a manner that enables financial benefit for all the main business stakeholders.

In our case, the creation of the solution took place during the value-based sales process and resulted in a set of requirements that were connected to firm offerings, needed operational capabilities, and processes. The value-based sales process focuses on specific, tangible and intangible customer problems. The method differs from the existing product and service sales in the way that it emphasizes co-creation, where the scope of the solution emerges during the different stages of the sales process as customer becomes more certain of the added value. As an outcome, the application of a new value-based sales process and tools, facilitating value creation between the buyer and the seller and considering also the broader ecosystem, has been developed in collaboration with Rebus clients and Åbo Akademi University researchers. The process is currently being piloted and further developed in several Rebus projects.

Theoretical Background

Solutions are a fairly recent phenomenon both in the business world and the academia. Several definitions of what implies a solution exist (see e.g., Cantù et al. 2011; Storbacka 2011). We adopt the definition provided by Storbacka et al. (2011, 699), which regards solutions as "longitudinal relational processes, during which a solution provider integrates goods, service and knowledge components into unique combinations that solve strategically important customer specific problems, and [is] compensated on the basis of the customer's value-in-use". The existing literature on solutions is helpful in a sense that it clarifies well the concept and covers well the process view for developing the solution and defines the common building blocks of the solution. However, it does not describe to a sufficient extent the mechanisms for formulating solutions. In particular, existing theories do not fully determine how sellers overcome the critical barriers and solve the set of customer business problems that emerge as the solution is formulated. Another issue that has not yet been comprehensively studied is how the supplier's value proposition and actions can impact on the customer's business and economic performance in terms of productivity enhancements, cost reductions or revenue increase.

In our research we attempted to tackle the aforementioned gaps, which resulted in a value-based sales approach presented in the next sections. As Terho et al. (2012) state, there is a need to study and conceptualize value-based selling as a sales approach that focuses on communicating the value creation on sales force levels. The value-based selling approach has emerged as both a field of research and an effective strategy for a subset of companies to succeed in competitive markets (see e.g., Ulaga et al. 2006; Liinamaa et al. 2016). However, many of the existing sales and solution development processes are drawn from the customer-centric business logic focusing on the customer's existing products and service needs (Davies et al. 2007). Such a focus hardly enhances the readiness of a customer to frame investment decisions due to the supplier not sufficiently providing fact-based arguments of the added value. In addition, the importance of so-called organization promoters (in the customer company) was noted. Rost et al. (2007) define promoters as "individuals who actively and enthusiastically promote innovation throughout the crucial organizational stages (p. 340)". The role of different promoters in our study was to communicate fact-based arguments of the value potential presented by the supplier within the customer organization and to lead the solution development with their specific intellectual capability.

From the beginning of our collaboration with the case company, it became clear that the qualitative and often abstract value propositions provided by the solution supplier do not remove the doubts that are caused by fuzziness of a long-term solution sales process. Based on these standpoints we soon understood that making a solution functional necessitates abductive problem-focused reasoning which is practical and takes place in situations where the direction and goals are influenced by diverse views (Buchanan 1992). Design thinking literature offers such kind of a context, which considers diverse views and works toward reaching a balance between those views. Therefore, the key factor that makes the design thinking relevant in the context of solution sales is that in design thinking the solution does not arise from the existing markets; instead, the act of designing seeks to identify new market and economic value (that does not exist yet, see e.g., Romme 2003).

Brown (2008, 88) metaphorically describes the design process "as a system of spaces rather than a predefined series of orderly steps". Thus, the process architecture is not linear, as in most of business activities (ibid.), but is abductive by moving back and forth between various tasks and allowing flexibility in solution development. This means that the design process does not start from market or customer analysis; instead, it begins from an investigation of sociocultural phenomena, triggered by the new technologies, products and services made available by the manufacturers. However, the solutions are not pushed only by new technologies, products or solutions—aiming to solve the explicit customer problem. Rather an idea of a solution pushes actions toward a new economic meaning: interpretation of how problems in customer's business should be changed to create value. For our case companies this meant that the solution developers, that is, sales force, were to adapt a new role as value designers.

Description of the Value-based Sales Process

In comparison to traditional solution sales, the approach we used to develop the value-based sales process has a more interactive, co-creative and customer-oriented character, and it represents an open-ended process of collaboration where the solution is designed. The solution design approach entails a step-wise value co-creation process, which increases customer's certainty in the proposed solution and enables gradual value creation through enhanced interaction, understanding of customer's logic and needs, and integration of business processes. The uncertainty of a solution was gradually diminished through points of customer–supplier interactions where the problems were overcome and changed into justified fact-based knowledge toward a functional solution—a value capture to a customer. The sales process (see Fig. 17.1) consists of the following steps:

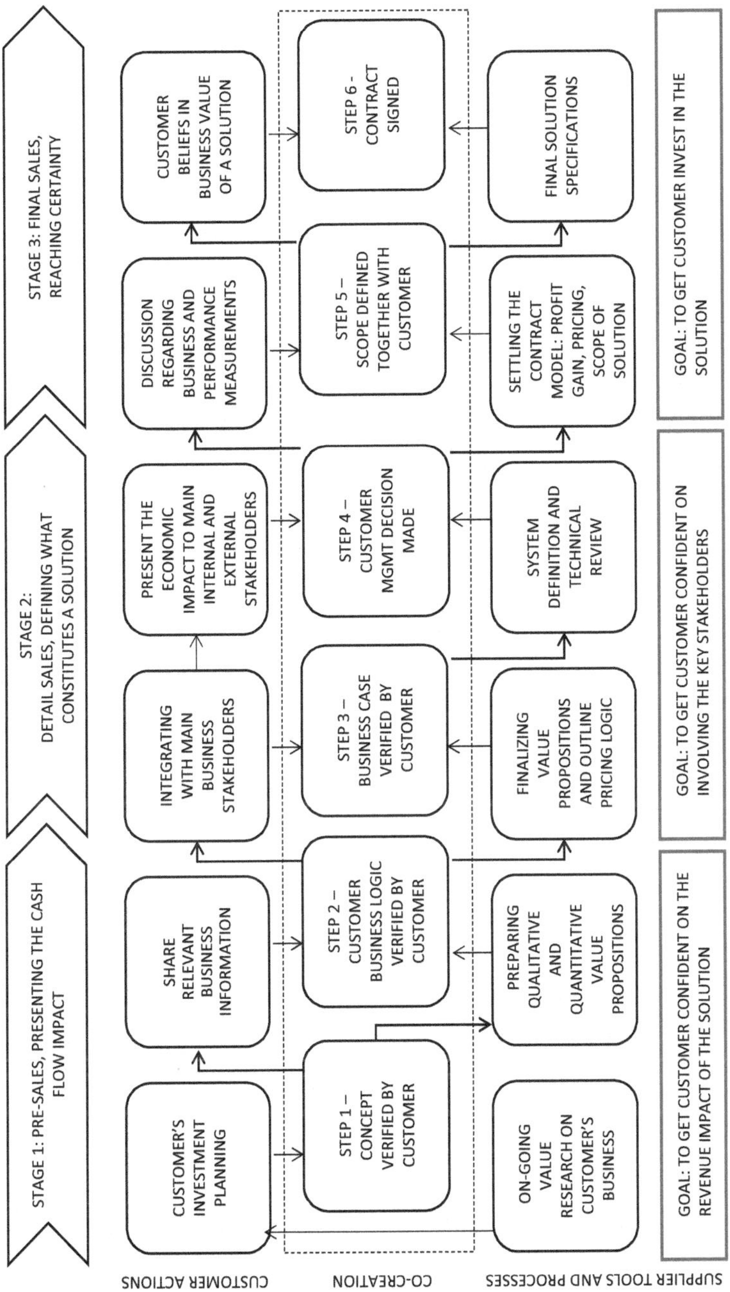

Fig. 17.1 The value-driven sales process

- Value definition (Pre-sales) involves the supplier and the customer setting the problem formulation and the interface together. The main aim is to make the customer certain about that the supplier can provide cash flow impact for its business model.
- Value commitment (Detail sales) involves increasing customer's commitment to the proposed solution by reaching the right promoters and decision makers within the customer organization. The aim is to present the customer with pricing models, which clearly outline customer's generated value from the proposed solution.
- Reaching certainty (Final sales) entails outlining the final scope and specifications of the solution together with the customer, outlining the final contract model, and signing it. Reaching such certainty highlights the role of the competent value designer/sales manager meaning that uncertainty and complexity of the solution are solved, and mutual confidence in the value of a solution is gained.

Case Example

We started active customer–supplier collaboration on the sales process, together with the focal company, in 2013. The study was collaborative in the sense that we as researchers not only acted as passive observers but also actively participated in the design of both the process and the outcome of the solution. The value creation in our case evolved during the value-based sales process, which took more than two years for the customer to sign the first solution contract. The process involved co-creation and intensive interaction between the customer and the supplier. The value-based sales process, tools, and capabilities to solve occurring problems are analyzed in the sections below.

Presenting the Cash Flow Impact (Pre-sales)

To make the customer aware of the cash flow potential, the supplier's sales force had to demonstrate the difference between the functional and the conventional solution. The main message was to convince the customer regarding the economic productivity that the supplier's solution can add. In turn, the customer was required to share necessary business data on their operation profile and revenue streams, with the supplier. This was a necessity, as the goal was to ensure that supplier's solution actually can increase the operational performance and the revenue side, and impact on the payback time of the investment. The common objection from the customer side was more than once that they did not believe the value impact of the solution. Thus, for tackling this barrier, the supplier calculated how their solution impacts on the customer's cumulative cash flow during the investment lifetime. For this purpose, a basic net present value chart, as shown in Fig. 17.2, was used.

For delivering the message of additional value to a customer, the sales manager was forced to act as a value designer, presenting and giving guarantees for the value to their business stakeholders. In other words, this means designing cash flows that support customers and the other stakeholder's earning logics. Therefore, the main capability of a sales force is to be able to recognize which actor harvests the main value, and how the value is divided between other key stakeholders. This included knowledge on the problems, market situation and verification on how the supplier's solution fits with the customer's business situation.

Defining What Constitutes a Solution (Detail-Sales)

Reaching the right persons and promoters in the customer organization was one of the main goals for the detail sales. The role of promoters was also relevant in the pre-sales stage, where the sales managers are supposed to target the message of the solution to the right stakeholders: commercial or technical personnel in the customer's organization. As departments often work in silos without being able to integrate between technical and business departments, the negotiations are often held with the people lacking on the business experience. This is causing major implications as the technical side of customer organizations is mostly not capable of promoting the value of an investment to the real decision makers.

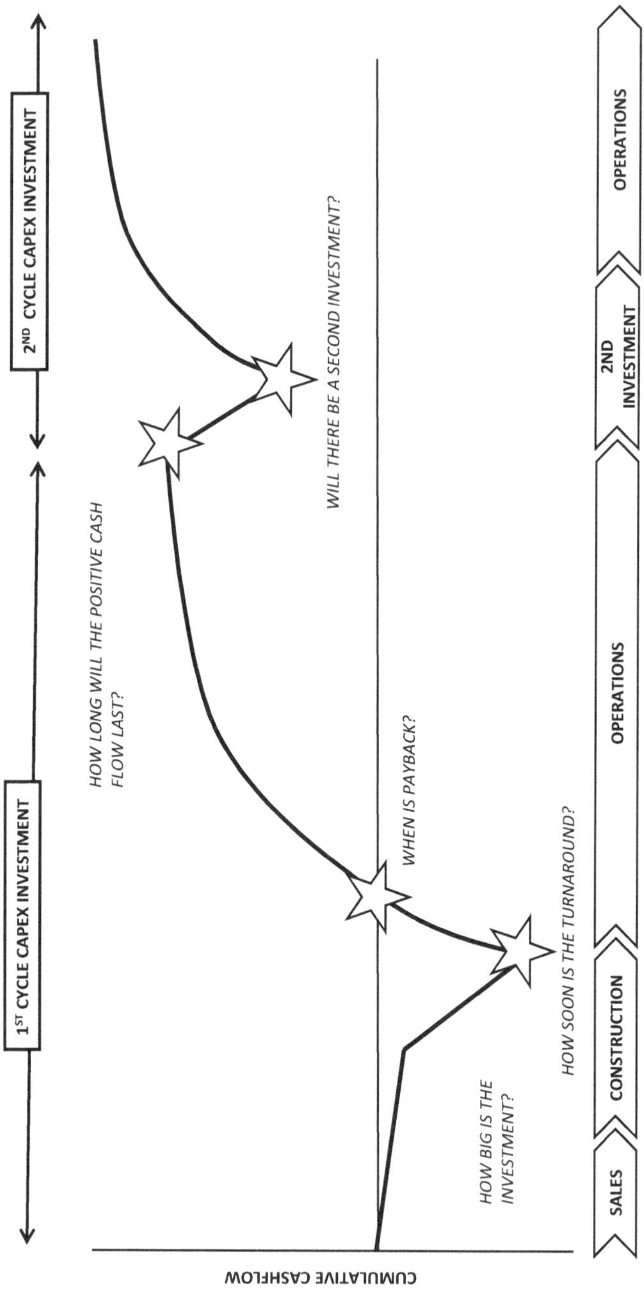

Fig. 17.2 Demonstrating the impact of the supplier's solution to the customers' investment

Reaching the Certainty (Final Sales)

In traditional product-based sales, a supplier company normally takes part in the sales negotiations after the customer has made a purchasing decision. The corresponding phase of solution sales is named final sales. In solution sales the supplier's sales team should impact on the customer's decisions at the very early stage of investment planning. In our model, when entering the final sales, the customer has already made an investment decision in collaboration with the sales team. During the final sales, the final scope of the solution and specifications are defined jointly, including verifications on the final contract model: profit gain, pricing, and scope of solution. In practice, the major customer problems were solved during the earlier stages, and uncertainties were thus tackled. Therefore, the parties were able to contract it.

Conclusions

Shifting toward value-based sales in solution business is a multifaceted and lengthy endeavor, which requires the supplier company to develop new capabilities, to engage in proactive sales, and to apply various tools in order to enable a value co-creation process with the customer. In order to aid companies with a solution to problems faced when engaging in solution sales, we developed the value-based sales approach further. The benefits a company can achieve by applying the developed approach are the following:

1. Gradual organizational change toward a more value-oriented mindset among the sales force and the rest of the company;
2. Ability to better understand industry and customer logics, and developing a de facto valuable solution;
3. Decreased customer uncertainty and improved business relationships by means of engaging in a value co-creation process and delivering a solution that meets customer needs (both implicit and explicit) and solves relevant market problems;

4. Improvement in supplier–customer interaction and ability to develop relevant arguments and pricing models based on solid verifiable data, considering the whole business ecosystem;
5. Possibility to break the predominant industry logic within the business ecosystem in which the customer and supplier operates. Industry logic in this case represents itself dominant assumptions within the industry that often create a barrier for the customer to understand the real value of the solution and
6. The modularity and step-by-step nature of the sales process allow gradually breaking the industry logic and ingraining the suppliers' innovative understanding of how the market should work.

To conclude, providing and selling solutions in the industrial business settings is the art of matching different components of what eventually makes a solution—into a design process. In practice, this requires capability to combine a commercially viable solution that unites elements of the customer's business model, supplier capabilities, business networks, and takes into account existing market, customer potential, and emerging technical and economic signals and trends. All of these components together create a solution (see Fig. 17.3).

During our collaboration with the companies, we understood that the challenges and problems of the value-based sales process were the result of deductive, product-oriented sales methods. In order to solve the challenges, companies need to apply abductive perspective on value creation. The reasoning in abductive solution sales begins with an incomplete set of observations of problems, and it proceeds to the likeliest possible explanation for the set. Moreover, abductive reasoning yields the kind of daily decision-making that does its best with the information at hand, which often is incomplete, and requires implementing a design approach to sales. The design approach impact on the traditional managerial thinking in two ways; first, encourage suppliers to make experiments, and second, handle with uncertain outcomes as there was no clear direction of action that eventually makes a solution. The potential value creation through design creates certainty, as emerging problems are tackled during the creative process.

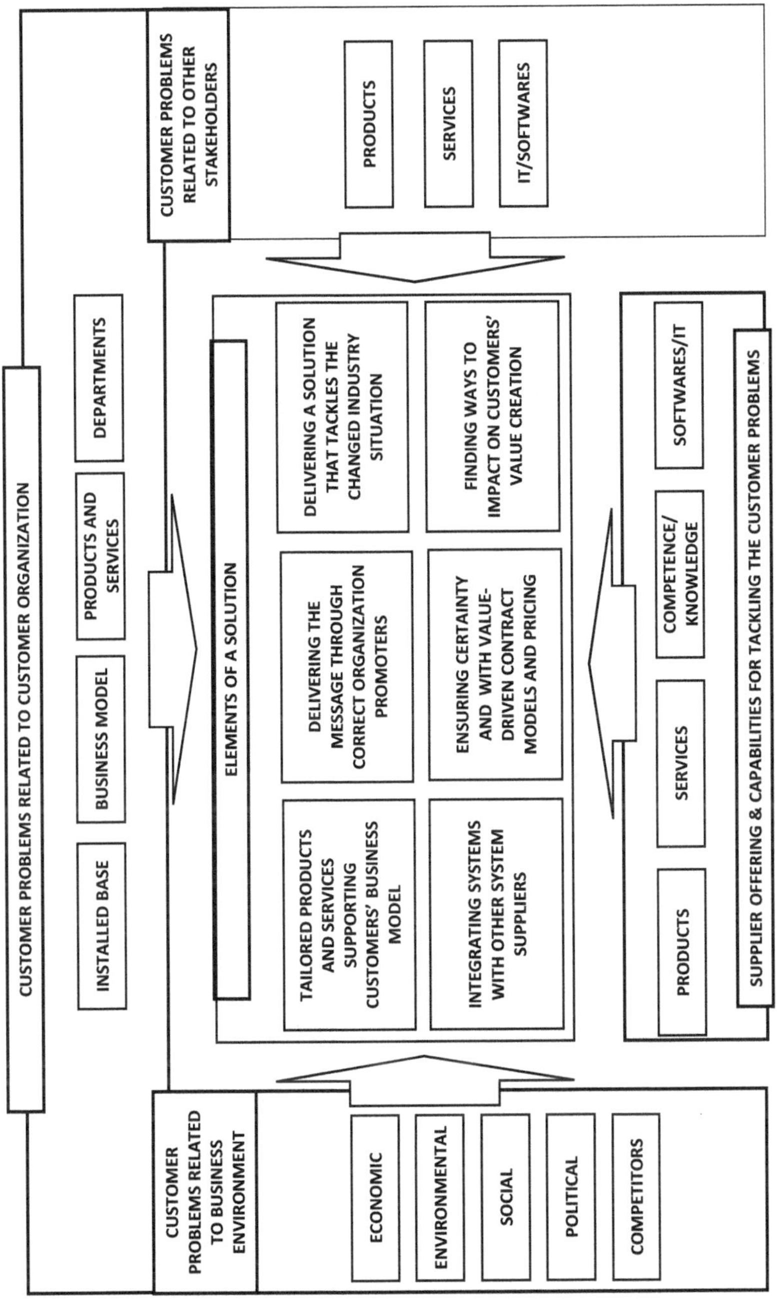

Fig. 17.3 Components of a solution

References

Buchanan, R. (1992). Wicked problems in design thinking. *Design Issues, 8*(2), 5–21.

Brown, T. (2008, June). Design thinking. *Harvard Business Review, 86*(6), 84–92.

Cantù, C., Corsaro, D., & Snehota, I. (2011). Roles of actors in combining resources into complex solutions. *Journal of Business Research, 65*(2), 139–150.

Dalziel, M. (2007). A systems-based approach to industry classification. *Research Policy, 36*(10), 1559–1574.

Davies, A., Brady, T., & Hobday, M. (2007). Organizing for solutions: Systems seller vs. systems integrator. *Industrial Marketing Management, 36*(2), 183–193.

Hellström, M., Wikström, R., Gustafsson, M., & Luotola, H. (2016). The value of project execution services: A problem and uncertainty perspective. *Construction Management & Economics, 34*(4–5), 272–285.

Liinamaa, J., Viljanen, M., Hurmerinta, A., Ivanova-Gongne, M., Luotola, H., & Gustafsson, M. (2016). Performance-based and functional contracting in value-based solution selling. *Industrial Marketing Management, 57*, 37–49. doi:10.1016/j.indmarman.2016.05.032.

Romme, A. (2003). Making a difference: Organization as design. *Organization Science, 14*(5), 558–577.

Rost, K., Hözle, K., & Gemünden, H. (2007). Promoters of champions? Pros and cons of role specialization for economic process. *Schmalenbach Business Review, 59*, 340–363.

Storbacka, K. (2011). A solution business model: Capabilities and management practices for integrated solutions. *Industrial Marketing Management, 40*(5), 699–711.

Terho, H., Haas, A., Eggert, A., & Ulaga, W. (2012). It's almost like taking the sales out of selling': Towards a conceptualization of value-based selling in business markets. *Industrial Marketing Management, 41*(1), 174–185.

Ulaga, W., & Eggert, A. (2006). Value-based differentiation in business relationships: Gaining and sustaining key supplier status. *Journal of Marketing, 70*(January), 119–136.

18

Value Co-creation Analysis in Customer–Supplier Network Relationships

Nina Helander and Vilma Vuori

Introduction

To have a successful business, companies must be able to create value through their sold products and services given to their customers and also capture part of that value by themselves. Value is, however, not merely tied to the actual object of exchange; instead, it is dependent on the successfulness of the entire relationship between the customer and the supplier (see, e.g., Lindgreen and Wynstra 2005). The value that the customer perceives is also relative to the competition, meaning the alternative solutions the customer is considering or has available for a particular need (Ulaga 2003). The supplier should be able to create more value than the customer can achieve by choosing another solution created by a different competitive supplier. This kind of differential value is very hard to

N. Helander (✉)
Tampere University of Technology, Tampere, Finland

V. Vuori
University of Vaasa, Vaasa, Finland

J. Vesalainen et al. (eds.), *Practices for Network Management*,
DOI 10.1007/978-3-319-49649-8_18

define and measure, however, because the expectations of customers are based on the alternatives available on the market (i.e., whether the impact of a similar or substitute product is remarkable). Thus, measuring of differential value always requires a mapping of other potential solutions as well and then a comparison of those with the one under consideration. Usually, it is not an easy task to identify which options are seen as potential and comparable solutions in the eyes of the customer.

For the supplier, it is essential to understand the alternatives that a customer considers to the supplier's offerings. In general, a false perception of value is more likely when there are intangible elements and services, systemic and complex goods, benefits that are not immediate, post-purchase costs, costs of consumables, products, and services that are new to the customer, and last, infrequently purchased goods (Parolini 1999). Essential to the current understanding of value is its subjectivity and the idea of perceived value. These areas refer to the basic nature of value for the customer; the value created by the supplier is in the end thus measured in the mind of the customer, which leads in most cases to a created value that is very hard to measure but still not a mission impossible.

In this chapter a value co-creation measurement tool is proposed for a dyadic level of interaction, specific to the customer–supplier boundary. The tool has three phases. The first two are its measurement parts: first, a measurement is carried out from the supplier perspective to identify the most valuable customers, and second, an analysis is carried out from the customer perspective to find out how value can be co-created in such a way that it maximizes the customer's value perception. The third phase is an actual value co-creation development (i.e., the encounter process) based on suitable relational business practices.

Theoretical Background

Taking a fairly broad perspective then, the concept of value can be seen in terms of a trade-off between benefits and sacrifices. These benefits and sacrifices can be understood in monetary terms, but also as including non-monetary rewards, such as competence, market position, and social rewards. Non-monetary costs can include, for example, the time, effort, energy, and amount of conflict that have to be engaged in by the customer to obtain the desired product or service.

Whether value is monetary or non-monetary, and whether absolute or differential, it always needs both a creator and a capturer. Sometimes these can be one and the same actor, and indeed, often there are several actors involved. However, in the methodology used for our study and in the context of networks, it is reasonable to differentiate between the value creator and the value capturer. It should be noted still, however, that each actor in the value network needs to both create and capture if she/he is to build a long-term and successful value network. Both value creation and value capture can also be viewed from a functional perspective. This kind of function-oriented viewpoint on value, which was introduced by Walter et al. (2001), offers a more complete view of the types of activities that actors can perform in order to create more value for the network members. According to the function-oriented value analysis, a company may gain value from its relationships through both direct and indirect functions. Direct functions bring value that is easier to measure financially and realize in the context of the relationship between the company and the customer. Indirect functions, in contrast, also require the input of third parties, and those outcomes are less easy to measure financially. The notion of value-creating functions of this kind can illuminate the discussion about which activities and functions are likely to create the most value (or any value in the first place).

Another important aspect in the value creation approach is that by understanding the customer's value creation process, the supplier can more thoroughly identify the problems that the customer has concerning his/her own business activities. It has been argued that by understanding the customer's value creation process, the supplier can notice problems and concerns that the customer organization itself does not know (Storbacka ct al. 1999). By providing a solution to these unrecognized problems, the supplier can offer a more valuable relationship to the customer than the competitive suppliers can, leading to a mutual value co-creation relationship between a seller and a buyer. All in all, value co-creation builds on good understanding and sound measurement of the supplier process, the customer process, and the encounter process (see, e.g., Payne et al. 2008).

Description of the Tool

Step 1: Supplier Value Creation Process

Measurement Objective: What Value Does the Company Receive from the Customer?

A potential way to analyze the value creation potential of a counterpart is presented by Walter et al. (2001). According to this function-based approach to value creation, value can be measured using seven value functions that can be related to a company's performance either directly or indirectly (Fig. 18.1). Indirect functions are created through network relationships and are usually non-monetary in nature, which makes them difficult to measure. Direct functions can materialize also in dyadic relationships and are therefore easier to measure.

The direct monetary functions are known as profit, volume, and safeguard functions. Profit function refers to the profit gained from selling product(s) to a customer. Volume function is about the selling volume of these products to customers, which helps to exceed the necessary minimum utilization of the supplier's capacities. Safeguard function is the possibility of "guaranteeing" a level of business that serves as insurance against crises or difficulties the supplier experiences with other customers.

The indirect value creation functions are innovation, market, scouting, and access. Innovation function refers to the possibility of product and

	Function	Example of measurement question
VOLUME	Securing a "break-even" volume	"How large projects / amount of purchases this customer has acquired from us in last year?"
PROFIT	Providing a positive cash flow	"How much revenue per sold item we got from this customer in last year?"
SAFEGUARD	Obtaining stability and control in sales terms within a dynamic marketplace	"How long contracts we have with this customer?"
INNOVATION	Obtaining technological knowhow and creative ideas	"How many successful shared R&D projects we have had within five last year with this customer?"
MARKET	Gaining access to new markets	"How many new global market entries we achieved through this customer?"
SCOUT	Providing possibility to gain critical information	"How useful information about competitors (e.g. pricing) we have gained from this customer?"
ACCESS	Allowing access to third parties	"How many contacts with government agencies leading to useful cooperation in new market areas we have gained from this customer?"

Fig. 18.1 Direct and indirect value functions (based on Walter et al. 2001)

process innovation with a particular customer. Market function is about the possibility of acquiring information about potential new customers, the initiation of contacts with new customers, and receiving referrals and/or recommendations to potential new customers from a particular customer. The scouting function refers to the market, competitor, and other information that can be acquired through a particular customer. The access function refers to gaining access to relevant other actors through a particular customer.

Each of these functions acts as a measure of the value creation potential of its counterpart. Under each function, more specific questions should be posed to enhance measurement. For example, under the profit function the exact measurement question might be, "How much revenue per sold item did we get from this customer in the last year?" For the market function, the measurement question could be, "How many new global market entries have we achieved through this customer?" For the innovation function, the measurement could be, for example, "How many successful shared R&D projects have we had within the last five last years with this customer?" Thus, the goals of these functions are to set more specific measurement questions through which the different customer relationships are rated and compared. It is possible to give the same weight to each function or give more weight to certain functions that are more relevant for a specific market area. Based on these ratings, the company is able to identify the most valuable customers to focus on in the next step of the analysis.

Step 2: The Customer Value Creation Process

Analysis Objective: What Kind of Value Can Be Created for the Customer?

This view underscores the importance of understanding value creation as a process during which the customer and supplier interact, and thus, not only the product, but also the overall value of the co-creation process through which the product is developed, marketed, and delivered tovthe customer should be considered (Kothandaraman and Wilson 2001). The process view is especially relevant in terms of service aspects, as the value a customer perceives may be different during the exchange process and afterward when the customer is able to evaluate the outcome of the process more thoroughly (Lapierre 2000).

The basis of the value creation process approach is to understand value creation from the customer's viewpoint and through understanding which kind of process phases that value is created and which kind of challenges occur from the customer's viewpoint. By offering solutions for these challenges, the supplier is able to support the customer in critical tasks and take a key step toward value co-creation (see Fig. 18.2).

The basic idea of the value creation process analysis is to divide the overall process into different phases. As seen in Fig. 18.2, these process phases are identification of needs, purchase, implementation, and, finally, utilization. In these process phases the boundary-spanning practices are carried out, and within these phases, the encounters, which are opened up in the next step of the analysis, play a critical role. Furthermore, in each of these phases the customer has its own problems and challenges. Usually also the supplier company focuses on only some of these phases—mainly the purchase phase, as they want to win the customer case, and naturally also the implementation phase. The customer, however, faces

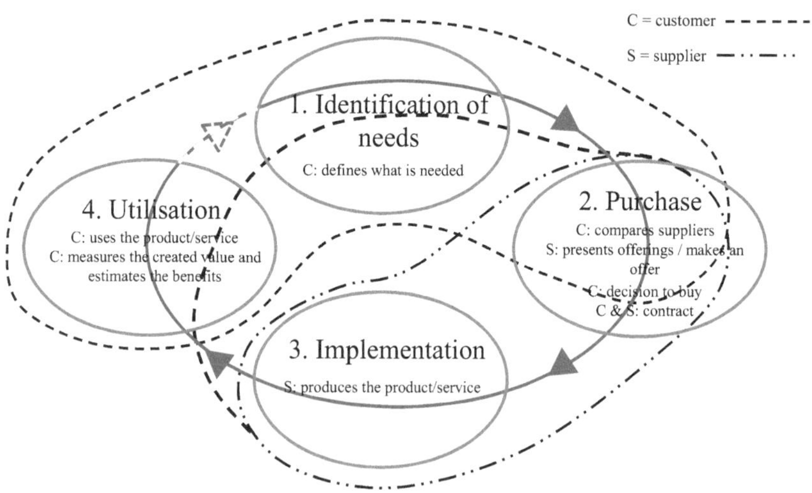

Fig. 18.2 Customer value creation process phases

usually most of the challenges in the need identification and the utilization phases. At the end, most of the value is perceived by the customer in the utilization phase. If the supplier is able to identify the key challenges and to support the customer to overcome those challenges in all of these phases, and especially in the need identification and utilization phases, then the co-creation of value is enhanced. In many cases, the customer's challenges in these process phases are so holistic that the supplier needs complementary resources and competences from other network actors. Thus, value co-creation usually does not happen only between the dyadic level of interaction and within the supplier–customer boundary, but must be leveraged to a wider network in order to achieve best possible value co-creation.

Step 3: The Encounter Process

Objective: How to Develop Value Co-creation

In order to really achieve the level of value co-creation, the processes of the supplier and the customer should be joint (see, e.g., Hirvonen and Helander 2001) as an encounter process (see e.g., Payne et al. 2008). The encounter process consists of a series of interactions between the supplier and the customer (Payne et al. 2008), and thus, it provides a continuation of touch points wherein the different representatives of both organizations of the dyad face each other. The encounter process also includes the physical elements enabling the interaction, such as the space and the IT systems. According to Payne et al. (2008), the encounter process is developed based upon the different types of encounters that each impacts the customers differently. Encounters can be emotion supporting encounters (such as stories and recognition), cognition supporting encounters (such as scripts and customer promises), and behavior and action supporting encounters (such as trials and know-how communication). These encounter types cover rather broadly the key aspects of value creation—symbolic, emotional, functional, and economic—as proposed in earlier research (see, e.g., Rintamäki et al. 2007). Based on the value creation analysis, those encounters that support the most value co-creation need to be identified and further developed. Even though the original research on the encounter process (Payne et al. 2008) concentrated only on the dyads between the customer and the supplier, they can also be used as tools to build the boundary practices and value co-creation between the broader networks.

As stated previously, the value creation process analysis usually reveals the need to cooperate with other network actors in order to be able to provide superior value for the customer. It is not usually feasible to try to create value for the customer merely through the company alone and the company's limited competencies when there is the option of allying with other companies that can complement the existing competencies and jointly create superior customer value. Thus, in a network, the value that is created for customers should be created within a web of actors, where each actor performs activities related to its core competence. The network operates in order to create value for the end customer, but each actor also contributes something to the creation process and in return captures something from the network. If the supplier tries to create superior value for the customer only, in the long run, the supplier might well also do things for the customer that are not related to its core competence, and thus, serving the customer may no longer be profitable. However, when the network is constructed of those complementary core competencies needed to create superior value for the end customer, then each supplier actor does not have to make major sacrifices. Instead, each actor can ultimately capture more value from the network than it originally contributed.

Case Description

The tool was applied in a B2B context, specifically in the ICT sector. First, the function-based value analysis was carried out to discover what kind of value the supplier is able to capture from its customer relationships. This part of the analysis was carried out by gathering internal data from the CRM system and other internal data sources, and then implementing a series of internal workshops where the key personnel responsible for customer relationships were involved. In the first workshop, the different value functions were weighted by their importance from the firm's perspective, and further still, additional specific measures under each of the functions were developed. In the second workshop, the key customers were evaluated based on these identified measures. Each customer received a value function rate, which indicated which customers were the most valuable for the firm. The representatives of the case firm perceived the measurement very useful, as it gave a more detailed, but, at the same time, a very holistic, view on the value capture potential of the customer portfolio. It also revealed which customer relationships should receive more emphasis.

In the second phase of the analysis, the most valuable key customers identified in the first analysis phase were chosen for further value analysis and under a development of relational practices. The purpose of the value process analysis was to understand the customer's needs better because this kind of understanding is necessary before relational practices can be further developed. In this second phase, five customer organizations were chosen, and from each at least two representatives were interviewed. Altogether, 13 thematic interviews were carried out, where all four value creation process phases were discussed thoroughly with the customer representative. These interviews not only discussed about the success factors and the biggest obstacles within all four phases, but also identified the softer "feelings" side of the interviewee in each phase. Using this approach, the overall value, including not only economic factors but also emotional and symbolic one, was then identified.

A process analysis enabled the measurement of the most valuable actions and practices that the supplier was able to carry out within its customer relationships. These were not monetary in nature; instead, they were related to the caring attitude and know-how of the supplier company and the agile methods that the company personnel used with the customer. As such, the supplier company seemed to already have potential for relational practices for managing and developing their customer relationships.

However, also based on the analysis, the key challenges in value creation were identified. It became evident that the supplier had almost totally neglected the need identification phase, even though all of the key customers had severe challenges in this phase. Furthermore, the customers also expected to receive more support in this phase, as they relied on the supplier's expertise on the subject. Another key finding was that the customers were most disappointed in the supplier's action (or in better terms, non-actions) in the utilization process. In many cases the customer felt that they were left alone with their problems in the utilization phase. Even with a little more input and concentration on this phase, the supplier would have grown the value creation to a new level. However, the biggest obstacle in supplier–customer relationship management was the shift between the different value creation process phases. For example, when moving from the acquisition phase to the implementation phase, the key personnel taking care of the project were usually changed in the supplier company. This action in turn caused feelings of non-trust and even a sense of neglect among the customers. Lack of trust was further hindering the potential of true value co-creation within the dyad. This was an interesting finding from the viewpoint of the boundary-spanning process; that is, more interaction was needed within the supplier company.

Based on these two phases of the value measurement analysis, the most important phase, the development of the relational practice and the value co-creation within the dyadic relationships, was started. This phase included the building of an encounter process between the supplier and the customer, where special emphasis was placed on solving the challenges identified in the analysis phases. First, a key account manager was named for each of the key customers so as to take care of the interaction and build trust (an emotion supporting encounter). This person took on the whole responsibility of taking care of the customer relationship and took care that the shifts between different value process phases were smooth ones. Second, continuous value measures (cognition supporting encounters) were developed and put into use in key customer relationships. These measurements were divided into strategic, tactic, and operational levels, including different kinds of measurement items and a varying sequence of measurement. Third, information and knowledge sharing practices (behavior and action supporting encounters) were taken under special consideration and development not only with the customer, but also within the supplier company's personnel who were participating in customer projects and the different value creation process phases. At the moment, the supplier company would also be building network cooperation with other supplier companies to create more value for the cooperating customer.

Conclusions

The tool presented in this chapter offers a path toward better understanding of value co-creation within customer–supplier boundary of network relationships. Its limitation is, however, that it takes the customer–supplier boundary as the unit of analysis, meaning that the analysis needs to be carried out for each customer–supplier relationship in the network and one by one at first. Only after that process can the measurement results be bundled. However, the value measurement usually reveals the commonalities within the different relationships, and thus, enables identifying and building the key encounters and relational business practices that do support value co-creation.

References

Hirvonen, P., & Helander, N. (2001). Towards joint value creation processes in professional services. *The TQM Magazine, 13*(4), 281–291.

Kothandaraman, P., & Wilson, D. T. (2001). The future of competition: Value-creating networks. *Industrial Marketing Management, 30*(4), 379–389.

Lapierre, J. (2000). Customer-perceived value in industrial contexts. *Journal of Business & Industrial Marketing, 15*(2/3), 122–145.

Lindgreen, A., & Wynstra, F. (2005). Value in business markets: What do we know? Where are we going? *Industrial Marketing Management, 34*(7), 732–748.

Parolini, C. (1999). *The value net. A tool for competitive strategy*. Chichester, UK: John Wiley & Sons Ltd.

Payne, A., Storbacka, K., & Frow, P. (2008). Managing the co-creation of value. *Journal of the Academy of Marketing Science, 36*(1), 83–96.

Rintamäki, T., Kuusela, H., & Mitronen, L. (2007). Identifying competitive customer value propositions in retailing. *Managing Service Quality, 17*(6), 621–634.

Storbacka, K., Blomqvist, R., Dahl, J., & Haeger, T. (1999). *Asiakkuuden arvon lähteillä*. CRM Finland Oy, WSOY Kirjapainoyksikkö: Juva (in Finnish).

Ulaga, W. (2003). Capturing value creation in business relationships: A customer perspective. *Industrial marketing management, 32*(8), 677–693.

Walter, A., Ritter, T., & Gemünden, H. G. (2001). Value creation in buyer-seller relationships. *Industrial Marketing Management, 30*(4), 365–377.

19

Value Curve as a Multipurpose Tool—From Self-assessment to Forming Collaborative Networks

Elisa Kallio and Antti Saurama

Introduction

This chapter introduces a novel approach to address a variety of strategic resource configuration problems, ranging from difficulties in differentiating one's business in the market, complications in unveiling existing levels of customer satisfaction or, for example, finding solutions on how to form network-level resource configurations which match the needs and wants of customers, by applying the practice lens on a strategic profiling and visualization tool, designed originally for organizations to assess their competitive advantage and current disadvantages in their operating environment. With specific focus on managing value creation in networks, we first introduce the theoretical foundations of the tool, after which a real-life case example will illustrate how the tool can be employed in practice.

E. Kallio (✉) • A. Saurama
University of Turku, Turku, Finland

J. Vesalainen et al. (eds.), *Practices for Network Management*,
DOI 10.1007/978-3-319-49649-8_19

While the ever-increasing competition in the global market is encouraging businesses to move from product-focused thinking to value-based operations in order to attract or retain customers (e.g. Vargo and Lusch 2004), in industries where firms are closely working together to create value in different parts of service ecosystems, even joint value proposals are co-created by different members of the network in order to attract buying parties (Tokman and Beitelspacher 2011). Problems managers often face in such situations are related to resource configurations; how to strategically combine the existing resources of the firm to fit the needs of the customers and are there other resources within the firm's network which could be adding value if acquired or combined? Through value co-creation, as a result of integration of interfirm resources, firms can enhance and facilitate value creation within their networks which provide benefits not only for themselves but also for the collaborating parties (e.g. Karpen et al. 2012; Wieland et al. 2012).

The value curve originates from Kim and Mauborgne's (2002, 2004, 2005a, 2005b) famous *Blue Ocean Strategy* in which the tool is introduced as part of strategy formation process in which value leaps are attempted to be created both for the customer and the for the value selling company. This section of the book first introduces a number of methods the value curve can be used to assess one's company or network after which it shows, by using a case study, how the tool is first used in practice, and second, how the tool is shaped into a new, more functional form for network management purposes as a result of the understandings and interpretations of the practitioners on the tool itself and by the context of its use (Jarzabkowski and Kaplan 2015). Furthermore, this practical example showcases the value curve's utility as a functional management tool for value co-creation within networks in which formation of joint value propositions from a number of ecosystem members to end-customers create increased levels of value in comparison to the more traditional two-party value creation (seller-buyer). By combining the traditional management tool with the practice approach (e.g. Jarzabkowski and Spee 2009), further understanding on how network-level value co-creation through joint value propositions occur can be developed, not forgetting very hands-on practical considerations for managers. The next section of this chapter outlines the key theoretical concepts behind the value curve.

Theoretical Background

Originally, the value curve is one of the tools used in Kim and Mauborgne's (2002) *Blue Ocean Strategy*, in which the process of creating strategy is viewed as reconstructionist (Kim and Mauborgne 2005a). In the reconstructionist's view on strategy, actions are perceived to create market structures in comparison to the more traditional structuralist view in which market structures determine the rules of the game in existing markets (Kim and Mauborgne 2009). In order to survive in existing markets or to create new markets, firms need to continuously integrate and reconfigure a competitive set of resources and capabilities (Prahalad and Hamel 1990; Teece et al. 1997; Eisenhardt and Martin 2000). As part of value creating systems, in which members of the value systems reconfigure resources and try to find right constellations to benefit all actors while co-creating value (Normann and Ramirez 1993; Maglio et al. 2009; Wieland et al. 2012), the burdensome task of managers becomes to ensure that the selected resource combinations are directed toward exploiting the core competences of the firm; otherwise, value creation can be hindered (Zenger 2013). That is, value creation is a dynamic process which can include not only numerous individuals and organizations but also information and technology (Maglio et al. 2009; Maglio and Spohrer 2013). In order to shed light on how such boundary spanning activity is done in business networks in practice, this chapter of the book explains the theoretical frameworks related to the task, after which a practical case example follows.

In the original use of the value curve, as described in the *Blue Oceans Strategy* (Kim and Mauborgne 2002, 2004, 2005a, 2005b), two curves are drawn; one portraying the competitor and another one the focal company. Each value curve is constructed and visualized using two dimensions: a horizontal dimension for the individual value elements (or competing factors if aiming to outline a new strategy) and a vertical dimension for the rating of each individual element/competing factor. The ratings, usually numerical values, are connected by drawing a curved graph. A figure containing multiple value graphs is referred as a value canvas.

Depending on the specific use of the tool, the same graphic can include several curves: for example, one or more of the focal companies or a comparison graph with several companies. Ratings can be made either by the firm itself or by the customer in cases in which customer satisfaction is measured. Once the value curve has been drawn, one can identify factors or elements on the horizontal axis which emphasis should be reduced when forming a value proposition for the customer (e.g. cutting costs to match industry standards) or eliminated altogether if considered moot. Also, a need for introducing new factors or elements that need to be added to the value proposition can be detected or factors or elements that should be more strongly emphasized to outdo the competition on the network level. (Kim and Mauborgne 2005a).

While the traditional use of the value curve tool emphasizes its usefulness in self-assessment or in customer assessment, our example shows how using the practice lens, the tool can be used for value co-creating purposes in business networks. Whereas value creation is often perceived as an abstract goal (e.g. Grönroos 2011), the practice lens encourage us to look at it as a set of actions executed by organizational members (e.g. Johnson et al. 2007). That is, value creation is something that people do while interacting, not something an organization possesses and passes on (cf Balogun and Johnson 2004; Chia and MacKay 2007). Nevertheless, it must not be forgotten that the actions of individuals carry outcomes on the organizational level. On the network level, this means that the sum of joint organizational value creating efforts is larger than those executed by single organizations: baking a larger cake to benefit the network instead of brawling over shares of the existing market.

Description of the Tool

This section describes various ways in which the value curve can be utilized in for different company and network purposes, including business performance, customer satisfaction, differentiation, value proposition redesign or constructing a business strategy. The curve and its elements as such are straightforward and easy to use whereas the selection of factors provides variety of possibilities for different practical outcomes and utilization.

In the business performance purpose, either a firm itself or its customer will numerically rate the firm's absolute performance in selected criteria. The selection of criteria (value elements) can be made by the company itself (what we think are the most important functions and characters of our performance, like quality, price, communication, and innovativeness) or these can be selected by the customer (what customers generally value as important elements of specific products or services). In this form, the value curve can also serve as a customer feedback tool.

In the comparative or relative performance purpose, a customer is asked to rate also one or several competitors against the same criteria/ elements. A firm can in such a case assess how it performs against its competitors in the market. This approach can be further extended to cover supplier network and its integrator and be assessed against other networks and integrators (see e.g. in Fig. 19.1).

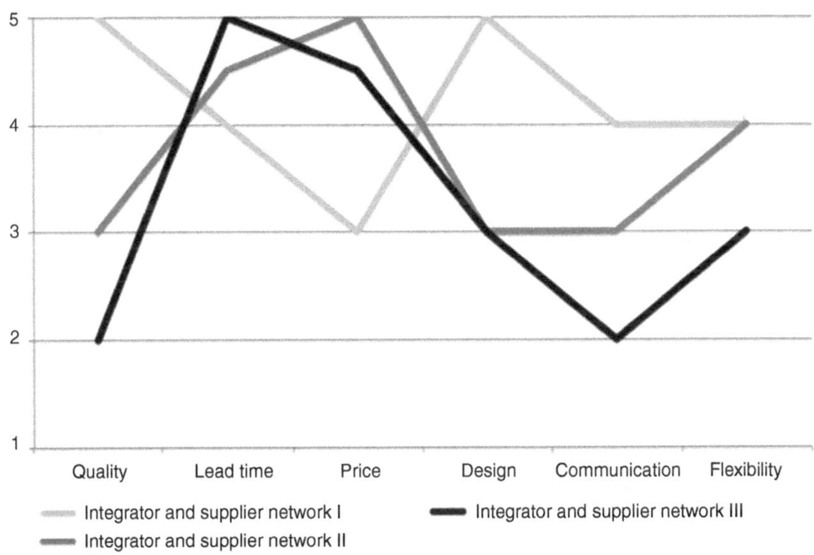

Fig. 19.1 Descriptive illustration of the value curve comparing three different supplier integrators according to their customer performance (1 = low, 5 = high). The gray pillars point the most distinctive differentiating factors between the networks

In the differentiation purpose, value curves or a value canvas can be created to identify the value profiles, differences and similarities between companies. This can reveal, for example, if all the competing firms have similar value elements and performance (all companies deliver excellent quality with a low price) or whether there are clear dissimilarities between the competitors (all companies deliver low price products, some accompany the low price with high quality and some others with excellent lead time) as descriptively illustrated in Fig. 19.1. This exercise helps firms to identify the competition profiles between the companies and to differentiate by changing their own performance preferences.

There are many possibilities in how to select the value elements and criteria in each of the cases listed above. For example:

- the firm itself could select criteria based on, for example, the firm's key performance criteria and request a customer to rate their performance;
- the firm could inquire a customer to identify, for example, factors that provide most value-added and ask the customer then to rate the firm's ability to create value in each of the selected elements;
- the firm could ask a customer similarly to identify factors that provide most value-added, and the firm compares its own key performance criteria against it; and
- the firm could first request a customer to rate its performance according to criteria set by the firm after which the customer would weigh the importance of each criteria.

Other firms'/networks' value curves can be added to visualize and understand the relative perspective.

All of the variations and modifications serve the firm's or network's understanding on how it succeeds to provide value for the customer, how value is perceived by the customer, and how the firm/network competes with other firms/networks in the market. Therefore, the value curve can be used as a solution method to multiple of analyses, for example:

- obtaining customer feedback;
- identifying competition factors;

- comparing available market offerings and choices;
- identifying differentiation factors;
- selecting new customer strategies; and
- setting new performance standards.

The case study explains next how the value curve tool was employed as a network management tool in practice and how a new method of using the tool was created as a result.

Case Study: Transformation from Performance and Value Perceptions of Asian Customers to Joint Value Propositions to End-Customers

This section introduces a case study in which the value curve tool was first applied to assess the business performance of a focal case company from the perspective of two of their Asian customers, which led to strengthening mutual cooperation in the network and encouraged the firms to consider forming a joint value proposition for an end-customer. The context of the study was the marine industry in which many companies are intertwined in value co-creating activities within their value systems. Massive vessels are constructed piece-by-piece; thus, the number of suppliers involved in producing and installing each part is vast. The two Asian customer companies mentioned above were both large scale manufacturers whose company profiles and wants and needs were considered to be identical to a large extent by the research group conducting the case study. This case study is part of a longitudinal action research project in which the research team conducting the case study has been closely cooperating with the focal case company for a number of years. The case study was completed by interviewing two Asian customers face-to-face, identifying jointly the key value elements and asking for a performance rating of the focal case company.

First, a list of value factors was drafted by the researchers based on their understanding on what the practitioners, the engineers and sales managers working in the focal case company, the supplier, considered as the most important from the perspective of the customer. This list was then shown to the interviewees, practitioners employed by the Asian customer companies of the focal company, and after a joint assessment conducted by the interviewers and company representatives, new factors were added according to the suggestions of the interviewees. The additions were additional performance criteria that customer companies also highly value besides the original suggested criteria and where they base their buying decisions from the various suppliers. In our case, for example, cooperation factor was added to be further evaluated according to customers' preferences, highlighting the importance of smooth interaction on the personal level collaboration during the whole lifetime of design, manufacturing and delivery.

As the process was repeated with two similar types of customers, it was possible to identify performance areas of excellence and areas of improvement potential. After the customer interviews, both the value factor mix and the value curves were analyzed against the focal company's own expectations. This process enabled the value curve tool to be used in collaboration with the customer which subsequently led to creation of deeper, mutual understanding of what the practitioners of the three firms (focal case firm and two customers) found highly important in their collaboration.

As a first round result, the analysis and assessment process provided for the supplier are the following:

1. important and structured information about the firm's performance and value profile toward the customer;
2. personal involvement and views of important customer stakeholder groups inside the customer organization which had never before been interviewed holistically;
3. a general agreement on improvement potential and concrete measures on how to better serve this customer group;
4. a deeper understanding of resource allocation while creating suitable resource configurations to create value for the customers; and
5. importantly, a shared agreement that the value proposition for the Asian customers has to be restructured to better meet the needs and value expectations of the customer.

This first round of assessment and analysis resulted in a process where the focal case firm's value proposition to the customer group was renewed and updated. This was followed by piloting a new value proposition in new sales cases. Equally importantly, the assessment resulted in a growing number of discussions between the supplier and the customers on how they could jointly guarantee the best possible value to the customer's customer, the end-customer (Fig. 19.2).

The second round of assessment of the value canvas resulted in the practitioners working for the supplier identifying factors that the interviewed practitioners of the Asian customer companies had completely overlooked and would be highly valued by the end-customer. Earlier business interaction between the focal case company and the end-customer had made the focal case company very aware of what the end-customer needed from its suppliers and contractors.

Some of the key value elements were completely missing and some shared factors had very different weights than what the end-customer would have placed.

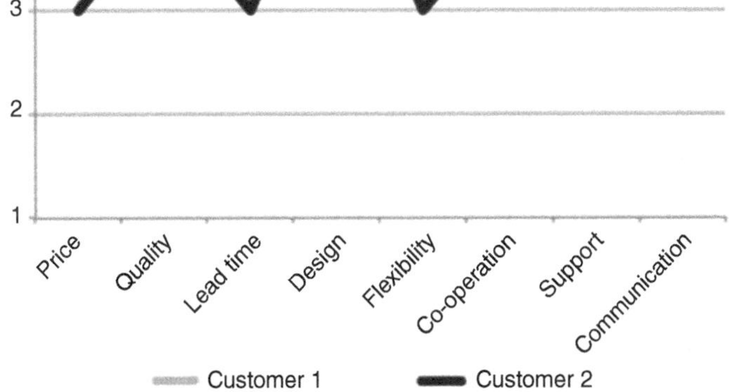

Fig. 19.2 Value profile compiled in two customer cases

A key result from using the value curve tool in practice was that the customer and supplier had begun serious discussions on the possibility of integrating offering and forming joint value propositions for the end-customer. Hence, as a result of using the value curve tool, the future business efforts of the focal case company and its two Asian customers lie more on combined resource and value configurations in comparison to before using the tool. By modifying the value curve tool to first further the understanding of the two separate practitioner parties on the manufacturing side of shipbuilding (focal case company and its two direct customers), the tool can be used to discover how two groups of practitioners in different parts of the value system can co-create value for an end-customer.

Conclusions

This section of the book introduced the value curve as a useful and highly versatile tool which can be used for a number of different value creating purposes not only on the firm level but also on the network level. Following are the key aspects to consider when utilizing the value curve: first, how I (and my resource network) intend to provide value for my customer, and does my customer have the same perception of my capabilities and available resources; and secondly, if I fail to possess all the required resources and capabilities needed to create value for my customers, who are the players in my value system I should collaborate with in order to co-create value using shared resource configurations?

By first introducing a number of more traditional ways of employing the value curve as a visualization tool and emphasizing its use in illustrating comparisons, we showed how the value curve and canvas provide a useful snapshot of the value profiles and offerings available in the market that sometimes, for example, complex and lengthy customer surveys fail to demonstrate in an easily comprehendible manner. Business managers can consider for example using the value curve and the value canvas by iterative steps: first assessing by themselves their firm's value-providing resources and capabilities, secondly asking customers for value assessments and thirdly, by adding competitor profiles to the canvas.

With our practical case study example, we illustrated the value curve's utility as a functional management tool for value co-creation within networks in which formation of joint value propositions from a number of ecosystem members to end-customers create increased levels of value in comparison to the more traditional two-party value creation (seller-buyer). As our case study showed, an increased level of value could be jointly offered to the end-customer by combining the forces of the practitioners from a supplier company and the practitioners of its two customer companies by using the tool in collaboration. Furthermore, by applying the practice lens both theoretically and empirically (Feldman and Orlikowski 2011), understanding of how network-level value co-creation through joint value propositions occur in practice was furthered.

References

Balogun, J., & Johnson, G. (2004). Organizational restructuring and middle manager sensemaking. *Academy of Management Journal, 47*(4), 523–549.

Chia, R., & MacKay, B. (2007). Post-processual challenges for the emerging strategy-as-practice perspective: Discovering strategy in the logic perspective. *Human Relations, 60*(1), 217–242.

Eisenhardt, K. M., & Martin, J. M. (2000). Dynamic capabilities: What are they. *Strategic Management Journal, 21*(10/11), 1105–1121.

Feldman, M. S., & Orlikowski, W. J. (2011). Theorizing practice and practicing theory. *Organization Science, 22*(5), 1240–1253.

Grönroos, C. (2011). A service perspective on business relationships: The value creation, interaction and marketing interface. *Industrial Marketing Management, 40*(2), 240–247.

Jarzabkowski, P., & Kaplan, S. (2015). Strategy tools-in-use: A framework for understanding "technologies of rationality" in practice. *Strategic Management Journal, 36*, 537–558.

Jarzabkowski, P., & Spee, A. P. (2009). Strategy-as-practice: A review and future directions for the field. *International Journal of Management Reviews, 11*(1), 69–95.

Johnson, G., Langley, A., Melin, L., & Whittington, R. (2007). *Strategy as practice, research directions and resources*. Cambridge: Cambridge University Press.

Karpen, I. O., Bove, L. L., & Lukas, B. A. (2012). Linking service-dominant logic and strategic business practice: A conceptual model of a service-dominant orientation. *Journal of Service Research, 15*(1), 21–38.
Kim, W. C., & Mauborgne, R. (2002). Charting your company's future. *Harvard Business Review, 80*(6), 76–83.
Kim, W. C., & Mauborgne, R. (2004). Blue Ocean strategy. *Harvard Business Review, 82*(10), 76–84.
Kim, W. C., & Mauborgne, R. (2005a). Blue Ocean strategy: From theory to practice. *California Management Review, 47*(3), 105–121.
Kim, W. C., & Mauborgne, R. (2005b). *Blue Ocean strategy. How to create uncontested market space and make the competition irrelevant*. Boston, MA: Harvard Business School Press.
Kim, W. C., & Mauborgne, R. (2009). How strategy shapes structure. *Harvard Business Review, 87*(9), 72–80.
Maglio, P. P., & Spohrer, J. (2013). A service science perspective on business model innovation. *Industrial Marketing Management, 42*(5), 665–670.
Maglio, P. P., Vargo, S. L., Caswell, N., & Spohrer, J. (2009). The service system is the basic abstraction of service science. *Information Systems and E-Business Management, 7*(4), 395–406.
Normann, R., & Ramirez, R. (1993). From value chain to value constellation: Designing interactive strategy. *Harvard Business Review, 71*(4), 65–77.
Prahalad, C. K., & Hamel, G. (1990). The core competence of the corporation. *Harvard Business Review, 68*(3), 79–91.
Teece, D. J., Pisano, G., & Shuen, A. (1997). Dynamic capabilities and strategic management. *Strategic Management Journal, 18*(7), 509–533.
Tokman, M., & Beitelspacher, L. S. (2011). Supply chain networks and service-dominant logic: Suggestions for future research. *International Journal of Physical Distribution & Logistics Management, 41*(7), 717–726.
Vargo, S. L., & Lusch, R. F. (2004). Evolving to a new dominant logic for marketing. *Journal of Marketing, 68*(1), 1–17.
Wieland, H., Polese, F., Vargo, S. L., & Lusch, R. F. (2012). Toward a service (ECO)systems perspective on value creation. *International Journal of Service Science, Management, Engineering, and Technology, 3*(3), 12–25.
Zenger, T. (2013). What is the theory of your firm? *Harvard Business Review, 91*(6), 72–78.

20

A Framework for Ecosystemic Strategizing and Change

Anastasia Tsvetkova, Tomi Nokelainen, Magnus Gustafsson, and Kent Eriksson

Introduction

Companies create value in interactions with other actors, including their suppliers and customers. Consequently, a company can be seen as an element in a functioning business ecosystem, where system value creation and company-specific value capturing, or appropriation, coevolve. As the supply chain in a mature industry fragments and innovativeness generally declines over time, the focus on systemic value creation tends to be replaced with local or company-specific efforts that sub-optimize system value creation (Utterback and Abernathy 1975). For instance, the focus of strategy-making tends to be placed on how to

A. Tsvetkova (✉) • T. Nokelainen • M. Gustafsson
Åbo Akademi University, Turku, Finland

K. Eriksson
Stanford University, Stanford, CA, USA

J. Vesalainen et al. (eds.), *Practices for Network Management*,
DOI 10.1007/978-3-319-49649-8_20

capture a larger share of the market (Bush and Sinclair 1992), and not on how to expand value creation in the market. Another example is that certain innovative companies can encounter obstacles while delivering their innovations if the current way of working inhibits them because of something like systemic historical lock-ins in terms of technology or institutionalized practices (Arthur 1989). Irrespective of the efforts to improve its own product or service, a company can find it difficult to affect a larger business ecosystem and the overall value creation logic within a given industry.

This chapter seeks to remedy these difficulties by presenting a framework for ecosystem-wide strategizing for improved value creation for the benefit of key actors. Put differently, the framework provides a general organizing outline for supra-organizational (ecosystemic) strategizing. As such, the framework can be seen as a *macro practice* for such inter-organizational strategizing, with several *micro practices* making an appearance and influencing specific strategizing episodes (c.f. Miettinen et al. 2009). Consequently, in this chapter, our focus is predominantly on the macro practice level, though throughout the text we present exemplary observations concerning micro practices as well.

The framework is concerned with redefining key ecosystem actors' strategic positions in a business ecosystem and increasing system value creation. Thus, it is intended to address the "tragedy of the commons"—like loss (Hardin 1968) of focus on system efficiency and company-level strategy-making; this latter factor is suboptimal with regard to the ecosystem-wide value creation and therefore, on average, suboptimal for the individual companies as well. The framework proposes a process through which key ecosystem actors can analyze the surrounding business ecosystem and its performance in terms of value creation, identify their strategic positions, and define and achieve new positions through affecting a positive change in the value creation and capturing logic in the ecosystem.

From a managerial point of view, the framework is useful for a number of reasons. Firstly, the business ecosystem perspective provides a lens to grasp the industry's complex, dynamic, and adaptive structure, which is crucial for formulating and implementing an informed strategy for any actor in it (c.f. Porter 2008). Instead of focusing on markets or traditional industry view, business ecosystems as a construct help to grasp the functional structure of an industry or a set of industries (Dalziel 2007). A business ecosystem has a goal or purpose, its *raison d'être*, which is determined by the needs and desires of the actors who pay for the ultimate products and/or services the ecosystem produces. This goal is fulfilled through a system of activities performed by various constituent actors; the changes in one part of it, such as exit or entrance of business actors, can affect the other actors as well as the overall value creation logic in the ecosystem and its performance in fulfilling the system goal. Each of the constituent ecosystem actors has a function within the activity system of the business ecosystem, and this can be either an opportunity or a challenge in realizing a strategic position for a focal company.

For example, the provisioning of taxi services for consumers is a result of a whole ecosystem of business actors, ranging from individual taxi entrepreneurs to manufacturers of automobiles and fuels. In this ecosystem, the relatively recent entry of Uber has created significant upheaval in several countries; for example, it has rearranged some of the key relationships between members as well as the ecosystem value creation and capturing models. Moreover, this change has, though somewhat controversially, increased the performance of the ecosystem in fulfilling its goal of provisioning taxi services to consumers (McGregor et al. 2015).

Furthermore, despite their dynamic character, business ecosystems are subject to inertial institutional barriers, such as regulations, social norms, and cognitive models (Scott 2008). Thus, in trying to change the value creation structure in a business ecosystem, it is crucial to be able to identify these boundaries and affect them through changing the status quo in terms of the distribution of roles and responsibilities, and appropriately altering the prevailing *industry mindset* or *industry recipe* (Spender 1986).

Acknowledging the interdependency between the elements of a system—business actors in a business ecosystem—we subscribe to a view that strategy-making also has to reflect the fact that the boundaries between different actors' activities are becoming more blurred (Gulati et al. 2012; Tsvetkova et al. 2014). Consequently, strategizing should move toward collective or supra-organizational strategy-making (Gadde et al. 2003). Companies can engage more easily in this movement by utilizing the framework presented in this chapter, which serves as an analytic tool.

The framework of ecosystemic strategizing and change has been developed and tested in the case of a short sea shipping ecosystem, in which key ecosystem actors have embarked on an ecosystem-wide effort to significantly improve the value creation capability of the focal ecosystem. The ecosystem comprises the shipping, shipbuilding, and other related industries that form a system for providing transportation of dry bulk cargo in the Baltic Sea. It includes a multitude of actors, such as ship operators, cargo owners, port operators, various technology providers, and so on, whose activities are interconnected and thus affect each other. In addition to being part of supra-organizational strategizing through which key ecosystem actors are reconfiguring the ecosystem for significant performance increase, we have also worked with two of these ecosystem actors throughout the whole process, including the organization-specific stages. Consequently, illustrative examples from this empirical case will be used throughout the chapter.

Theoretical Foundation for the Framework

Value Creation and Capturing in Business Ecosystems

Business ecosystems have been defined as economic communities supported by a foundation of interacting organizations and individuals, which produce goods and services of value to customers, who are themselves members of the ecosystem. Ecosystem members or actors tend to coevolve in terms of their capabilities and roles and align themselves with the directions set by one or more central companies (Moore 1996).

General systems research argues that the whole of the system is more than the sum of its parts (Simon 1996). A business ecosystem, in its complexity, can also be characterized by the fact that as a whole, it creates more value compared to the aggregate value that all the actors would create independently (Tsvetkova 2014). System value creation is usually at the heart of emerging ecosystems, while more mature or stagnating industries can find themselves in a situation when efforts of individual actors or clusters of actors compromise the achievement of the system goal (i.e., delivering value to the customer). Understanding of the value creation structure in a business ecosystem, as well as roles and responsibilities of business and non-business actors in relation to it, can shed light on whether system value creation can be increased or achieved more efficiently. Thus, business ecosystems can be analyzed with the explicit purpose of improving the value-creation performance of the system (Santos and Eisenhardt 2009). Asking whether there is potential for affecting value creation on a business ecosystem level needs to serve as a starting point for any company defining or redefining its strategic position, because value creation does not wholly reside at the company level.

As noted by Järvi (2013), most research on business ecosystems has emphasized organization-specific value capturing over systemic value creation. That is, the focus of exploring system "shaping" efforts revolves mostly around the way companies profit from system innovations by appropriating a larger share of total value creation (Teece 1986). Naturally, value capturing plays a crucial role in strategy formulation and implementation, since it ultimately determines a company's survival and growth (Hannan and Freeman 1977). The framework presented in this chapter focuses both on the way system value creation can be increased through a joint, or supra-organizational, effort by key ecosystem actors and on the way value can be captured by each of the actors so that the ecosystem is resilient and self-sustaining.

Such a view challenges the traditional perspective on competitive advantage, which emphasizes the maximization of the benefit for an individual company. The framework we propose, in turn, implies that both value creation and value capturing models at the ecosystem level are to be considered when attempting to shape ecosystems that have a sustainable competitive advantage over incumbent or other competing ecosystems. The reason for this is the fact that, as Moore (1996) noted, competition has shifted from the level of individual species (i.e., company level) to the level of entire business ecosystems.

Strategic Management

Strategic management—both as an academic discipline and as a practical organizational undertaking—still usually concerns one organization, maximizing the performance of that organization as the phenomenon of interest (Furrer et al. 2008; Nag et al. 2007). Therefore, while this traditional view acknowledges the existence and performance implications of inter-organizational phenomena such as cooperation (Gulati and Singh 1998), co-opetition (Brandenburger and Nalebuff 1998), and complementorship (Yoffie and Kwak 2006), the point of view predominantly remains at the level of a performance-maximizing organization.

Within strategic management literature, one influential view to conceptualize and understand the essence of strategy is perceiving it as a set of activities (Porter 1996) instead of the more traditional view of a general plan toward the performance (or other) goals of the organization (Mintzberg et al. 1998). In this conception, the strategy of an organization *is* the set of activities and especially their configuration that enables the organization to offer unique products and/or services, or to do so in a unique manner. What is more, in such an activity system-based view of strategy, there are no particular sources of competitive advantage as such, but rather the competitive advantage of an organization is embedded in or arises from the way the activities are put together (Porter 1996). In a way, this resembles the above-described view of an ecosystem consisting of components (actors), each of which contribute in a certain manner to the fulfillment of the ultimate task, but in this case within a single organization.

The unique feature of our framework is to apply the activity-based view on strategy not only at the organizational level, but also—and just as importantly—at the ecosystem level. Thus, the "strategy" of an ecosystem *is* the set of activities and their configuration with which the ecosystem performs its ultimate task, such as provisioning a taxi service. And if an ecosystem can be viewed in this manner, following Porter (1996), to *have* a strategy, then the ecosystem (i.e., its constituent actors collectively) can equally as meaningfully be seen as capable of *strategizing* (i.e., intentionally reconfiguring this activity system) as well.

Strategizing, in contemporary strategic management parlance, refers to strategy work or making of strategy (Whittington 2003). While there are differences in terms of how such work is understood, (e.g., in terms of its temporal duration, actors involved, or the end result [Vaara and Whittington 2012]), in virtually all conceptions, strategizing refers to deliberately (or relatively deliberately) shaping the organization's long-term direction and, ultimately, performance (ibid.).

In our case, if an ecosystem can be viewed as having a strategy in terms of the activity system it comprises, then strategizing at this level takes the form of collective strategy work by and among the constituent ecosystem members (or at least the most consequential or influential key actors capable of affecting a meaningful change in the activity system). Since this is an inter-organizational undertaking that intends to bring about a positive change at the ecosystem level (with intended positive implications for the constituent actors as well, of course), we refer to this strategy work as *supra-organizational strategizing*. Currently, this perspective is virtually absent in existing strategic management literature (Vaara and Whittington 2012).

Such strategizing is peculiar in that it is not guided and mediated by a uniform set of norms as in organizational strategy work, at least to a significant degree. Instead, the strategists—those who engage in the strategy work (Jarzabkowski and Spee 2009)—represent different organizational cultures, are subject to different performance goals and pressures, and may even apply different industry recipes (Spender 1986) in the case that they represent different industries as traditionally construed.

Description of the Framework

The framework consists of three main stages, which proceed from the ecosystem level to the organizational level:

- Stage 1. Analysis of business ecosystem
- Stage 2. Strategic (ecosystem) position and strategy formulation for each focal company
- Stage 3. Strategy implementation by each focal company

The process is reminiscent of a traditional view of a strategy process of analysis, formulation, and implementation (de Wit and Meyer 2010), but essentially concerns the ecosystem level as the starting point. Furthermore, while stages 2 and 3 are concerned with the organizational level, inter-organizational strategizing will be present and/or will affect all the stages. For example, establishing an ecosystem position—and consequently a strategy for a particular ecosystem actor—is highly dependent upon corresponding choices by other companies; the ecosystem activities performed by each of the companies must be compatible and interface with those performed by others. Moreover, to maintain inter-organizational cohesion and trust (hopefully) established at the first stage, organization-specific strategizing must honor and be compatible with mutual agreements already made, or iteratively engage supra-organizational strategizing practices again.

Thus, the framework constitutes a macro-level supra-organizational strategy practice, with three relatively distinct phases, all of which include a number of stage-specific micro-level practices. The framework has been employed in our case context in just such a manner, as a supra-organizational macro practice to formulate and implement (1) a jointly constructed strategic vision of a short sea shipping ecosystem and (2) corresponding company-specific positions and organizational strategies.

According to our experience, it is unreasonable to assume that this macro practice would unfold linearly stage-wise. Instead, the process appears to be rather messy by nature, requiring frequent iterations between the stages. Nonetheless, each stage in the overall supra-organizational practice is further described in detail (Fig. 20.1).

Stage 1: Business Ecosystem Analysis

To begin with, the focal business ecosystem must be analyzed jointly by the key ecosystem actors. Key aspects include system value creation logic and current structure of relationships and interactions among the actors, particularly the activities they perform with respect to the ultimate task of the ecosystem. Furthermore, problems and opportunities related to system value creation must be identified. Based on the results, it is possible to develop a detailed shared understanding of the current business ecosystem and envision the target business ecosystem, with increased ecosystem value creation with regard to its ultimate task as the main aspect of interest.

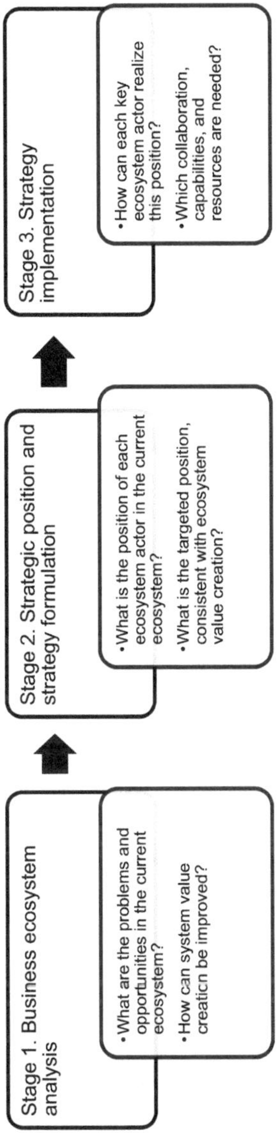

Fig. 20.1 The three stages of ecosystemic strategizing and change

However, according to our experience, such analysis requires an organizing framework to structure praxis and provide participants with a shared terminology to codify their thoughts. Moreover, a neutral facilitator (a non-member of the ecosystem) and neutral premises for the conduct of the practice are quite likely to catalyze joint strategizing both at this stage and at subsequent stages (c.f. e.g., Johnson et al. 2010).

An appropriate organizing framework for this stage may be obtained by combining *activity-based* and *function-based* views of business ecosystems. On the one hand, an ecosystem can comprise various functions to produce systemic value. For example, in the short sea shipping context, the ship must be navigated during a voyage, which in turn affects fuel consumption, safety, timeliness, and so on. However, such navigation can be performed, for example, by a ship operator itself (the captain onboard), or in the case of an autonomous (unmanned) ship, it may be performed remotely by a specific voyage execution service provider. In other words, an ecosystem function can be realized by alternative activity and/or actor configurations.

With such an organizing principle, the practice of analyzing a business ecosystem can be split in two sub-stages: (1) analysis of the current business ecosystem and each actor's position in it, and (2) envisioning the future ecosystem and each actor's position in it.

Analysis of the Current Business Ecosystem and Each Actor's Position in It

At this sub-stage, the participating actors need to analyze what the performances of the current ecosystem and its constituent actors are and how the current configuration of functions, activities, and actors work to bring about such performances. In other words, the analysis concerns both ecosystem-wide value creation and company-specific value capturing as a proportion of the ecosystem-wide value.

More specifically, the following questions need to be answered at this sub-stage:

- What is the basic task of the business ecosystem? Such a task can be, for example, to transport cargo or to supply energy to remote places.

- What are the major ecosystem functions required to perform this task?
- Which activities are currently performed to realize those functions, and which actors currently perform the activities?
- What are the interfaces between different functions and activities? How do they affect each other in terms of the flow of goods, information, and money?
- How much (end user) value is currently created by the ecosystem and by which functions, activities, and actors, and how is this value being captured by each actor?
- How are each of the actors currently incentivized?

Equipped with answers to these questions, a few types of problems can typically be somewhat effortlessly identified:

- Some actors are incentivized in a way that is detrimental to the performance of the ecosystem task—usually in a classic sub-optimizing manner. For example, in the short sea shipping context, several actors involved in vessel construction are incentivized with cost minimization to drive down the initial capital outlay for a new vessel, which leads to vessels that are affordable, but not built for high-capacity utilization, in-use performance, and lifetime profitability. As a consequence, ecosystemic performance is significantly undermined by inappropriate incentives by certain actors.
- The interfaces between certain business ecosystem functions and activities do not exist or are inadequate, which harms the overall ecosystem efficiency. For example, in the short sea shipping context, cargo owners (shippers) are usually not involved in designing new vessels, even though it is precisely their needs the ships are aiming to satisfy. As a result, inefficiencies of old ships are carried over to new ships in the form of suboptimal dominant designs because end customers' needs are not adequately heard.
- Certain actors do not fulfill their functions in the best possible way, or they create bottlenecks for system value creation. Often this is linked to the lack of incentives or disincentives to act differently. For example, in the short sea shipping context, cargo brokers typically earn through obstructing the flow of information between cargo owners

(demand) and ship operators (supply). In other words, more efficient and direct matching of supply and demand would hurt cargo brokers by making them less necessary, even though the ecosystem as a whole would enjoy significant performance increase.
- There are unfulfilled business ecosystem functions. For example, in short sea shipping, capacity utilization could be notably improved with computerized optimization of how ships and cargoes move in the system. Today, however, such systemic optimization function is by and large absent in most short sea shipping contexts.

Such identified problems lay the foundation for the next stage, envisioning the future business ecosystem and each actor's position in it.

It is important at this stage to keep the discussion fairly abstract in order to avoid blaming participating actors or to let any actor fall into defending their existing incentives. Again, a neutral facilitator and the practice conducted on neutral premises are likely to assist in this.

Envisioning the Future Business Ecosystem and the Company's Position in It

By addressing problems identified in the previous stage, it is possible to outline a conceivably better-performing ecosystem. Better performance, in turn, implies increased value creation through increased end-user value and/or lower costs.

In a nutshell, this comprises

1. designing a coherently configured set of activities to perform essential ecosystem functions, which would bring about an increase in ecosystem-wide value creation (i.e., an activity-based strategy [Porter 1996]) for the ecosystem; and
2. designing a future ecosystem position for each of the key ecosystem actors, in terms of the position's activities within the ecosystemic configuration (i.e., an activity-based strategy) for each of the key actors.

Quite obviously, the future ecosystem should fulfill (at least) the following criteria:

- Exhibit better performance potential than is currently the case (i.e., create more value through efficiency or effectiveness, or both)
- Provide all key actors (i.e., those who are capable of affecting the transition from the current to the new state, either positively or negatively) with sufficient incentives to embrace the change, with perceived equitability of value distribution as a particular concern
- Be realistic (credible) so as to capture the imagination of the key actors

According to our experience, these criteria are highly important, quite challenging to meet, and likely to require several iterations before satisfactory configuration is found. It is of particular importance to find efficient and effective ways, or practices, to codify and illustrate how each candidate configuration satisfies these criteria. In our case, transparently prepared business case calculations, graphical inter-organizational relationship depictions (flow of goods, information, and money), and graphical computer simulations have turned out to be efficient means toward this end.

With regard to inter-organizational relationships and the overall configuration of the ecosystem in particular, the future ecosystem can be described in terms of the interfaces between, and functions performed by, the constituent actors. Based on that, a roadmap for arriving at a new ecosystem can be drawn. The analysis within this stage can be performed, to continue the preceding list, using the following steps:

3. Preparing a graphical ecosystem activity map, which demonstrates value creation logic in the strategy of the ecosystem
4. Detailing each key actor's impact on system value creation in terms of its activities and their interfacing with activities performed by others
5. Developing a roadmap "from here to there," which explicates the actors' key actions required to achieve the envisioned state of the business ecosystem

While presented as a chronologically proceeding set of steps, according to our experience, these steps are highly iterative and intertwined. Also, the tools referred to above (such as the ecosystem activity map) are means, or practices, of facilitating and structuring the analytical process and communication of results instead of templates that enable a mechanistic analysis of ecosystems step by step.

Nonetheless, to highlight a practical tool, a graphical ecosystem activity map (see Fig. 20.2) is, in our experience, a useful summary means for formulating and depicting how value will be created in the envisioned ecosystem. For that, only the key activities required for the renewed business ecosystem need to be outlined for a meaningful depiction. The analysis starts from formulating what the ultimate ecosystem goal or task is, and which functional outputs are required to fulfill it (the area labeled "functional output" in Fig. 20.2). Then, key activities contributing to those outputs are mapped (the area labeled "ecosystem activities" in Fig. 20.2). It is possible that most activities are more or less the same in the current and future ecosystems, except for newly introduced activities, but there are likely to be significant differences in terms of how they are configured: which actors perform them and how they interface with each other.

The last layer in the ecosystem activity map (the area labeled "ecosystem governance" in Fig. 20.2) depicts the implications for governance changes. In the exemplary case depicted in Fig. 20.2, for instance, the highlighted company (a cargo handling solution provider) is to be involved in more activities: that is, to not only provide cargo handling solutions for cargo vessels based on predetermined requirements, but also to affect other activities such as fast cargo hold cleaning, fast vessel loading and unloading, and so on. This is because of the interdependency between those activities identified earlier in the process.

Co-created by the participating ecosystem actors through the above-described practice of supra-organizational strategizing, the ecosystem map serves as the basis for organization-specific strategizing. In other words, at the next stage, strategizing practice shifts largely to the organizational level—toward the more widely discussed concepts found in the strategy-as-practice literature (Vaara and Whittington 2012). Nonetheless, organizational strategizing must conform to the outcomes of the supra-organizational practice, or alternatively engage the supra-organizational practice again if changes are sought. According to our experience, the latter is highly likely in most organizations, resulting in multiple iterative rounds between the supra-organizational and organizational levels. This,

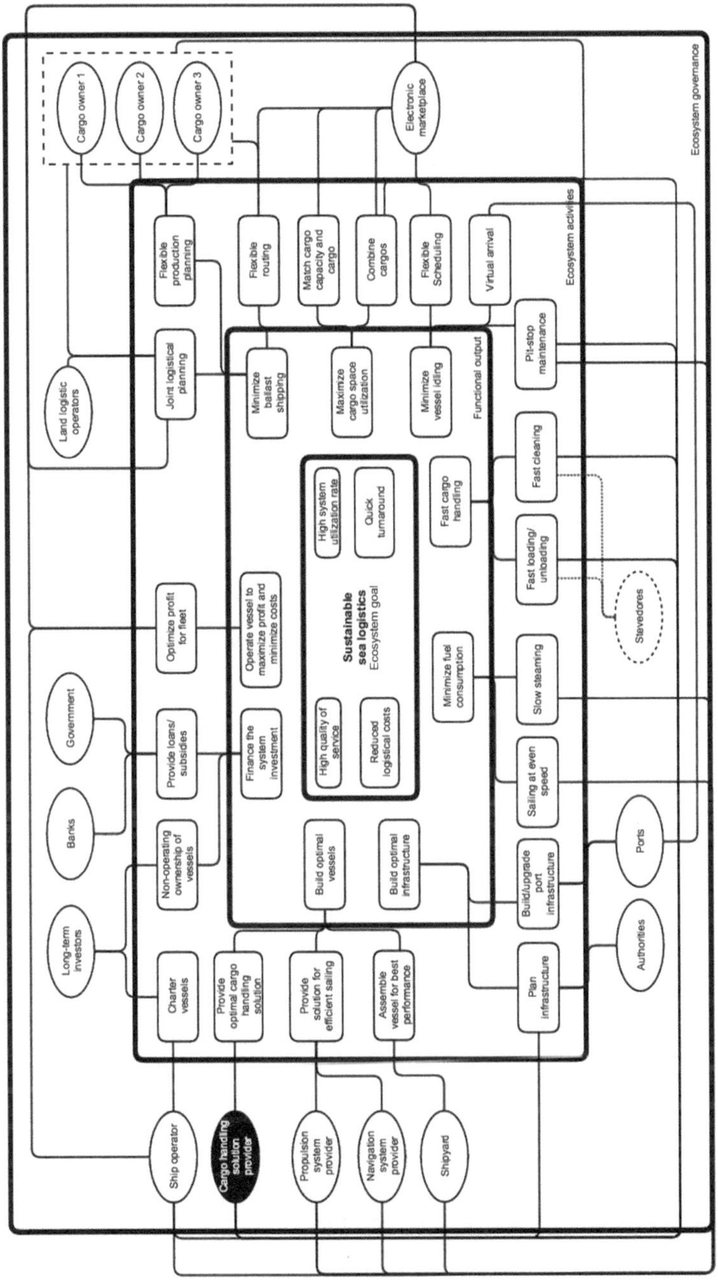

Fig. 20.2 An ecosystem activity map (an exemplary focal company is highlighted)

in turn, calls for efficient supra-organizational micro practices, especially with regard to codifying, analyzing, and illustrating any chances to avoid participant frustration.

Stage 2: Strategic Position and Strategy Formulation

The second stage is about formulating and describing the strategic position of each of the key ecosystem actors based on the opportunities identified during the previous stage and consistent with the co-constructed vision of the configuration of the future ecosystem.

In contrast to traditional strategic management prescriptions, however, the organizational position is not about defending against market forces or distancing the company from them (Kim and Mauborgne 2005), but rather about integrating each of the key actors into the envisioned ecosystem in a value-creating (and appropriately capturing) manner.

The method employed in the description of the aspired strategic position is, like at the ecosystem level, that of activity system mapping, though in accordance to its original intended organization-specific use (Porter 1996). As noted earlier, the aim of activity system mapping is to graphically represent the cornerstones of an organizational strategy and especially to show the interconnections between its elements: how all the elements reinforce each other and together constitute core contents and the logic of the strategy.

Because of the ecosystem-based nature of strategy formulation, a corresponding organizational strategy always needs to include three fundamental elements in its core (Bowman and Ambrosini 2000; Lepak et al. 2007; Barney and Clark 2007):

1. Creating added ecosystem value
2. Capturing added ecosystem value
3. Sustaining the organization's position in the ecosystem

Of these, elements 1 and 2 already have their outlines set at the previous supra-organizational strategizing stage.

Creating added ecosystem value. This should be the starting point of an organizational strategy in an ecosystem-based setting. Otherwise, "the pie does not grow" (i.e., the ecosystem does not create increased economic value to be enjoyed by the ecosystem members), and the aim of corporate strategy is relegated to merely trying to incrementally increase the organization's share of that "existing pie." Though already addressed at the previous stage with regard to future ecosystem design, it should be borne in mind that for any actor to substantially positively affect the ecosystem, increased value must be introduced into it, and, consequently, the strategy of the focal company and its depiction must be premised on this goal.

Thus, in the activity map of each of the key actors, the first segment of the map should concentrate on explicating the logic (i.e., the *organizational* activities and their interrelations) by which the focal organization introduces added value to the ecosystem. This constitutes the value-creation strategy of the focal organization.

Capturing added ecosystem value. To benefit the focal company in particular, it is evident that the strategy must also be premised on how the focal company itself can capture, or appropriate, a substantial proportion of that added value. In comparison to the previous aspect, this one is closer to the traditional notions of competitive strategy.

However, it is of the utmost importance to emphasize that in contrast to much traditional strategic management thinking (Bowman and Ambrosini 2000; Lepak et al. 2007), the aim is not to maximize value capturing in the usual sense, but rather to capture an equitable and mutually agreeable share of the ecosystem-wide value creation. In other words, prescriptions by equity theory (Carrell and Dittrich 1978) are very applicable at this as well as at the previous stage. Put simply, in a social setting, actors are highly sensitive to perceived equitability in benefit (value, payoff) distribution even beyond what their self-interests would warrant. A significant body of relatively recent research in experimental economics corroborates this view (Sanfey et al. 2003; Kirchsteiger 1994) beyond reasonable doubt. Thus, each of the ecosystem actors must be highly sensitive to what they have mutually agreed to in the supra-organizational strategizing stage and invoke the collective practices at that stage in all cases of doubt or change.

Consequently, the second segment in the activity map of each of the ecosystem actors should focus on detailing the activities through which the focal organization may capture *its fair and mutually agreeable share* of the expected value created in the envisioned future ecosystem. In any case of disagreement, likely the most feasible way to resolve it is to assess the relative *contribution* of the focal organization to the ecosystem-wide value creation (Greenberg 1986).

Sustaining one's own position. In order to ensure that the advantageous strategic position endures over time, both for the ecosystem as a whole and for the focal organization, each of the ecosystem actors must take into account the ways (or in the language of activity system mapping, the activities) through which the actor aims to sustain its position against competition and imitation in the future. This notion of advantage sustainability is a prime concern in mainstream competitive strategy as well (Barney 1991; Barney and Clark 2007), and not really constrained by supra-organizational strategizing. In other words, each ecosystem actor has substantial freedom of strategic choice with regard to this element.

In mainstream strategic management thinking in general—and in the competitive dynamics perspective in particular (Williams 2007)—sustainability is perceived as resilience toward hostile actions by competitors and other such actors, but sustainability in an ecosytemic setting refers to sustained contribution capability for ecosystemic value creation and therefore continued relevance for the ecosystem. Thus, the threat toward sustainability is more about becoming irrelevant than about defending against imminent opportunistic attacks by other ecosystem actors. And in an ecosystemic setting, arguably the best way to pre-empt any opportunistic attack is to ensure that the ecosystem as a whole, and thereby most likely the attacker itself, would be worse off as a result of having replaced a superior ecosystem value contributor.

More traditional sustainable competitive advantage in relation to immediate competitors within an ecosystem (i.e., the companies that can take on the role of the focal company) still needs to be maintained, for example through locking customers in or developing a particular fit with the overall ecosystem structure so that the focal company would not be easily replaceable. This, however, should not compromise the sustainable competitive advantage of the overall ecosystem and its capacity to remain flexible and adaptive in order to retain it.

Hence, the third and final segment in the activity map of the focal organization depicts those activities that aim at ensuring that the position outlined by the first two segments (value creation and value capturing) can be sustained over time.

Figure 20.3 illustrates the basic setup of the organization-specific activity map. It departs to a degree from Porter's (1996) original depiction, but according to our experience with two organization-specific cases in the short sea shipping ecosystem change initiative, it is better suited to ecosystem-based organizational strategy work, consistent with what is described earlier.

As shown in Fig. 20.3, the activity system map describes not only the activities themselves, but also the key corporate initiatives which actualize the activities and their intended organizational and ecosystemic outcomes as actualized in the initiatives. Especially the ecosystemic outcomes serve as points of interfacing with other actors in the ecosystem-wide activity map, since often such outcomes are not solely dependent on the undertakings of one organization alone, but instead are a result of activities by several actors performed in concert.

It is likely, however, that any attempted change in corporate strategy as well as disruptions in the status quo of the current ecosystem will elicit both support and, importantly, resistance. The sources for such support and resistance are both internal (employees) and external (stakeholders, other ecosystem members) to the focal company (Pardo del Val and Martínez Fuentes 2003; Barnett and Pontikes 2008).

Therefore, in order to proactively leverage and mitigate these reactions, each ecosystem actor must evaluate all the elements (i.e., activities) in its strategy in terms of

- which ecosystem actors stand to win and how; and
- which ecosystem actors stand to lose and how.

This evaluation serves as a feasibility assessment for the aspired strategic position and thereby allows one to identify

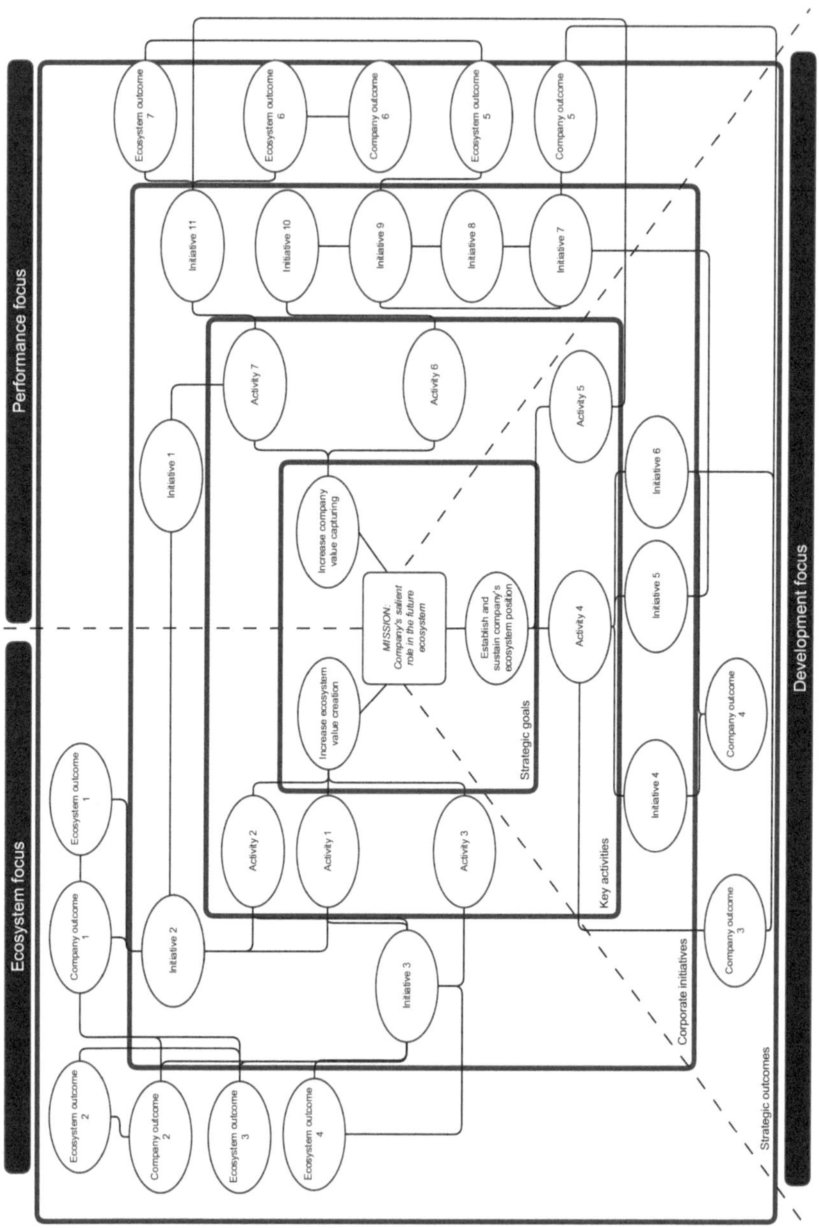

Fig. 20.3 The starting point of the activity system mapping-based organizational strategic position

1. if the strategy violates the agreements made among the participating ecosystem actors at the supra-organizational strategy; and
2. if the strategy is likely to encounter such overwhelming resistance from internal or other ecosystem actors that revision of the strategy is required.

In utilizing the framework, it is not necessary to meticulously "fill in" detailed enumerations of likely support and resistance, but rather to identify the most salient ones that probably are the most beneficial (support) and detrimental (resistance) with regard to the envisioned strategy. Of essence is a mindful and insightful assessment of these aspects, not a laborious production of itemized lists.

This assessment provides the basis for preparing the plan for strategy implementation, which should take both the ecosystemic and the organizational considerations into account in order to result in a feasible plan of action in bringing about the aspired future ecosystem, including the desired position of each of the focal organizations in it.

Stage 3: Strategy Implementation

Based on previous analysis, each ecosystem actor defines a detailed plan for strategy implementation. Of the stages in our overall framework, each of the focal organizations here can exercise the most individual judgment and choice, since organization-specific implementation is relatively little concerned with the supra-organizational setting and mutual agreements therein.

Thus, practice-wise, established literature on strategy-as-practice is generally very applicable (see Vaara and Whittington 2012 for a review), especially that concerning the critical role of middle management (e.g., Woolridge ct al. 2008; Rouleau 2005).

To summarize the key points in outline, implementation requires understanding about organizational (re)structuring, staffing, setting up governance structures, and resourcing within the company in order to implement the strategy. The key products, services, and capabilities for creating and delivering ecosystem value, as discussed earlier, also need to be identified.

Once the organization is appropriately set up, the strategy implementation can be perceived as a diffusion process (Noble 1999), whereby the intended strategy should permeate throughout the organization and manifest itself in behavior according to this strategy.

In essence, this requires *translation* (i.e., sense-giving and sense-making practices) at every organizational level, and in the end at the individual level (Rouleau 2005). Translation is, of course, heavily specific in case, strategy, and organization, but in the end it should always answer the following questions: what does the strategy mean for X, and what kind of behavior should the strategy elicit in the case of X (where "X" stands for the organizational unit in question)?

The latter question is significant for two reasons: first, it makes the (perhaps otherwise abstract) corporate strategy concrete and specific. And second, it serves as the foundation of measuring the progress of the implementation in the organization, because if strategy-specified behavior is observed (or not), the strategy implementation can be perceived successful (or not).

Managerial Implications and Conclusions

The framework of ecosystemic strategizing and change has been developed and tested in the case of a short sea shipping context, in which key actors have embarked on an ecosystem-wide effort to significantly improve the value creation capability of the focal ecosystem. Furthermore, we have worked with two of these ecosystem actors throughout the whole process, including in the organization-specific stages.

According to the experiences and observations accumulated during this work, we have found the framework quite applicable for initiating, organizing, and facilitating intentional ecosystem change. However, it has become exceedingly evident that the general framework constitutes only the general organizing template for actual work and that the tangible micro-level practices within each of the stages within the overall framework are highly important and consequential. In this sense, our work affirms the basic position of the strategy-as-practice school of thought: practices matter in—if not wholly determine the outcome of—organizational strategy/strategizing (Vaara and Whittington 2012).

Thus, we wholly subscribe to and have witnessed the importance of such considerations as terminology; language and other discursive practices (Mantere 2013); practices or working with numbers such as business case, cash flow, and investment calculations (c.f. Ezzamel and Willmott 2008); narrative; and other practices of describing "us" and "our common future" (c.f. Brown and Thompson 2013). Moreover, practices concerning analytical tools and their in-situ use (Molloy and Whittington 2005) seem to be highly consequential in a supra-organizational setting, too. For example, in our case, simulation models have proven to be highly efficient means of analyzing and illustrating various future scenarios as well as providing a common point of reference for the strategists from different organizations in supra-organizational strategizing episodes, which is consistent with Schrange's (1999) notion of "serious play."

Moreover, as in organizational settings, we have found that in supra-organizational strategy, setting appropriate meeting practices from the very beginning is important because such practices tend to be rapidly instituted or "ritualized" (c.f. Johnson et al. 2010) and subsequently laborious to change. Thus, it is important to mindfully plan the supra-organizational strategizing episodes in advance, including the physical environment (Jarzabkowski et al. 2013). In this, a neutral facilitator and neutral premises are, we maintain, conducive to a power-neutral basic setting.

All in all, in this chapter, we have focused on and presented a general organizing framework for ecosystemic strategizing and change. We have developed and refined this framework in a concrete ecosystemic change effort with a set of key ecosystem actors and have found it to be productive in organizing both inter- and intra-organizational strategizing. However, as suggested earlier, this framework constitutes a macro practice. Actual strategizing, both within and outside of specific strategizing episodes, comprises and is determined by a host of micro practices, which are highly consequential for flow and eventual success. For organizational strategy practices, there is already reasonably well-established knowledge about what works (Vaara and Whittington 2012). However, such knowledge is by and large lacking at the supra-organizational level, which is the necessary starting point in intentional ecosystem change initiatives.

In this chapter, we have provided some tentative insights about what we have found to be important in supra-organizational strategizing, but this is clearly an avenue worthy of more systematic research for strategy-as-practice scholars in the future.

Acknowledgments We wish to cordially acknowledge the financial support provided by DIMECC (Digital, Internet, Materials & Engineering Co-Creation) within the REBUS (Towards Relational Business Networks) program, Project 2 Logistics Networks, and Tekes (the Finnish Funding Agency for Innovation) within the Redesigning Ecosystems project.

References

Arthur, W. B. (1989). Competing technologies, increasing returns, and lock-in by historical events. *The Economic Journal, 99*(394), 116–131.
Barnett, W. P., & Pontikes, E. G. (2008). The red queen, success bias, and organizational inertia. *Management Science, 54*(7), 1237–1251.
Barney, J. B. (1991). Firm resources and sustained competitive advantage. *Journal of Management, 17*(1), 99–120.
Barney, J. B., & Clark, D. N. (2007). *Resource-based theory: Creating and sustaining competitive advantage*. Oxford: Oxford University Press.
Bowman, C., & Ambrosini, V. (2000). Value creation versus value capture: Towards a coherent definition of value in strategy—An exploratory study. *British Journal of Management, 11*(1), 1–15.
Brandenburger, A., & Nalebuff, B. (1998). *Co-opetition*. New York: Doubleday.
Brown, A. D., & Thompson, E. R. (2013). A narrative approach to strategy-as-practice. *Business History, 55*(7), 1143–1167.
Bush, R. J., & Sinclair, S. A. (1992). Changing strategies in mature industries: A case study. *Journal of Business & Industrial Marketing, 7*(4), 63–72.
Carrell, M., & Dittrich, J. (1978). Equity theory: The recent literature, methodological considerations, and new directions. *Academy of Management Review, 3*(2), 202–210.
Dalziel, M. (2007). A systems-based approach to industry classification. *Research Policy, 36*(10), 1559–1574.
Ezzamel, M., & Willmott, H. (2008). Strategy as discourse in a global retailer: A supplement to rationalist and interpretive accounts. *Organization Studies, 29*(2), 191–217.

Furrer, O., Thomas, H., & Goussevskaia, A. (2008). The structure and evolution of the strategic management field: A content analysis of 26 years of strategic management research. *International Journal of Management Reviews, 10*(1), 1–23.
Gadde, L. E., Huemer, L., & Håkansson, H. (2003). Strategizing in industrial networks. *Industrial Marketing Management, 32*(5), 357–364.
Greenberg, J. (1986). Determinants of perceived fairness of performance evaluations. *Journal of Applied Psychology, 71*(2), 340–342.
Gulati, R., Puranam, P., & Tushman, M. (2012). Meta-organization design: Rethinking design in interorganizational and community contexts. *Strategic Management Journal, 33*(6), 571–586.
Gulati, R., & Singh, H. (1998). The architecture of cooperation: Managing coordination costs and appropriation concerns in strategic alliances. *Administrative Science Quarterly, 43*, 781–814.
Hannan, M. T., & Freeman, J. (1977). The population ecology of organizations. *American Journal of Sociology, 82*(5), 929–964.
Hardin, G. (1968). The tragedy of the commons. *Science, 162*(3859), 1243–1248.
Järvi, K. (2013). *Ecosystem architecture design: Endogenous and exogenous structural properties*. Lappeenranta: Lappeenranta University of Technology.
Jarzabkowski, P., & Spee, A. P. (2009). Strategy-as-practice: A review and future directions for the field. *International Journal of Management Reviews, 11*(1), 69–95.
Jarzabkowski, P., Spee, A. P., & Smets, M. (2013). Material artifacts: Practices for doing strategy with 'stuff'. *European Management Journal, 31*(1), 41–54.
Johnson, G., Prashantham, S., Floyd, S. W., & Bourque, N. (2010). The ritualization of strategy workshops. *Organization Studies, 31*(12), 1589–1618.
Katz, M. L., & Shapiro, C. (1994). Systems competition and network effects. *Journal of Economic Perspectives, 8*(2), 93–115.
Kim, W. C., & Mauborgne, R. (2005). *Blue ocean strategy*. Boston: Harvard Business Review Press.
Kirchsteiger, G. (1994). The role of envy in ultimatum games. *Journal of Economic Behavior and Organization, 25*(3), 373–389.
Lepak, D. P., Smith, K. G., & Taylor, M. S. (2007). Value creation and value capture: A multilevel perspective. *Academy of Management Review, 32*(1), 180–194.
Mantere, S. (2013). What is organizational strategy? A language-based view. *Journal of Management Studies, 50*(8), 1408–1426.

McGregor, M., Brown, B., & Glöss, M. (2015). Disrupting the cab: Uber, ridesharing and the taxi industry. *Journal of Peer Production*. Retrieved from http://peerproduction.net/issues/issue-6-disruption-and-the-law/essays/disrupting-the-cab-uber-ridesharing-and-the-taxi-industry/

Miettinen, R., Samra-Fredericks, D., & Yanow, D. (2009). Re-turn to practice: An introductory essay. *Organization Studies, 30*(12), 1309–1327.

Mintzberg, H., Ahlstrand, B., & Lampel, J. (1998). *Strategy safari: A guided tour through the wilds of strategic management*. New York: Free Press.

Molloy, E., & Whittington, R. (2005). Practices of organising: Inside and outside the processes of change. *Advances in Strategic Management, 22*, 491–515.

Moore, J. F. (1996). *The death of competition: Leadership & strategy in the age of business ecosystems*. New York: Harper Business.

Nag, R., Hambrick, D. C., & Chen, M. J. (2007). What is strategic management, really? Inductive derivation of a consensus definition of the field. *Strategic Management Journal, 28*(9), 935–955.

Noble, C. H. (1999). The eclectic roots of strategy implementation research. *Journal of Business Research, 45*, 119–134.

Pardo del Val, M., & Martínez Fuentes, C. (2003). Resistance to change: A literature review and empirical study. *Management Decision, 41*(2), 148–155.

Porter, M. E. (1996, November–December). What is strategy? *Harvard Business Review, 74*, 61–78.

Porter, M. E. (2008). The five competitive forces that shape strategy. *Harvard Business Review, 86*(1), 78–93.

Rouleau, L. (2005). Micro-practices of strategic sensemaking and sensegiving: How middle managers interpret and sell change every day. *Journal of Management Studies, 42*(7), 1413–1441.

Sanfey, A. G., Rilling, J. K., Aronson, J. A., Nystrom, L. E., & Cohen, J. D. (2003). The neural basis of economic decision-making in the ultimatum game. *Science, 300*(5626), 1755–1758.

Santos, F., & Eisenhardt, K. (2009). Constructing markets and shaping boundaries: Entrepreneurial power in nascent fields. *Academy of Management Journal, 52*(4), 643–671.

Schrance, M. (1999). *Serious play: How the world's best companies simulate to innovate*. Cambridge: Harvard Business School Press.

Scott, W. R. (2008). *Institutions and organizations: Ideas and interests*. Thousand Oaks, CA: Sage Publications.

Simon, H. A. (1996). *The sciences of the artificial*. Cambridge, MA: MIT Press.

Spender, J.-C. (1986). *Industry recipes: An enquiry into the nature and sources of managerial judgment*. Cambridge: Basil Blackwell.

Teece, D. J. (1986). Profiting from technological innovation: Implications for integration, collaboration, licensing and public policy. *Research Policy, 15*, 286–305.

Tsvetkova, A. (2014). *Designing sustainable industrial ecosystems: The case of a biogas-for-traffic solution*. Turku: Åbo Akademi University.

Tsvetkova, A., Gustafsson, M., & Wikström, K. (2014). Business model innovation for eco-innovation: Developing a boundary-spanning business model of an ecosystem integrator. In S. G. Azevedo, M. Brandenburg, H. Carvalho, & V. Cruz-Machado (Eds.), *Eco-innovation and the development of business models* (pp. 221–241). Dordrecht: Springer.

Utterback, J. M., & Abernathy, W. J. (1975). A dynamic model of process and product innovation. *Omega, 3*(6), 639–656.

Vaara, E., & Whittington, R. (2012). Strategy-as-practice: Taking social practices seriously. *Academy of Management Annals, 6*(1), 285–336.

Whittington, R. (2003). The work of strategizing and organizing: For a practice perspective. *Strategic Organization, 1*(1), 117–125.

Williams, S. D. (2007). Gaining and losing market share and returns: A competitive dynamics model. *Journal of Strategic Marketing, 15*(2), 139–148.

de Wit, B., & Meyer, R. (2010). *Strategy: Process, content, context*. Hampshire: Cengage Learning.

Woolridge, B., Schmid, T., & Floyd, S. W. (2008). The middle management perspective on strategy process: Contributions, synthesis, and future research. *Journal of Management, 34*(6), 1190–1221.

Yoffie, D. B., & Kwak, M. (2006). With friends like these: The art of managing complementors. *Harvard Business Review, 84*(9), 88–98.

21

Network Performance Management: Measurement, Scorecard, and Boundary Processes

Jukka Vesalainen and Sampo Autio

The Challenge of Managing Network-Level Performance

The idea of strategic networks was first presented in 1980s when Jarillo (1988) and others argued that rather than between firms, competition is something that occurs between networks. After all these years there still seems to be one question unanswered: How does one define and capture what is good or excellent level of performance for a network? The lack of comprehensive frameworks and models is obvious concerning both academic research and managerial practices.

The core idea of networking rests on the pursuit of collaborative advantage (Dyer and Singh 1998). It is assumed that firms can improve their competitiveness by allying closely with partners and manage relationships in a way that brings about gains for the firm itself as well as

J. Vesalainen (✉) • S. Autio
University of Vaasa, Vaasa, Finland

J. Vesalainen et al. (eds.), *Practices for Network Management*,
DOI 10.1007/978-3-319-49649-8_21

its partners. The main logic of collaborative advantage stems from relationship-specific investments, complementary resources, knowledge-sharing routines, and effective relationship governance, which bring about distinctive advantages into a relationship, and as a consequence, to the parties of the relationship.

Managers responsible for business relationships continuously bring up the difficulty of having fruitful interaction with their partners in terms of strategic development. They may arrange 'strategic' development sessions, but very often the content of these sessions shift from the strategy level to current operational issues between the parties. It seems that the practices in business relationships are not strategic in the sense that boundary role persons would stick to the intended point.

Managers highlight the importance of networks, but seldom refer to any practical tools and approaches by which the entire network's performance would be possible to measure and manage. The problem is partly linked to the difficulty to effectively measure network-level performance. This makes managers worry about the gains that can be achieved through a massive data collection. Thus, the problem is both theoretical (what constitutes network performance) and practical (what information is managerially relevant, how to collect data, analyze it, and use knowledge acquired for managerial purposes).

From the managerial perspective, it is clear that mere information about how a network performs and what the underlying prerequisites are for performance is not a sufficient goal. The point of departure for this development project was our partner firm's (hereafter 'Delta') interest to get a comprehensive view on its network's (Delta Network) current state, different suppliers' relative position in the network and different relationships' nature as well as their performance. The original idea was to use the measurement results for supply chain management purposes by using the information as a starting point and inspiration for network-level and relationship-level discussions. The value sought refers to the network-level development by making explicit the current network-level performance and the mechanisms that have an effect on that performance. It was also important to gather relevant comparative data[1] to figure out the relative performance level of the focal supply network.

Our solution to the *theoretical problem* is an analytical model, which is based on the resource-based view (RBV) of strategy. The framework defines factors that together represent the underlying mechanisms that generate network performance. In order to choose the most important factors of networking, we leaned on recent theoretical knowledge on network mechanisms and the factors that most clearly can be connected with performance outcomes in interorganizational contexts. In our solution, network performance is measured on dyadic supplier–customer basis and the approach allows both network-level and relationship-level analyses. The theoretically grounded framework is presented in the following section.

What comes to the practical challenge, the collection of data was arranged so that both the suppliers and the representatives of the customer firm participated in the evaluation. Evaluation was carried out by taking each relationship as an object of investigation. Second, in order to improve the usability of the massive data gathered, we developed a specific *network performance scorecard*, by which the actors involved can figure out the big picture as well as drill down to the pieces of more specific information in terms of different measures as well as relationships. Third, in order to use the information collected, we planned and tested a scheduled plan for relationship-specific development discussions so that within a year they (relationship owners) should arrange supplier–customer discussions that deal with different themes derived from the network performance framework.

Modeling Network Performance

Applying the RBV to Network Performance Analysis

The better resources a firm has and the wiser it uses them, the better it performs as compared to competitors. Applying this simple principle to

[1] We are here able to use data from Delta Network and three other networks together consisting of 65 supplier–customer relationships.

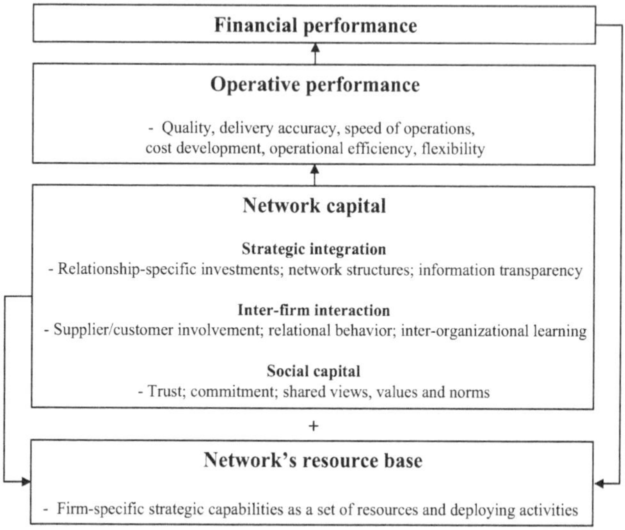

Fig. 21.1 A resource-based model of network performance

networks means that a network outperforms its competing networks if its resource base is stronger and it uses it more effectively. Network's resource base refers to the network members' resources and capabilities. If a network comprises of 'world class companies', it probably outperforms a network formed by more average firms. In a similar vein, if two networks have equal resource bases, but the other uses its resources more effectively, it will probably outperform the other network. Thus, in order to measure network-level performance by using the RBV, one has to define measures for network member capabilities and network activities. Both of these tasks are challenging because of the amount of information needed.[2] The theoretical foundation for network performance consists of four elements (Fig. 21.1). Following the RBV, the first 'ground' level of the performance framework focuses on network members' capabilities and the second on

[2] We constructed a measure for firm-specific capability evaluation and it was used in the pilot study; when collecting comparative data from other networks, we had to abandon this part of the evaluation due to the length of the questionnaire; we suggest that firms would gather supplier-specific capability information in connection to, e.g. auditing activities.

the mechanisms by which a network deploys[3] firm-specific resources in the best possible way. We propose this mechanism to include three different but intertwined elements: *strategic integration, interfirm interaction, and social capital.* In the model, we use the term 'network capital' to highlight the fact that well-functioning network mechanisms are something that develop slowly and once developed they can be considered as a network-specific asset. Network's resource base and network capital together form the foundation for network performance. The rest two levels consist of performance measures addressing different outcomes made possible by the resource/activity interaction. The first of the two outcome measures focuses on operative performance (quality, delivery accuracy, speed of operations, cost development, operational efficiency, and flexibility). The upmost outcome level measure relates to the network's financial performance on the basis of weighted firm-based financial measures drawn from financial statements. To sum up, the RBV-based model for network performance (Fig. 21.1):

- highlights firm-specific capabilities as the base for network performance
- assumes network capital as a means for deploying effectively network's resource base
- assumes operative performance as a consequence of high level of network capital
- assumes financial performance to be (partly) a product of operational performance
- assumes network capital to have a positive effect on the development of network's resource base, and
- assumes financial performance to have an effect on network's resource base

[3] A network can hardly be considered as an entity and/or an actor as such; the term 'network deploys' refers to activities that the members of a network alone and together do in order to achieve strategic and operational excellence.

Network Capital as the Key to Increase Network Performance

Research on interorganizational relationships has found numerous relationship-related factors to affect positively on firm-specific or relationship-level performance. Based on an extensive theoretical knowledge, we chose a group of the most important relationship factors to be measured as the main antecedents for network-level performance. These factors constitute an important capability of a network, and as pointed out earlier, we call it network capital. As a conceptual construct, network capital comprises three types of elements, which again consist of 15 more specified and measurable factors.

Network's *strategic integration* consists of four factors: suppliers' and customer's *relationship-specific investments*, *network structures* (organizational integration, integrated processes and systems), and *information transparency* (from suppliers' as well as customer's side). Network's *social capital* consists of *trust*, *commitment*, and *unity* (shared values and goals). Together, strategic integration and social capital form the benign interorganizational environment or 'enabling structure' (Kohtamäki et al. 2012) for a network within which *interfirm interaction* gets valuable forms to achieve collaborative advantage and network-level performance. Interaction can take many forms. In the model, we chose to measure *supplier and customer involvement* on each other's development activities, *relational behavior styles* of boundary role persons, various dimensions of *interfirm learning*, and *customer's value profile* as the most important elements of interfirm interaction.

Prior research on networking and interorganizational relationships gives a lot of support to the positive effects of various network mechanisms to operative and strategic performance at both firm and relationship level of investigations (Vesalainen and Kohtamäki 2015). Trust has been found to facilitate cooperation, effective interaction, innovation, or value creation and thus indirectly to increase operative and financial performance (McEvily et al. 2003). There is also a connection between relational capital and interorganizational learning (Chang and Gotcher

2007). Further, trust is connected to decreasing transaction costs as well as increasing openness between the parties of a relationship. Supply chain integration (interface structures, systems, and processes) facilitates information sharing between parties (Bensaou and Venkatraman 1995), and interorganizational IT systems affect performance positively if communication and openness are good enough (Paulraj et al. 2008).

Relationship-specific investments have found to positively affect customer commitment to a seller by making the relationship more important to the customer (Anderson and Weitz 1992). Moreover, relationship-specific investments represent idiosyncratic resources generating sustainable competitive advantage and superior outcomes (Palmatier et al. 2007). Structural integration in the form of system, process, or organizational integration may have a direct positive effect on relationship performance, but it seems that in connection to social capital the positive effect is stronger (Kohtamäki et al. 2012). In a similar vein, social capital seems to increase the effect of relationship-specific investments on relationship performance (Chang and Gotcher 2007).

Based on an extensive review of supplier–customer relationships from the point of view of new product development, Johnsen (2009) found strong evidence on the positive effect of supplier involvement in various success factors. The advantages relate to shorter times to market, improved product quality, and reduced development and production costs of new products. Along with the new product development collaboration, supplier–customer collaboration is suggested to be also beneficial in continuous improvement practices (Chapman and Corso 2005).

Information transparency in a supply chain has found to improve operational performance such as increased flexibility and product availability, reduced inventories, and improved quality and responsiveness (Barratt and Oke 2007). Moreover, high-quality information in a supply chain seems to have a positive effect on delivery performance in terms of delivery accuracy and order fulfillment (Zhou and Benton 2007). Information transparency achieved by integrated information systems seems to improve supply chain performance in terms of cost efficiency, process improvements, and increased profitability (Lee et al. 2014). Furthermore, transparent cost information in the buyer–supplier relationships has found to provide cost reductions in products and operational processes (Kajüter and Kulmala 2005).

Multilevel Scorecard as an Effective Boundary Object

In the development of this managerial tool, we paid much attention to the quality of output in order to maximize the utility value of information produced. We developed a specific multilevel scorecard which was expected to serve as an effective boundary object. The goals set for the scorecard as a boundary object were:

- easy readability through visualization
- possibility to see a comprehensive picture and to drill down to details
- clarity of concepts so that all the users involved would understand various concepts similarly

The network performance measurement produces a large amount of information concerning the focal network's as well as its separate relationships' performance. It is thus very important to offer the information in a form which is possibly easy to use for the practitioners. We developed an Excel-based network performance scorecard which follows structurally the framework presented earlier (Fig. 21.1). The first sheet of Excel is a dashboard view of focal network's performance in comparison to the comparative network data. The first layer in the dashboard displays a network's financial performance[4] in terms of profitability (earnings before interests and taxes, (EBIT)), equity ratio, and investment ratio. The second layer displays a network's operative performance in comparison to other networks in three settings: compared to networks in average, lowest network-specific values, and highest network-specific values. The third layer in the dashboard displays the network capital in terms of social capital, integration, and interaction compared to networks in average. From the

[4]The comparative data for financial performance is the industrial average drawn from public sources; all the other comparative data are based on the measurement of three other networks.

dashboard view, users can navigate into a list view, which displays more accurate results of the analysis. This setting is also comparative; that is, the focal network's results are related to the comparative data. From the list view one can drill down to the relationship-specific view, which displays all the relationships of the focal network in a two-dimensional setting with operative performance (a sum scale) and network capital (a sum scale) as the dimensions. From this view, the users can navigate (by clicking the relationship button) to relationship-specific scorecard. The whole scorecard is thus a four-level system, which is supposed to display all the relevant information in a form that is easy to adopt. Additionally, we used the Excel's 'view option' (the text pops up when the cursor is put on the specific cell) to explain the concepts and terminology as well as to give detailed information about how the measurement was done.

Network Delta's Performance

In the following, we show how the Network Delta's performance looks like when it is viewed by the Network Scorecard. Figure 21.2 displays a comprehensive dashboard view where the Network Delta is evaluated against the comparative data. It seems that Network Delta's profitability sunk in 2014 due to the decrease in customer firm's profitability. Suppliers' profitability has decreased continuously from 2011 to 2014 and it has all the time been weaker than the industrial average in Finland. Network Delta's suppliers are, however, quite strong in terms of equity ratio when compared to the industrial average. The investment ratio of Network Delta also exceeds the industrial average with the exception that suppliers' investment per turnover has sunk in 2014 below the industrial average.

As can be seen in Fig. 21.2, Network Delta's operative performance seems to be good in all the measured areas as the performance exceeds the lowest network-specific values[5] in all the performance measures. Network Delta's performance seems to be especially high in flexibility and the speed of operations, where it has the highest values of all the net-

[5] The lowest network-specific value among the four networks in the data.

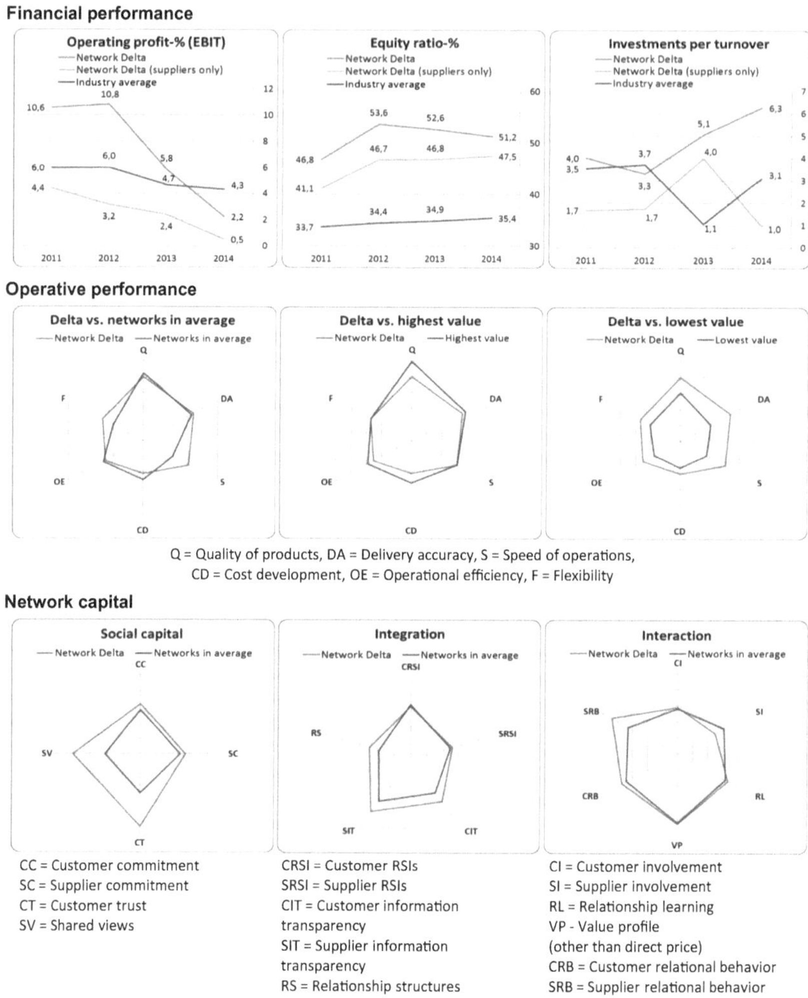

Fig. 21.2 Network performance scorecard: The dashboard view

works evaluated. Moreover, delivery accuracy and quality are good and much better compared with the lowest network-specific values. The main development area is cost development whose value is below the average but still better than the lowest network-specific value.

As can also be seen in Fig. 21.2, Network Delta possesses a high level of social capital. The levels of trust and unity are particularly high when compared to other networks. Also both customers' and suppliers' commitments are higher compared to other networks. Network Delta also seems to be a more structurally integrated and transparent supply network than any other network in the comparative data. Concerning supplier and customer commitment the network is at average level. When it comes to interaction, Network Delta does not differ so much from an average network. Only 'suppliers' relational behavior' seems to be well developed when it is compared to other networks. On the other hand, suppliers' involvement in Network Delta seem to be even lower than in an average. Considering high social capital in the network, there seems to be potential to add supplier involvement.

All in all, Network Delta seems to be less well-performing if one looks at the profitability of the firms in the network. Especially the supplier part of the network is less profitable than firms in the industry in average. This may affect network firms' willingness to invest in development. This seems to be the case as the investment ratio of the suppliers dropped in 2014. Network Delta's operative performance still exceeds other networks and is especially good in terms of flexibility and speed of operations.

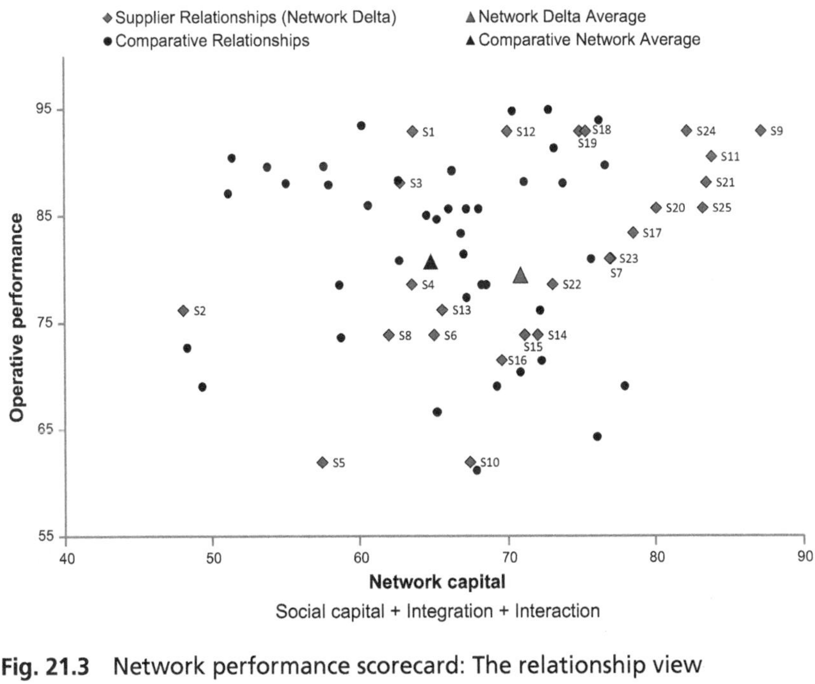

Fig. 21.3 Network performance scorecard: The relationship view

Delta is clearly a trust-based network with good supplier–customer relationships. However, the social capital does not lead to effective interaction as both supplier and customer involvement and interorganizational learning are quite low. Network Delta may benefit from more deliberate interaction in the form of customer and supplier involvement and learning practices.

When Network Delta is viewed at relationships' level (Fig. 21.3), one can see that most customer–supplier relationships in Network Delta are both well-performing and highly relational in terms of network capital (social capital + integration + interaction). It is also evident that the assumption 'the benign the network atmosphere, the better the operative performance' is true (the correlation between operative performance and network capital is 0.54 and it is statistically significant at the 0.002 level for Network Delta).[6] There are, however, some relationships in the network which must be considered more closely. For example, the relationships S2, S5, and S10 are either very low performing or low in network capital or both. These relationships must be viewed in more detail in order to find reasons for such a low performance and network capital.

In the scorecard, it is possible to drill down to the relationship level[7] to study the performance and activity of specific relationships. For example, the more detailed view (not shown here) shows the reasons why the relationships S2 and S5 have low performance and network capital. The relationship S2 scores low in supplier relationship-specific investments, supplier involvement, supplier commitment, and supplier relational behavior. The relationship S5 scores low in supplier relationship-specific investments and involvement from both sides. Furthermore, both relationships score low in relationship structures as well as in information transparency from both sides (S2) or from the customer's side (S5). This kind of result can be expected because of low level of structural ties in the relationships. Moreover, the transactional type of the relationship does not foster parties to increase transparency in the relationship. The crucial question concerning these relationships is: is there anything one can do

[6] Concerning the whole data the correlation between performance and network capital is 0.35 and it is statistically significant at the 0.002 level, which may indicate that network capital does have some explanatory power on relationship-level operative performance.

[7] In the original scorecard view, the real names of the suppliers in Network Delta are shown and they also function as buttons to open the supplier-specific scorecards.

to improve network capital in these relationships in order to improve operational performance?

Purposeful Use of Information: The Boundary Processes

The analysis produces valuable information to be used in network management. It compares the values of the focal network to overall network data and in that way gives relevant benchmark information of the current performance of the network. From the managerial point of view, however, the crucial question is, what has this information to do with network management? In the development process with Delta, we also touched upon this issue by planning and experimenting ways to manage the supplier network by using the above analysis as a framework and source of inspiration.

Intra-organizational Use

Network management is always based on intra-organizational strategy-making as it defines firm-specific goals and principles for networking. Even though firms cannot build relationships one-sidedly, their strategic principles have a strong impact on what kind of relationships and networks they aim to develop. The framework developed in this project may very well serve as a framework for overall network strategy for a firm. Our case represents a supply chain-type of a network, but the framework is not restricted to supply chains only, but is applicable for other types of networks (e.g. delivery chains) as well. From a firm's perspective, the framework offers a platform to define and decide what kinds of relationships its network constitutes. The framework specifically focuses on network capital and challenges firms to decide how relational or close are relationships they try to achieve and what the network mechanisms are that they believe are relevant in improving network performance. It is, thus, important to tie the analysis framework with the chosen network strategy. By doing so, the factors in the framework get a meaning and the results of an analysis reveal if the objectives are met or not. Say, for example, that a firm believes supplier involvement to have a positive impact on decreasing cost level due to better manufacturability of products. It sets a strategic goal to increase supplier involvement in its supplier relationships. The firm may also have found very low level of trust and commitment in its supplier network and due to that it understands that in order to increase the level of supplier involvement it has first to improve the level of trust and commitment in the network. In that way, the framework and the information it offers get a meaning when it is tied to strategic objectives of the firm.

Dyadic Interorganizational Use

Along with the intra-organizational use, the framework and the information based on the analysis of the evaluation data serve as a boundary-spanning tool in dyadic interorganizational relationships. Still, it is not enough to just present the information as it is, but there have to be deliberate managerial purpose in the background. The drivers for managerial consideration could be both backward-looking and forward-looking. The relationship-level analysis (Fig. 21.3) revealed, for example, that the relationship S2 does not show good performance and the network capital in the relationship is very low. This is clearly an indication that has to be dealt with in a meeting with the supplier S2. If both parties agree the low level of network capital to be harmful, they may set up a plan to improve the situation. The forward-looking drivers for relationship development originate themselves from the firm-specific goals (as, e.g. the one presented earlier) and these can be raised as issues related to the framework presented earlier.

A certain amount of transparency may be beneficial for network management. The issue was discussed also with Delta, and they saw it important. It was decided that all the analyses conducted would be transparent so that each firm in the network can see its own figures in a comparative setting with other relationships. Each supplier may get the information in Fig. 21.3 in a way that only its own position is identified openly. The others are hidden, but the distribution of relationships offers an overall benchmark to consider.

As pointed out in the introductory part of this section, one challenge for network management is the difficulty to stay at the strategic-level discussion. It tends to be so easy to leave the strategic level of discussion and focus on more operative issues. In order to avoid this problem, we developed a simple interaction schedule for dyadic interorganizational relationships. It schedules certain planned meetings in a relationship on yearly basis. The interaction schedule consists of two layers. The operative layer consists of continuous daily interaction, and the meetings at that layer can be both ad hoc and scheduled (e.g. a weekly Skype meeting to coordinate production). The strategic layer may consist of three scheduled meetings in a year. The first one deals with commercial/contract issues. The second meeting focuses on relationship development, and the network performance scorecard forms the structure and offers information for this session. The last scheduled session would address firm-specific capability development and can be related to, for example, auditing activities.

Managerial Value Generated

An important feature of a tool like this is the comparative data that serves as a yardstick when interpreting a network's performance level. A comparative setting is clear when concerning financial and operative measures as there exists a general understanding what is good and what is not. The 'soft' issues of network capital, instead, need to have a comparative data in order to 'calibrate' the measure. Thus, a measurement system like this must offer comparative data in order to be valuable for managerial purposes.

Transparent network information may foster firms' self-control as network members. The idea of self-control stems from the idea that firms are not explicitly managed by some other firm, but get managed as a network member. Network analysis and information offered by tools like the one presented here may increase firms' self-awareness. If, for example, a firm finds itself to be 'low' in relational orientation compared to the others in a network, the notion may lead it to revise its practices.

Tools in general are beneficial because they force people out from their customary practices and mindsets. Thus, the managerial value of a tool like this is related to learning outcomes. This tool particularly forces the boundary role persons to focus on the relationships, which is a product of both firms and all boundary role persons' conduct. If networks are supposed to be developed, it is essential to focus on relationships.

Managerial value of this kind of tools must be related to the time and effort used for the activity. The use of a network performance measurement system like this must be effective concerning evaluation practices, analysis, reporting, and use of information. In the first pilot the representatives of the customer firm allocated approximately two man-days to the evaluation of 24 supplier relationships. They wanted to involve as many boundary role persons as possible in the process, which made the process quite heavy. In the later evaluations the representatives of the customer firm used less than one man-day for the evaluation of 15 to 31 supplier relationships.

References

Anderson, E., & Weitz, B. A. (1992). The use of pledges to build and sustain commitment in distribution channels. *Journal of Marketing Research, 29*(1), 18–34.

Barratt, M., & Oke, A. (2007). Antecedents of supply chain visibility in retail supply chains: A resource-based theory perspective. *Journal of Operations Management, 25*(6), 1217–1233.

Bensaou, M., & Venkatraman, N. (1995). Configurations of inter-organizational relationships: A comparison between U.S. and Japanese automakers. *Management Science, 41*(9), 1471–1492.

Chang, K. H., & Gotcher, D. F. (2007). Safeguarding investments and creation of transaction value in asymmetric international subcontracting relationships: The role of relationship learning and relational capital. *Journal of World Business, 42*(4), 477–488.

Chapman, R. L., & Corso, M. (2005). From continuous improvement to collaborative innovation: The next challenge in supply chain management. *Production Planning & Control, 16*(4), 339–344.

Dyer, J. H., & Singh, H. (1998). The relational view: Cooperative strategy and the sources of interorganizational competitive advantage. *Academy of Management Review, 23*(4), 660–679.

Jarillo, C. J. (1988). On strategic networks. *Strategic Management Journal, 9*(1), 31–41.

Johnsen, T. E. (2009). Supplier involvement in new product development and innovation: Taking stock and looking to the future. *Journal of Purchasing & Supply Management, 15*(3), 187–197.

Kajüter, P., & Kulmala, H. I. (2005). Open-book accounting in networks: Potential achievements and reasons for failures. *Management Accounting Research, 16*(2), 179–204.

Kohtamäki, M., Vesalainen, J., Henneberg, S., Naude, P., & Ventresca, M. (2012). Enabling relationship structures and relationship performance improvement: The moderating role of relational capital. *Industrial Marketing Management, 41*(8), 1298–1309.

Lee, H., Kim, M. S., & Kim, K. K. (2014). Interorganizational information systems visibility and supply chain performance. *International Journal of Information Management, 34*(2), 285–295.

McEvily, B., Perrone, V., & Zaheer, A. (2003). Trust as an organizing principle. *Organization Science, 14*(1), 91–106.

Palmatier, R. W., Dant, R. P., & Grewal, D. (2007). A comparative longitudinal analysis of theoretical perspectives of interorganizational relationship performance. *Journal of Marketing, 71*(4), 172–194.

Paulraj, A., Lado, A. A., & Chen, I. J. (2008). Inter-organizational communication as a relational competency: Antecedents and performance outcomes in collaborative buyer–supplier relationships. *Journal of Operations Management, 26*(1), 45–64.

Song, M., & Di Benedetto, C. A. (2008). Supplier's involvement and success of radical new product development in new ventures. *Journal of Operations Management, 26*(1), 1–22.

Vesalainen, J., & Kohtamäki, M. (2015). Toward a typological view of buyer–supplier relationships: Challenging the unidimensional relationship continuum. *Industrial Marketing Management, 49*, 105–115.

Zhou, H., & Benton Jr., W. C. (2007). Supply chain practice and information sharing. *Journal of Operations Management, 25*(6), 1348–1365.

Part IV

Concluding Remarks

22

Managerial Tools and the Network-as-Practice Perspective

Jukka Vesalainen, Magnus Hellström, and Katri Valkokari

The main goal for the DIMECC REBUS program was to develop and study relational business practices in industrial networks. Researchers from seven research institutes worked closely together with managers from 22 different firms to find new ways to make networking easier and an even more useful means for firm- and network-specific success. From the beginning, the program leaned on the participatory design science approach, striving to achieve findings that would have practical managerial value for network management. This choice was supported by a par-

J. Vesalainen (✉)
University of Vaasa, Vaasa, Finland

M. Hellström
Åbo Akademi University, Turku, Finland

K. Valkokari
VTT Technical Research Center of Finland, Tampere, Finland

J. Vesalainen et al. (eds.), *Practices for Network Management*,
DOI 10.1007/978-3-319-49649-8_22

ticular focus on managerial tools and the notion of boundary-spanning issues that firms face when building and acting within interorganizational relationships and networks. During the project, we started to realize the importance of the practice-based approach known as strategy-as-practice in the ongoing studies of organization. As the mainstream strategy-as-practice approach focuses on intra-organizational strategy-making practices, there appeared to be a gap in the knowledge on interorganizational or networking practices. Some scholars have brought up the issue as being an important future task for interorganizational research (Berthod et al. 2016; Chakrabarti et al. 2013). Inspired by these new study openings, we have presented here the tools for network management within a framework that introduces them as three types of interorganizational practices: networks-as-coordinated social systems, networks-as-knowledge creating platforms, and networks-as-value creating entities (see Fig. 1.2). In accordance with practice theory (Whittington 2006), when the tools represent *practice*, *praxis* is what boundary-spanning personnel do when actually managing and interacting in network contexts. In other words, when the strategy-as-practice approach asks what people do when they are strategizing, we then ask **what people do when they are networking**.

Our approach also includes the idea of intentional action, namely, why boundary-spanning practitioners do the things they do. From a more deliberate managerial perspective, the answer is: these practitioners act in certain ways to seek collaborative advantage and firm-specific success. Rationality is a normative ideal that manifests in the practices of individuals intending to be rational, as they create strategy (Jarzabkowski and Kaplan 2015). We assume this aspect also holds true in business networks.

In order to highlight the rationality perspective, we use the resource-based view (RBV) of strategy as another important theoretical base for developing our view. RBV tries to explain the competitiveness of a firm by analyzing its firm-specific strategic capabilities, which are the product of resources and activities that deploy resources. Interestingly, as resources are treated as the base for competitiveness, the activities that *deploy* and *develop* those resources are needed in order to realize and develop organizational excellence. Thus, the intertwining of resources and activities in

RBV represents a similar kind of interlinkage as the duality of practice and praxis does in practice theory.

In the discussion that follows, we elaborate the framework we presented in the introduction of this book as a combined model that adopts certain ideas from both practice theory and RBV. We call it the combined *network-as-practice* model. That model refinement is followed by a discussion of the position of managerial tools in the actual network-as-practice perspective. Finally, we offer suggestions on what is important for practitioners to consider when they act as boundary spanners in interorganizational settings.

Building a Combined Practice-Based Model for Collaborative Advantage

The framework we presented in the introductory chapter of this book basically follows the RBV approach, as the defined practices represent activities that deploy and/or develop resources, based on the view of co-exploration and co-exploitation as two basic purposes for various network forms (Parmigiani and Rivera-Santos 2011). By adopting the RBV approach, we highlight networks as goal-oriented actors that possess competitiveness as an entity. The discussion below aims to bring this theoretical mix together; the two approaches—the practice theory and RBV—thus form the basis for the network-as-practice perspective, which we believe captures most of the key practices in interorganizational interaction.

Analyzing networks as multilevel resource configurations makes it possible to perceive them as competitive entities. A multilevel understanding of competitiveness also makes it possible to focus on resource-deploying and resource-developing activities as part of the "competitiveness formula" of a network in addition to its bare resources and knowledge. From this point of view, network competitiveness depends on the quality of its resources and the quality of the interorganizational activities by which those resources are used and/or developed. Thus, the practice perspective offers a fresh angle on network studies by highlighting three important aspects of networking: (1) the wider industrial, the network-specific, and the organization-specific practices of interorganizational interaction; (2) the real everyday praxis of boundary-spanning personnel, as they interact; and (3) the role of boundary spanners as acknowledgeable practitioners who both reproduce and transform interorganizational practices. From this perspective, the praxis of network management and interorganizational interaction is guided by the networking practices, and at the same time, these practices are reproduced and transformed by the daily activities of the practitioners.

The connecting feature between the two approaches (the practice theory and RBV) is the concept of *practice*. In the practice theory it is linked to everyday praxis, and in the RBV theory it is linked to resources, as illustrated in Fig. 22.1. Referring to the framework of this book, the cornerstones of social capital, knowledge, and tangible resources (see Fig. 1.2) represent different forms of network resources, while the practices for network building, knowledge creation, and value generation represent the forms of activity that deploy as well as develop them. Together, the resources and these forms of activity form the basis for network-level strategic competence.

From a structurationist perspective (Giddens 1984), networks can be understood as being configured by actual practices. This perspective sees reality as an emerging phenomenon based within the network and its interorganizational relationships (Berthod et al. 2016; Chakrabarti et al.

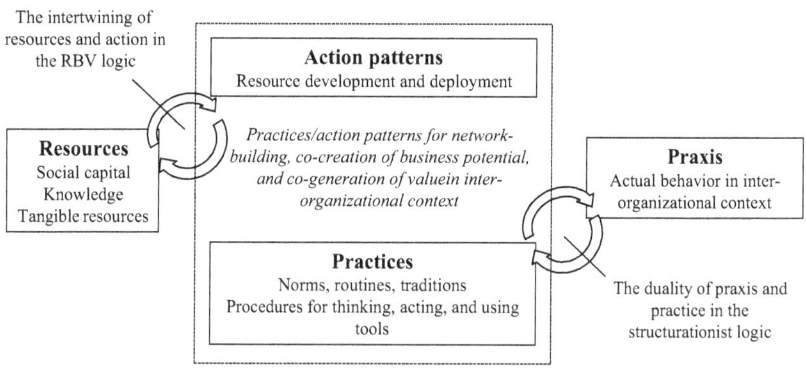

Fig. 22.1 Combining practice theory with RBV logic

2013). Network practices are maintained and reinforced by the daily actions of their users and reproduced by subsequent reflexive monitoring and rationalization. While network structures are produced by network-related action, the structure defines limits and enables, legitimizes, and guides action. This duality is the basic idea behind structuration theory, and we use it here as a main conceptual idea to define the practical nature of networks and their interorganizational relationships.

According to Whittington (2006), *practices* refer to shared routines of behavior, including the traditions, norms, and procedures for thinking, acting, and using "things" (e.g., tools). *Praxis*, again, refers to actual activities that people do in reality. In strategy research, scholars have followed the practice approach by defining organizational and/or wider institutionalized *practices* as the source from which actors draw when they act in daily (business) life. Taking one example from the network context, *early supplier involvement* refers to a wider sectoral or organizational practice by which supplier-specific knowledge is deployed for developing better products, while the way people actually apply this practice refers to the praxis or the way the procedure is implemented in time and space.

The essence of RBV logic is simple: the better resources an entity has and the wiser ways it uses them, the more competitive that entity is (Barney 1991). In order to understand a network's strategic capability, it is crucial to define the general conceptual architecture of the RBV. Two different types of capability can be found in the literature, the first referring to resources and the second referring to activities that deploy and develop resources. The firm-specific RBV approach has currently been developed also to address interorganizational and network settings (Lavie 2006). These new openings are congruent with Dyer and Singh's (1998) collaborative advantage view that shifts the perspective from firm-specific to a relationship- and network-specific perspective by highlighting the mechanisms through which the collaborative advantage can actually be achieved. They refer to relationship-specific assets, knowledge-sharing routines, complementary resources and capabilities, and effective governance as the means for collaborative advantage. Interorganizational relationships and networks are thus understood as entities, which makes it possible to analyze them from the RBV point of view.

The two basic organizational purposes of activity inferred earlier—resource development and resource deployment—are key concepts in our combined model. They represent the most important manifestations of networking practices from the RBV perspective. In the introductory chapter, we referred to co-exploration and co-exploitation as the two profound interorganizational activities. As Parmigiani and Rivera-Santos (2011) found in their meta-analysis, these two types of activities also represent the main purpose of interorganizational cooperation. In our framework (see Fig. 1.2), the dimension known as *networks-as-knowledge creating platforms* refers to practices for co-exploration. These practices create and integrate knowledge to develop new business potential and make it possible for a network to adapt to or even induce changes in the business environment. The dimension *networks-as-value -generating entities* again represents those practices by which firms cocreate value. This dimension is, thus, linked to co-exploitation, and as an output, the corresponding practices generate value for all network members and stakeholders.

The combined model we put forward in this concluding chapter integrates certain aspects of RBV with practice theory. From the RBV, it adopts the idea of distinguishing between bare resources, on the one hand, and activities that deploy and develop them, on the other. Practices herein are understood in a similar vein as interpreted in practice theory. They represent general, sectoral, network- or relationship-specific and firm-specific interorganizational business practices that guide the actual praxis for network management and interorganizational interaction. Thus, RBV-oriented thinking contributes to the model by stressing the importance of resources and highlighting both resource deployment and development as the basic purposes of practices. Practice theory, in turn, contributes to the model by bringing in the idea of praxis as a contrast to practice. The connecting link for both approaches is *practice* (i.e., activities) as a theoretical concept having a role in both theories. Figure 22.2 illustrates the combined model, and the circular arrows refer to the two reciprocal elements in the model—network practice/praxis and network resources/activities, and further, we propose these practices to be categorized as the aforementioned three types (see also the sides of the triangle in Fig. 22.2).

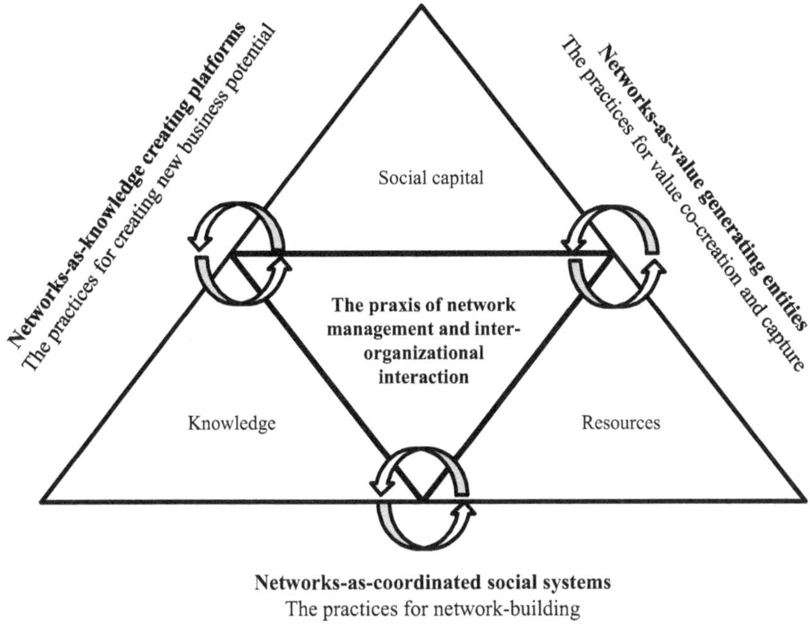

Fig. 22.2 Network-as-practice: The combined model

Practice theory also highlights the importance of *practitioners*. They represent different roles and some are more powerful than others, but together, this social network of actors represents network management and they do undertake network managerial actions. In this book, network management tools and practices are highlighted as important means for this particular type of social network to achieve collaborative advantage.

Tools as Practices of Network Management

Among others, interorganizational practices consist of procedures for thinking, acting, and using "things". The term "thing" can be interpreted as a materialized object with a managerial purpose (Whittington 2006). In terms of the design science approach utilized in our research work here, these can be called artifacts, that is, a "means to an end" that researchers have developed together with the practitioners to solve a practical problem in network management (Holmström et al. 2009). Whereas practice theory emphasizes the use of tools (for the *tools-in-use* aspect, see Chap. 1), design science can generally be described as a *tools-in-development* approach. A tool can also be treated as a boundary object with the purpose to overcome knowledge boundaries that occur in inter-organizational interfaces. This book is about developing these "things" or the boundary objects and procedures by which these objects can be used to manage networks and business relationships. When developing these managerial tools, we actually tried to build new network management practices through collaborating with company managers already close to their praxis. By adopting the collaborative design science approach, we (as researchers) became actors in the daily praxis of our partner firms' interorganizational practitioners, the boundary-spanning personnel responsible for interorganizational management and interaction. The tools presented in Parts I, II, and III of this book have a deliberate role to play in the praxis of network management and interorganizational interaction, as the summary Table 22.1 illustrates.

The tools presented in Part I relate to those practices that strive for network building. As institutionalized practices, they guide the daily activities boundary-spanning personnel undertake when trying to build and maintain relationships. Typically, firms have various codes of conduct that direct their personnel in how to act in customer/supplier relationships. These practices also develop by praxis, as, for example, in those cases where people adopt new ways to interact using social media. This category of practices is usually interlinked with social capital. As an example, a typical interorganizational practice is a "supplier day," when a customer invites a group of the most important suppliers to a gathering with the intention to coordinate the network of suppliers and improve both the relational (trust, commitment, and unity) and cognitive (shared understanding of key goals and each other's roles in achieving those goals) social capital. In Part I of this book, we provided other examples of practices that build shared understanding between network members at the company level (Chaps. 5 and 6) and the individual levels (Chaps. 4 and 7), and with other stakeholders (Chap. 3).

Tools presented in Part II relate to practices used to build new business potential. They thus implement the concept of co-exploration. One

Table 22.1 Summary of the tools: Theoretical grounding and links to prior literature

	The general focus and intent of the tools introduced in the book	The function of the tools and their grounding in theory	Examples of practices defined in the networking literature related to the tools
PART I: Networks-as-coordinated social systems: The practices for network building	• Strategic intents of stakeholders • Human values as social connectors • Joint sense-making of network structures and positions • Functional contracting for trust-based networks • Rhetoric and persuasion in cross-border interaction	The tools in this category are mostly related to the development of social capital (Nahapiet and Ghoshal 1998). Some are clearly linked to *relational social* capital in terms of building trust, unity, openness, and relational norms. Others relate more to *cognitive social* capital, addressing the building of shared understanding of the network structure, common activity, and goals	Practices related to socialization mechanisms, such as social events, joint workshops, site visits, supplier conferences, and team-building exercises (Cousins and Lawson 2007; Dyer and Nobeoka 2000)
PART II: Networks-as-knowledge-creating platforms: The practices for developing new business potential	• Systematic integration of knowledge • Third party supported benchmarking • Co-developing a value proposition • Evaluation of supplier–customer fit	The tools in this category use social capital as a resource to develop new knowledge. These processes represent interactive learning (described, e.g., by Nonaka and Takeuchi 1995). Knowledge sharing, integration, and the joint conceptualization of new knowledge are characteristic of the tools in this category. New knowledge is supposed to be an important trigger for improved business potential	Interactive learning (Ballantyne et al. 2011), supplier involvement (Freytag and Ritter 2005), customer involvement (Nicolajsen and Scupola 2011), Co-development of value propositions (Truong et al. 2012)

(*continued*)

Table 22.1 (continued)

	The general focus and intent of the tools introduced in the book	The function of the tools and their grounding in theory	Examples of practices defined in the networking literature related to the tools
PART III: Networks-as-value generating entities: The practices of value generation and capture	• Product life cycle cost calculation in business relationships • Co-configuring project offerings • Value-driven sales process to meet customer expectations • The use of the value-curve tool to build joint value propositions • Performance-improving change in a business ecosystem • Joint value creation • Measuring network performance	The tools in this category relate to co-deployment and coordinated use of both tangible and intangible resources in networks. Value chain integration is the key concept highlighting co-production of value, effective coordination, smooth flow of operations, and customer–supplier fit in terms of value generation and complementarities. The tools introduced make visible network members' positions in the network or business relationship thus help the networks to plan and coordinate value co-production	Co-production of value (Ramírez and Ramirez 1999), co-creation of value (Grönroos 2011) Supply chain integration (Cousins and Lawson 2007) Use of interorganizational information systems for improved information transparency (Hultman and Axelsson 2007). Gain-sharing and open-books accounting (Kajüter and Kulmala 2005)

of the most widely used activities in this category of networking practices is early supplier involvement, a practice that tries to use suppliers' manufacturing-related knowledge, as it relates to the customer firm's R&D process. Part II introduces the tools that enable the practices of knowledge integration (Chap. 9), joint benchmarking (Chap. 10), and co-development of value proposition (Chap. 11), as well as practices related to supplier involvement (Chaps. 12 and 13). These practices are primarily expected to develop knowledge and tangible resources. For early supplier involvement-practice, the suppliers share their specific manufacturing knowledge in order to improve the manufacturability of their customer's new product. That is how this particular cooperative practice should deploy supplier knowledge and develop the customer's product.

Part III of this book includes the tools and practices by which firms jointly can create value. One of the most common practices of this kind is a relationship-specific investment. For example, in a case of a supplier's relationship-specific investment, there may be sectoral or network-wide norms of long-term orientation that prohibit opportunistic behavior and in that way diminish the risks for increased dependency. Relationship-specific investments are typically based on trust and a deep commitment between the parties in a relationship. In that way, this networking practice deploys social capital as a resource. On the other hand, a relationship-specific investment develops a supplier's resources especially in connection to a certain customer, who may then also benefit from the investment through the more effective and high-quality production by the supplier. Part III presents tools that support the practices required for joint value creation (i.e., value co-creation) and especially those for developing and communicating different value elements in a sales situation (Chaps. 15–17) as well as tools that support strategic planning by measuring and elucidating the value position or benefits from the viewpoint of different network or ecosystem members (Chaps. 18–21).

In each of the three parts (I–III), there are stronger connections to different research streams of network management, from sourcing and supplier involvement in Part II to industrial marketing and the service paradigm in Part III, to management or even the social sciences in Part I. Thus, in line with the research on networks and interorganizational relationships (Håkansson and Snehota 1995), all these approaches highlight the importance of *interaction* between the involved actors, which range from individuals to networks of organizations. Interaction, then, manifests itself as various *cooperative behaviors* (Johnston et al. 2004) and *action patterns* (Lui and Ngo 2005) that occur at interorganizational interfaces. Table 22.1 presents how the tools presented in this book are actual manifestations of several forms of interorganizational action patterns, such as interactive learning (Ballantyne et al. 2011), co-creation of value (Grönroos 2011), joint decision-making (Piercy 2009), joint problem solving (Stanko et al. 2007), supplier involvement (Freytag and Ritter 2005), customer involvement (Nicolajsen and Scupola 2011), and co-development of value `propositions (Truong et al. 2012), which have been identified in the empirical research on networks and interorganizational relationships. These cooperative behaviors can be interpreted as practices for interorganizational interaction, thereby our contribution to these practices and earlier literature is offered and defined in Table 22.1.

Managerial Implications for Boundary Spanners

Practice theory sees practitioners as intentional and knowledgeable actors. This view means that actors are aware of the goals and the means, and they know how and why specific actions will lead to certain outcomes in certain situations and contexts. The network-as-practice model outlined in this book offers a framework for analyzing the work and role of boundary spanners, as they "do network management" and interact with colleagues from partner firms. In this regard, the book has the following specific implications for managers.

Firstly, tools constitute a way to make academic knowledge accessible and actionable. However, most available tools offer help for firm-internal strategizing and thus inevitably represent a one-sided (sometimes even inward-looking) view on relationships and networking. The tools presented in this book have their point of departure the quest for mutual benefits and collaboration. Hence, they offer help in situations where the wish is to adopt an external perspective on various activities or even to doing things in common (i.e., collaborating by two or more parties using tools together).

Secondly, managers should acknowledge the difference between actual interaction—the praxis—and the principles they say are their strategic guidelines when cooperating with partners. Too often, one runs into situations where a partner says they follow "partnership principles" in their business relationships but the actual behavior is not congruent with their strategic declaration. Interorganizational interfaces consist of several boundary spanners from various firms with the challenge being to ensure that the overall praxis corresponds with the practices already strategically declared. Knowledgeable network practitioners understand the power of praxis in reproducing as well as transforming practices. In a business relationship we studied earlier, the customer firm started a design-for-manufacture practice. Originally, the idea was to use supplier knowledge to lower the manufacturing costs of new products. The actual discussions in the meetings with suppliers, however, dealt with anything from their suppliers' sourcing problems to their investment decisions. The issues relating to new product development were very few. This example shows how the actual action did not fit the intended practice. A knowledgeable boundary spanner pays attention to this gap and either tries to stay with the original idea or transform the practice. In this particular example, the proper description of the practice should have been something like "network-level continuous improvement". The fact that the function of tools forms and changes during their use indeed calls for more regular reflection on their actual purpose.

Thirdly, network actors will benefit if they acknowledge the idea of resource deployment and resource development when interacting in network contexts. The idea stemming from the RBV is that competitiveness is not only a question of high-class resources, but also the way resources are used. The idea is especially useful in network contexts when boundary spanners try to coordinate resource use and development. Therefore, it is important to understand whether a tool primarily has an exploitative or explorative character, and then balance these forces so as to foster actual ambidexterity in the network, that is, the ability to pursue both exploration and exploitation in the long run (or in more concrete terms both growth and development, or flexibility and efficiency).

Fourthly, the often obscure field of network management may get more structured content if network actors define it as the three areas of practices we outlined in our network-as-practice model (see Fig. 22.2). In other words, boundary spanners can define their work in terms of its relationship to network building, co-creation of business potential, and value generation and capture. Each of these is important for a truly comprehensive understanding of networks as systems and entities, and acknowledged boundary spanners should have a role in both finding and developing new practices as well as taking care that the actual behavior (i.e., praxis) corresponds to the practice or, if not, transforms and defines new practices in line with the emergent new activities, as indicated earlier.

Finally, boundary spanners need to know how to use boundary objects. In this book, we introduced 17 tools for network management. As said earlier, this is by no means an exhaustive or an ideal package of network management tools, but rather a collection of new tools that have been developed from close interaction with network managers. What we particularly want to stress is the fact that the practitioners themselves "make the tools" in the way that they use them in their professional daily lives (i.e., in praxis). Tools are basically only artificial conceptualizations, and so the crucial skill and task of a boundary spanner is to fit the tool being used into culturally different interorganizational relationships. At its best, a tool may function as a "discursive template" that helps boundary role persons to achieve shared understanding of the best ways to develop collaborative advantage.

Limitations and Future Research

Basically, all the chapters presented in this book represent tools that have been developed for use but not necessarily yet been taken into wider use. This is not a problem as such, but it does adhere to a *tools-in-development* stage that is in line with the design science approach that served as a premise for our program and also this book. Nevertheless, to complete the "practice turn" in studies on networks and interorganizational relationships, a *tools-in-use* view seems the natural continuation for this emerging perspective. As contended in the introduction, research on *tools-in-use* may enhance our understanding of what is considered to be important when crossing interorganizational boundaries at the network level.

Just as the RBV and practice theory form the **theoretical frames** for our combined model, the literature of interorganizational relationships provided the network-oriented **content** for the model. In extant literature, networks and business relationships have been studied from the point of view of several theoretical models, including transaction cost theory, social capital theory, agency theory, interaction theory, and the resource dependency approach. This rich body of knowledge includes a significant amount of varied descriptions of networking and/or interorganizational practices that are anchored in marketing, logistics, industrial management, strategic management, and sociology. Further, the three main parts of our book offer different interlinkages to these earlier studies (see Table 22.1). The literature does not necessarily refer to these practices literally as *practices* (at least in the specific meaning that term has in practice theory), but rather treats them as interaction types, action patterns, or cooperative behaviors.

The grand aim of the book, therefore, was to take the first steps toward something we term *network-as-practice*. In the spirit of engaged scholarship, we hope this book and its idea will inspire other academics to explore the approach further as well as develop better tools, working together with boundary spanners to explore and institute different and more effective network management practices.

References

Ballantyne, D., Frow, P., Varey, R. J., & Payne, A. (2011). Value propositions as communication practice: Taking a wider view. *Industrial Marketing Management, 40*(2), 202–210. doi:10.1016/j.indmarman.2010.06.032.

Barney, J. (1991). Firm resources and sustained competitive advantage. *Journal of Management, 17*(1), 99–120.

Berthod, O., Grothe-Hammer, M., & Sydow, J. (2016). Network ethnography: A mixed-method approach for the study of practices in interorganizational settings. *Organizational Research Methods*. doi:10.1177/1094428116633872.

Chakrabarti, R., Ramos, C., & Henneberg, S. (2013). Network dynamics in the UK pharmaceutical network—A network-as-practice perspective. *Industrial Marketing Management, 42*(3), 356–371. doi:10.1016/j.indmarman.2012.12.009.

Cousins, P. D., & Lawson, B. (2007). The effect of socialization mechanisms and performance measurement on supplier integration in new product development. *British Journal of Management, 18*(3), 311–326. doi:10.1111/j.1467-8551.2007.00514.x.

Dyer, J. H., & Nobeoka, K. (2000). Creating and managing a high-performance knowledge-sharing network: The Toyota case. *Strategic Management Journal, 21*(3), 345–367.

Dyer, J. H., & Singh, H. (1998). The relational view: Cooperative strategy and sources of interorganizational competitive advantage. *Academy of Management Review, 23*(4), 660–679. doi:10.5465/AMR.1998.1255632.

Freytag, P. V., & Ritter, T. (2005). Dynamics of relationships and networks—Creation, maintenance and destruction as managerial challenges. *Industrial Marketing Management, 34*(7), 644–647. doi:10.1016/j.indmarman.2005.06.002.

Giddens, A. (1984). *The constitution of society: Outline of the theory of structuration*. Cambridge, UK: Polity Press.

Grönroos, C. (2011). Value co-creation in service logic: A critical analysis. *Marketing Theory, 11*(3), 279–301. doi:10.1177/1470593111408177.

Håkansson, H., & Snehota, I. (1995). *Developing relationships in business networks*. London: Routledge.

Holmström, J., Ketokivi, M., & Hameri, A.-P. (2009). Bridging practice and theory: A design science approach. *Decision Sciences, 40*(1), 65–87. doi:10.1111/j.1540-5915.2008.00221.x.

Hultman, J., & Axelsson, B. (2007). Towards a typology of transparency for marketing management research. *Industrial Marketing Management, 36*(5), 627–635. doi:10.1016/j.indmarman.2006.04.001.

Jarzabkowski, P., & Kaplan, S. (2015). Strategy tools-in-use: A framework for understanding "technologies of rationality" in practice. *Strategic Management Journal, 36*(4), 537–558. doi:10.1002/smj.2270.

Johnston, D. A., McCutcheon, D. M., Stuart, F. I., & Kerwood, H. (2004). Effects of supplier trust on performance of cooperative supplier relationships. *Journal of Operations Management, 22*(1), 23–38. doi:10.1016/j.jom.2003.12.001.

Kajüter, P., & Kulmala, H. I. (2005). Open-book accounting in networks. Potential achievement and reasons for failures. *Management Accounting Research, 16*(2), 179–204. doi:10.1016/j.mar.2005.01.003.

Lavie, D. (2006). The competitive advantage of interconnected firms: An extension of the resource-based view. *Academy of Management Review, 31*(3), 638–658.

Lui, S. S., & Ngo, H. (2005). An action pattern model of inter-firm cooperation. *Journal of Management Studies, 42*(6), 1123–1153. doi:10.1111/j.1467-6486.2005.00536.x.

Nahapiet, J., & Ghoshal, S. (1998). Social capital, intellectual capital, and the organizational advantage. *The Academy of Management Review, 23*(2), 242–266. doi:10.2307/259373.

Nicolajsen, H. W., & Scupola, A. (2011). Investigating issues and challenges for customer involvement in business services innovation. *Journal of Business & Industrial Marketing, 26*(5), 368–376. doi:10.1108/08858621111144424.

Nonaka, I., & Takeuchi, H. (1995). *The knowledge-creating company how Japanese companies create the dynamics of innovation*. New York: Oxford University Press.

Parmigiani, A., & Rivera-Santos, M. (2011). Clearing a path through the forest: A meta-review of interorganizational relationships. *Journal of Management, 37*(4), 1108–1136. doi:10.1177/0149206311407507.

Piercy, N. F. (2009). Strategic relationships between boundary-spanning functions: Aligning customer relationship management with supplier relationship management. *Industrial Marketing Management, 38*(8), 857–864. doi:10.1016/j.indmarman.2009.03.015.

Ramírez, R., & Ramirez, R. (1999). Value co-production: Intellectual origins and implications for practice and research. *Strategic Management Journal, 20*(1), 49–65. doi:10.1002/(SICI)1097-0266(199901)20:1<49::AID-SMJ20>3.0.CO;2-2.

Stanko, M. A., Bonner, J. M., & Calantone, R. J. (2007). Building commitment in buyer–seller relationships: A tie strength perspective. *Industrial Marketing Management, 36*(8), 1094–1103. doi:10.1016/j.indmarman.2006.10.001.

Truong, Y., Simmons, G., & Palmer, M. (2012). Reciprocal value propositions in practice: Constraints in digital markets. *Industrial Marketing Management, 41*(1), 197–206. doi:10.1016/j.indmarman.2011.11.007.

Whittington, R. (2006). Completing the practice turn in strategy research. *Organization Studies, 27*(5), 613–634. doi:10.1177/0170840606064101.

Index

Note: Page numbers followed by 'n' refer to notes.

J. Vesalainen et al. (eds.), *Practices for Network Management*,
DOI 10.1007/978-3-319-49649-8

R

S

Kolibri 360 GmbH
Ferdinand-Jühlke-Straße 7
99095 Erfurt, Deutschland
produktsicherheit@kolibri360.de